MICHAEL BAWTREE

THE BEST
FOOLING

ADVENTURES IN CANADIAN THEATRE

MEMOIRS VOLUME II

MICHAEL BAWTREE

THE BEST FOOLING

ADVENTURES IN CANADIAN THEATRE

MEMOIRS VOLUME II

MEREO
Cirencester

Mereo Books

1A The Wool Market Dyer Street Cirencester Gloucestershire GL7 2PR
An imprint of Memoirs Publishing www.mereobooks.com

THE BEST FOOLING: 978-1-86151-666-4

First published in Great Britain in 2017
by Mereo Books, an imprint of Memoirs Publishing

Copyright ©2017

Michael Bawtree has asserted his right under the Copyright Designs and Patents Act 1988 to be identified as the author of this work.

A CIP catalogue record for this book is available from the British Library.

This book is sold subject to the condition that it shall not by way of trade or otherwise be lent, resold, hired out or otherwise circulated without the publisher's prior consent in any form of binding or cover, other than that in which it is published and without a similar condition, including this condition being imposed on the subsequent purchaser.

The address for Memoirs Publishing Group Limited can be found at
www.memoirspublishing.com

The Memoirs Publishing Group Ltd Reg. No. 7834348

Cover design and artwork - Ray Lipscombe

The Memoirs Publishing Group supports both The Forest Stewardship Council® (FSC®) and the PEFC® leading international forest-certification organisations. Our books carrying both the FSC label and the PEFC® and are printed on FSC®-certified paper. FSC® is the only forest-certification scheme supported by the leading environmental organisations including Greenpeace. Our paper procurement policy can be found at
www.memoirspublishing.com/environment

Typeset in 10/15pt Bembo
by Wiltshire Associates Publisher Services Ltd. Printed and bound in Great Britain by Printondemand-Worldwide, Peterborough PE2 6XD

Dedicated to
HELEN (BURNS) LANGHAM
1916 -
and to the memory of
MICHAEL LANGHAM
1919 - 2011

"Why, this is the best fooling, when all is done."
Andrew Aguecheek, Twelfth Night Act 2, sc. 3

PREFACE

These adventures begin as I step off the boat in Halifax, Canada, having left England to embark on my new life as an immigrant, with the intention of staying no more than a year. A first volume, As Far As I Remember, published in 2015, covered my first twenty-five years, and was written almost entirely out of my memory, because nearly all my early papers and records in the UK had been disposed of as a result of a misunderstanding. But once in Canada I rarely threw anything away, and am now awash in letters, photographs, programs and every other kind of record of life in my new country. In spite of all this mass of documentation, I was advised by a good friend to keep relying on memory, so that the tone of the writing would stay the same, and the same selective principle keep operating. Once my first draft was written, I could always go back to my letters and other papers, to check and occasionally to correct. This I have done, throughout the years covered in this volume.

However for 1973 onward I decided on a change of gear, because in January of that year I had begun to keep a diary. It was an irregular affair – sometimes weeks or even months went by without an entry. But I realized that the diary opened a clear window on my thoughts and feelings at the time I wrote in it, and that this might give a new impetus and interest to the story. So extracts from the diary start taking a minor, and occasionally major, role in the telling – which I have continued to supplement with my own recall of events.

I have also felt it only fair to intersperse an account of my public doings with some reference to the private life that ran alongside them, because for some reason the world continues to act surprised and shocked when the personal areas of people's lives are suddenly exposed, as though the respectable majority of us have no private world of any kind. I have tried to balance discretion with truthfulness as I trace this tumultuous, sexually active and now distant part of my life. All these years, after all, fell within what has been called the 'sexual revolution,' when doors suddenly opened up for millions of people in the Western world into all sorts of new experiences, sometimes transcendent and life-affirming, sometimes seedy – and occasionally both.

My theatre career has seen remarkable peaks of success. It has also witnessed spectacular crashes, as my various heady dreams ran into the rocks of personal let-down or envy, or financial stress, or my own loss of confidence, or sometimes my fatal politesse.

In spite of everything I have been extraordinarily blessed in Canada, as will be seen: finding great things to do, a wide circle of friends and colleagues from east to west, and above all an abiding love. My year in the country turned out to be somewhat longer.

MB
Wolfville, Nova Scotia
February 2017

CONTENTS

	Preface	
Chapter 1	Beginning Life Over	P. 1
Chapter 2	A Magic Door Opens	P. 22
Chapter 3	Branching Out	P. 38
Chapter 4	A Summer at Stratford	P. 51
Chapter 5	Shall I Stay?	P. 72
Chapter 6	Home Again	P. 85
Chapter 7	Gone West	P. 100
Chapter 8	Russian Interlude	P. 113
Chapter 9	Sea Changes	P. 127
Chapter 10	My New Country	P. 148
Chapter 11	Latin America	P. 167
Chapter 12	Transitions	P. 191
Chapter 13	Back To Stratford	P. 221
Chapter 14	'And Away He Shall Again'	P. 245
Chapter 15	To The USA	P. 277
Chapter 16	Britten to Bernstein	P. 292
Chapter 17	COMUS Music Theatre: a Splashy Launch	P. 312
	Index	P. 347

ACKNOWLEDGMENTS

To the New York Public Library for the Performing Arts for permission to make use of two photographs © Martha Swope, from my production of The Rivals in New York (1974-5); to photographer Robert C. Ragsdale for permission to use his photographs from my productions at the Stratford Festival, 1972-4; to Roundabout Theatre Archives for the portrait of Gene Feist; to Gill Evans for the portrait of Grant Glassco; to Library and Archives Canada for permission to use three photographs in the Walter Curtin collection, from my production of The Beggar's Opera at the Guelph Spring Festival 1977.

Photographs from my play The Last of the Tsars (Stratford 1966) are reproduced from the original slides given to me by photographer Douglas Spillane. I have made unsuccessful efforts to trace the origin of one or two other photographs I have used. The rest come from my own collection.

I would like to thank my good friend Christopher Langham for permission to share stories about his parents Michael and Helen, to whom, as will be seen, this book is dedicated. Thanks also to old friends Bill and Marie Clarke, John Weston and Jonathan Harlow for reading and critiquing my first drafts; and to Chris Newton for his sensitive editing skills.

MB
May 2017

CHAPTER ONE

BEGINNING LIFE OVER

With most of us crowded on deck to catch our first view, the coastline of North America appeared hauntingly on the horizon. We were steaming towards Nova Scotia after a smooth five-day passage, and three or four hours later, with the rocky shore now close and misty but plainly in sight, we nosed up the narrow channel towards Halifax, past George's and McNab's Islands, to tie up at Pier 21. A Red Ensign of Canada flew high above the long, chunky building. I have hazy memories of entering the vast hall of the Pier along with hundreds of my fellow travellers and waiting until my turn came to stand before an immigration officer, who checked my papers and stamped my British passport. I was now a Canadian Landed Immigrant. The date was September 26, 1962.

Some of our passengers disembarked here. But many, like myself, returned on board, and a few hours later the *Arkadia* went slowly about and headed out again to the open sea. The next two days saw us rounding the Gaspé Peninsula and ploughing up into the vast mouth of the St. Lawrence. As we approached Quebec City the shoreline edged closer on each side, and we could see settlements of red wooden houses, and docks, the grey spires of churches and deciduous trees without number, their leaves just beginning to turn.

Quebec City, when we finally reached it, was a wonder, beetling on the hill above us like a mediaeval walled town. We were allowed to land and stroll about for a few hours, and I remember being amazed at how unlike it was to the modern Canada I was expecting. An old city, and a French city. I was glad I had spent that year in France, and felt oddly at home.

A few hours more back on board, and we reached our final destination: the Port of Montreal. We disembarked around eight in the morning. There must have been friendly goodbyes, especially with Andrès my Polish cabin-mate, with whom I had done some entertaining on board, accompanying his saxophone on the ship's piano. I can't think what music we had in common. Perhaps *Blue Moon*.

An hour or two later, my baggage rounded up and transported to the station – I suppose by taxi – I had boarded my first Canadian train, wondering at its sleek silver sides and high platform. I remember nothing of the rail journey except our arrival at Toronto's Union Station, where I was relieved to be met by my dear and only Canadian friends, Bill and Jane Glassco. Coming up into the main concourse I was startled by the assured massiveness, the stone-clad classicism of the place with its almost absurdly high, coffered ceiling.

Bill drove us back in his Volkswagen Beetle to their apartment on the ground floor of a redbrick house on Madison Avenue in Toronto's Annex, a cluster of quiet, leafy streets north of Bloor Street and east and west of Spadina Avenue. I was shown to their guest room, and Bill carried in my two large suitcases. I had arrived.

Bill had been at Worcester College Oxford with me back in 1958, where we had been part of the Worcester Buskins, the

College's drama club. A couple of years ahead of me, and like me reading English, he was treasured among our troupe because of his superb piano-playing and his ability to write catchy tunes. Because of our musical interests we had become good friends, and it was Bill who earlier in the summer had suggested to me that I should come to Canada for a year, and try my luck.

Bill generously assured me I could stay with them until I found other accommodation. But their son Benjamin was less than a year old, and his parents were coping with all the usual stresses of dealing with a first-born. So a week or so later I set off down the street, having seen a 'Room for Rent' sign in the window of a massive house not fifty yards away from Bill and Jane's. The room I was shown into was tucked under the eaves at the top of two flights of stairs, its window looking straight into another one in the next-door house not more than four feet away (I remember having been already amazed at how these large Victorian houses in Toronto were all sitting cheek by jowl with one another on narrow lots). I would be sharing the bathroom. The kitchen, which I would also share with the other roomers, was far away down in the basement. The arrangement was not perfect. But the landlord and his wife were Italian, warm and friendly, and the rent was modest: $8 a week, payable in advance. I took the room, and in less than twenty-four hours had moved out of the Glasscos and into my own place.

It was at this still point, established in my own space for the first time on this vast new continent, and thousands of miles away from the life I had been living, that I experienced what immigrants throughout history must have felt. In the Britain I had left I had known and been known by countless people. I could find my way with ease through many of its counties and towns and cities. I knew its politics, its accents, its ways of dressing, its class preoccupations, its weather, and the price of a pint. I felt confident in the love of my family and friends. And now, in what seemed little more than a blink of an eye (I was glad it had been a sea-journey and not a flight), I found myself alone in a strange country, in a city where I knew just two people. I understood nothing more of Canada than the lumberjack caricature I had picked up over the years. Everything was to explore and to discover.

But there was something more. The realization hit me that if I did nothing in this new world I found myself in, if I stayed alone in the cocoon of this little room, I would slowly rot away, and no one the wiser or sadder. The existential idea that persons had no essence and were identifiable only by their deeds became suddenly relevant and real. As far as Canada was concerned, at this moment I was nothing. I did not exist. My life to come in this place, and the way it would be shaped, lay entirely in my own hands.

It was perhaps in response to this sense of isolation that I almost immediately ordered a telephone, which arrived two days later. I also enlisted with a message company – in those days, when you went out, you had to call the company and ask them to take your line and its messages. An extravagance, yes, but if I was to be in touch with my new country it was the only way.

And now for the first time, from my new viewpoint outside it, I saw the world of my life up to this moment as a single traveller's bundle: like Dick Whittington's as he trudges towards London carrying his scant belongings at the end of a stick over his shoulder. Whatever I was able to do here, to make my way, would have to come out of whatever skills and knowledge and will I had acquired and brought with me. What was in my bundle? What were the resources I was bringing to this new land? It was time for what in later years we would call a diagnostic.

I had experience as an actor, with apparently some superior

talent in the comic line – an ability to make audiences laugh. I was musical, had written songs and sung them, could read music and play the piano at a modest level. I had - so I had often enough been told - a melodious speaking voice as well as a good singing voice. But these skills and talents had been tested only in the world of school and university – or the army! I had no professional training as an actor or musician: no professional credentials of any sort.

I had a fair capacity in the English language, and could speak and write it more or less articulately. I even had some reputation at home as a wit, although I was soon to find out that wit in one culture can be downright rudery in another.

I retained small Latin and less Greek from my years studying the classics, but could sketch for you the histories of ancient Greece and Rome and their literatures. I also had a fair grasp of the canon of English literature, from Beowulf to Eliot. I had read widely, although I think not deeply.

I could speak French ('French French' as opposed to québecois) with reasonable competence, and could read it comfortably, though with a somewhat restricted vocabulary.

On the social level, I was perhaps especially lucky, in that my life experience – my parents' hotel, my many years of boarding school, my two years in the army, and my year in France – had enabled me to be very comfortable with people of all kinds. I could meet strangers and know how to speak to them. I was able to make friends. I smiled easily, and enjoyed laughing. I had been told, often enough to believe it, that I had 'charm': that capacity, picked up maybe from my school at Radley, for sensing the feelings and thoughts of others and responding with care and attention. It could be said too that I had 'taste', if by this is meant a sense of proportion, an avoidance of unseemliness, an ear for the right moment. That kind of taste, like charm, could of course be an impediment as well as a gift.

I was, I believe, good-looking in an English way – high forehead, big nose – and had a fair amount of physical and mental energy, determination and tenacity. I had some confidence in myself: a belief that I could make something of my life. And I believed that whatever I did not know I could easily learn.

These were some of my qualities. It is interesting that the one I am putting last – that I had a Bachelor of Arts degree in English Literature from the renowned University of Oxford – would now be considered my only qualification, because it was the only one that could be recorded on a piece of paper. The rest were vague, numinous gifts, which I could reveal and test only by displaying them.

And what were my deficits – as we should now say?

My rarefied upbringing had made me unworldly. I had little knowledge of business or finance. I had no experience of salesmanship and in fact found the whole idea of pushing a product – even, or perhaps especially, when the product was myself – wholly distasteful. I was not by nature a hustler: at least, not yet.

Brought up among so many people of kindness and generosity, I believed that everyone was well intentioned, that all lies were white. I had no real knowledge of practised malevolence among men or women, no experience of the demonic. That was to come.

For all my vaunted self-confidence, I had moments of crippling self-doubt, when my world entirely caved in on me. I would wake up at three in the morning and be beset by nightmares of disaster and shame, in which all hopes and plans would be blasted, and I would want to sink into the floor. By dawn, I was usually myself again.

Sexually I was still a conundrum even to myself, although I had determined as part of my new life in the New World to put my confusion behind me and find the girl of at least some of my dreams. For all this willed planning, I still found myself beset by the sight of beauty in both sexes, and this rattled me, though not to the point of paralysis.

So, Canada, this is what I am offering you, warts and all: not a bad bundle of possibilities, all things considered! Thus I thought. I also realized what an enormous advantage I already had in knowing English, and how much of a burden my cabin mate Andrès — and hundreds of our fellow immigrants on the *Arkadia* — had to take on before they could pick up anything more than manual or service work.

But my advantages didn't stop there. My brief time at Bill and Jane Glassco's — and I continued to see them regularly after I moved out — had already taught me that though I knew only these two people in all of Canada, they were extremely valuable people to know. Jane was the daughter of chartered accountant Walter Gordon, senior partner in the family accounting firm of Clarkson, Gordon, who had just launched himself on a political career. He and his wife lived on Chestnut Park in Rosedale, which I soon learned was one of the most expensive and desirable districts in Toronto. They also owned a farm outside the city, with fields and lakes. Bill's father Grant Glassco, also an accountant, was president of Brazilian Traction (soon to be Brascan), the old and wealthy Canadian company which at that time owned and ran Brazil's transportation and hydro networks. He had been commissioned in 1960 by the reigning Diefenbaker government to head up a commission: the Glassco Royal Commission on Government Administration. Grant and his wife Willa lived in a spacious apartment on Poplar Plains Road. They also had a farm outside Toronto, with a couple of hundred acres, a fine herd of Aberdeen Angus cattle, a swimming pool, and two houses.

Interestingly, the Glasscos were a prominent Progressive

Conservative family, and the Gordons were equally prominent Liberals. So the marriage of Bill and Jane, at which Liberal leader Lester Pearson had proposed the toast to the bridal couple, had been something of a Montague-Capulet affair. Party loyalties in Canada at this social level, I learned, were almost ancestral.

Bill was cast somewhat out of the mould of his wealthy and business-oriented family. When he had returned from Oxford in 1959 he had enrolled in a Ph.D. program in English, which was now nearing completion: he was writing a dissertation on the mediaeval poet John Skelton. He was also attached to Victoria College at the University of Toronto, where he taught a course or two, and it wasn't long before he invited me to eat with him at the College's High Table. There I had a chance to meet several of the English faculty, including Victoria's celebrated principal, Northrop Frye – at that time Canada's most famous English scholar, and indeed a most famous Canadian, whose work on criticism and on Blake I had studied at Oxford.

Before long Bill took me to meet his parents for dinner on Poplar Plains, and a week or two later drove me out to the Glassco farm, nestled in a happy valley near King, and closed in on each side by maple woods turning now into their fall glory. At some point too we visited Jane's family in their country retreat, and I had my first encounter with Walter Gordon, whose wit and charm were immediately apparent. Mrs Gordon's qualities in that direction were less obvious, and I later learned that Jane and her mother were often at odds. 'Two queen bees', as my mother used to say. They were both powerful, even willful personalities. Jane, though, had the most enchanting smile, and was kind and generous.

Having urged me to come to Canada, Bill evidently felt almost an obligation to help me get into the swim of things. It was soon clear that his connections went beyond Toronto's high society, and

I was introduced to friends of his at the CBC radio building on Jarvis Street, including Bob Weaver, who ran a literary program, was interested in new writers, and edited an important literary journal, *The Tamarack Review*; and also the formidable Esse Jungh, radio drama's most accomplished producer. Somehow I also found my way to CBC Television's music and drama department, which occupied the second floor above Basil's Restaurant and Grill, on the southeast corner of Gerrard Street and Yonge. This was a buzzing hive of activity: the CBC at that time presented an astonishing number of television dramas and concerts, all performed live in front of the cameras. The large, low-ceilinged central area was lined with the offices of the Corporation's television director/producers, their distinguished (and all male) names on the doors: Mario Prisek, George McCowan, Norman Campbell, Daryl Duke, David Gardner and Perry Rosemond, among others. Outside each man's office sat his (female) assistant hurriedly typing away at a new play script, to be ready for rehearsing the next day or the next week. The noise of clacking typewriters was almost deafening – I only now realize how long ago that sound disappeared from our office worlds. The script assistant also served as her producer's guard-dog, keeping eager actors at bay. The trick I soon learned was to try and make friends not with the bosses but with their guard-dogs, who in their quiet way wielded considerable influence: "You might like to take a look at so-and-so – she seems just right for that small part…"

The place was abuzz with would-be performers, who were allowed to rove around and socialize. I soon got to know some of the regulars, and we would gather together below in Basil's for coffee after our visits, swopping news of the latest possibilities. "I hear Daryl Duke is looking for burly young guys for his battle scenes…" – that kind of thing.

I suppose Bill was peddling me as an actor and reader, but also as a writer, editor and even as a very green Oxford scholar. He also knew that I had brought very little money with me to Canada, and that I was increasingly in need of employment. So it was after these many introductions, and entirely due to Bill, that some time in October I landed my first Canadian job.

Bill called one day to tell me that his father wanted me to meet with him at his office in downtown Toronto, somewhere midway up the flagship building of the Canadian Imperial Bank of Commerce. The CIBC tower was at that time the tallest building in Canada – and also, it was said, in the whole British Commonwealth. As you look at it now, nestling like a humble stone puppy-dog among the dizzily high glass towers of Bay Street, you wonder how that could ever have been so. But it was, and I was properly awed to be entering its revolving doors and ascending its sleek, old-fashioned brass elevators. I think they even had human operators.

Grant Glassco was a tall, big-built and paunchy businessman in his late sixties, with reddish face, small grey moustache and receding hair, and with a formidable aura about him that made even his son Bill nervous. He had a natural air of authority, and there was a gleam in his eye that told you he had a temper and would not suffer fools too gladly. But he had fine manners and considerable old-fashioned charm when so disposed. He took little time to let me know the reason for my visit. He was in the final stages of putting together his Royal Commission report, and needed an editor for two of the six volumes. One of these dealt with agriculture, the other with the CBC, and both needed to be trimmed down and checked for spelling, grammar and style. Bill had suggested I could do the job: would I like to work with him on the volumes?

I readily accepted the offer, especially after he asked me whether I would find $25 a day an acceptable wage. I secretly hugged myself with amazement at the generous stipend, which more or less corresponded to what I earned in a laborious five-day week driving my builder's-merchant truck back in Oxford during the summer vacation. I left the office with two large bundles of galley proofs, and with an agreement to meet again in a week's time. As a humble suitor begging for the Corporation's favour on my regular jaunts to her office above Basil's, I was amused now to be collaborating in a report that was intensely critical of the way the whole enterprise was being run. I was, of course, sworn to confidentiality.

My visit to Victoria College also paid off. An English professor, a Shakespeare scholar named David Hoeniger, needed someone to help read and grade his students' written work. Bill put me in touch with him, and I visited him at his house round the corner from the College, emerging with my first package of twenty or thirty essays, to be assessed and commented on at $3 an essay. Not a lordly amount, but it added up, and since a dollar in those days bought you a beer or a loaf of bread or even a bowl of soup in a restaurant, I considered myself, with my two jobs, more or less in clover.

Meanwhile, I was getting to know my way round Toronto by bus and streetcar, and by the one subway line which ran up and down Yonge Street – the Bloor Street line was still under construction. The city at that time, for me at least, ended more or less at Eglinton Avenue in the north, at Jane in the west, and at the newly completed Bayview Expressway in the east. I remember marvelling when Mr Glassco told me he was in discussion with City Hall about how to preserve his farm outside King as parkland when Toronto grew to swallow it up: it seemed inconceivable to me that the city could ever expand so far. In the words of the Queen of Sheba, "The half was not told me" – his farm might now be almost considered downtown.

I became very familiar with the area around Bloor Street and Spadina Avenue, the intersection that was no more than five minutes' walk away from my room. There was a small grocery there, and a hardware store. On the corner was a branch of the Bank of Nova Scotia, and it was not long before I dropped in and opened an account to deposit my modest earnings. A few yards down Spadina stood the red-brick headquarters of the YMHA. I had never heard of the Hebrew Association, and assumed it was off limits to me as a Gentile, but a few months later found I was able to join, and regularly played squash at its two courts. Next to the grocery was the local restaurant, the Varsity Grill, and since my cooking skills at that time never went beyond breakfast I soon became a regular there, enjoying the vast portions which were served up at all Canadian eating-places in those days, and which amazed anyone coming from still ration-conscious England. Huge piles of potato chips, which I was learning to call French fries; hamburgers two or three inches high 'with everything'; mounds of greasily-battered cod, and all dishes accompanied by the statutory 'tangy cole slaw.' A hefty slice of apple pie, with a square of Cheddar and a globe of vanilla ice cream, finished off the meal – and all for four or five dollars if I remember. I did not starve.

It's worth noting that Toronto in 1962 had many eateries of the 'greasy spoon' variety, like the Varsity Grill, but very few restaurants offering what now would be called fine dining. You could eat well and cheaply at the Chinese restaurants west of Spadina below College. But if you wanted to eat more expensive fare you went to the hotels, like the Prince Arthur Room at the Park Plaza. The only ethnic restaurants I remember were the Chez Paris on Bloor Street (also a night-club and open until the shockingly late hour of eleven), La Chaumière in a charming old house somewhere off Jarvis, the gloomy Balkan on Elm just west of Yonge, and the freshly-opened Viking Restaurant at Yonge and Wellesley, where you could be served Danish open sandwiches and good coffee. When you look today at the bemusing wealth of eating-places in Toronto (or any other large city), you realize how people nowadays spend their money in ways which were simply not available then. Even then, though, things were beginning to change. The Italian influence was starting to make itself felt in the west and northwest of the city; the Greeks were beginning to enliven Danforth. And as early as 1948 Honest Ed Mirvish had opened his cheerfully vulgar store on the edge of downtown, at Bloor and Bathurst, drawing folks like a magnet from all walks of life for his astonishing deals and the shouting, self-mocking slogans plastered over his building: "DON'T GO SOMEWHERE ELSE AND GET ROOKED: COME TO HONEST ED'S!!!"

For the prosperous old Toronto families among whom I had by chance landed, this vulgarity was a source of contempt. But then Toronto still at that time belonged to them, and was a very restrained, God-fearing and even dull place – and more or less (as they say) closed on Sundays. They had their private clubs – like the conservative York Club on Bloor of which Mr Glassco was a member: but eating out even for them was something of a luxury, and shopping for clothes meant going to department stores: Holt Renfrew on Bloor, or more democratically to Eatons or Simpsons at Yonge and Adelaide – or to the other Eatons at College and Yonge. Summer weekends were spent at their hobby farms outside the city, or in cottage country up north.

As a new immigrant trying to make his way, I lived in something of a schizoid world. Through the Glasscos I was privileged to rub shoulders from time to time with the wealthy and highly anglophile circles which still ruled Toronto, among whom I was the engaging young Oxford man who could charm and entertain them, and whom they welcomed into their houses. But I was also making friends among the down-and-out actors at Basil's: mostly (but by no means all) young people who were struggling to find a toehold in the entertainment world, and living in rooms, or in cheap apartments in shabby, Bohemian places like Yorkville. There was no unemployment insurance for actors, only the dole: I remember one who had himself listed as a 'shepherd', searching diligently but unsuccessfully for work in this line at the Employment Exchange each week, and therefore successfully drawing assistance until such time as the next leaderless flock happened to clatter in to the city.

Over breakfast I also got to know my two fellow roomers at 6, Madison Avenue. They were both simple old fellows, and I think had been there for some years. One was Cyril, a sweet little man, very kindly, very grey and very poor. The other, a Second World War veteran with a steely crew cut, was somewhat strange. We shared pots and pans in the communal basement kitchen, and I had noticed that before using the huge cast-iron frying pan he would clean it very carefully. Then he would clean it again. And again. The same with every knife, fork and spoon. A few months later he started taking showers in the middle of the night - for as long as an hour and a half at a time. One night an ambulance came and took him away. I had met my first anal obsessive-compulsive, though it was years before I knew such a phrase. Psychological disorders of that kind had not yet made their way into the general consciousness: at least not into mine.

I soon became aware that while the good people of Victoria College, and also the circles in which the Glasscos moved, had respect for the young Oxford man with his articulacy and smartish English accent, there were other less privileged Canadians by 1962 who were becoming increasingly resentful of the way Englishmen had been making their way to 'the colonies' for a couple of centuries, and then strutting around as though the place owed them a living. There were of course British doctors, teachers and other professional men, whom Canadians certainly had need of. These were generally appreciated, since for a long time there had been so few opportunities for Canadians to gain the required training in their home country, and there was a perpetual shortage. But there were also bounders who seemed to think that the mere fact that they were Englishmen was enough for them to be looked up to. And, worse, there were some well-educated Canadians who unconsciously or not thought of themselves as intellectually inferior to someone from the old country. The year I arrived, though, things were definitely on the move, and in fact I had turned up just at the moment when Canadian cultural nationalism was beginning to make headway. There were pockets of it at the CBC, and I was aware that my accent was an impediment when the one or two Canadian dramas being produced were looking for actors. But there was still a heavy dose of British and European classics being served up to the Canadian public, and English vowel sounds and clipped syllables were for some reason thought perfectly acceptable, not just in British plays but in the works of Ibsen or Chekhov.

The live theatre was something different again. Less than ten years before, Canada had begun to play host to one of the most remarkable theatrical enterprises ever launched anywhere. Tyrone Guthrie had been inveigled over the Atlantic to the little railway and market town of Stratford, three hours' drive west of Toronto, and in the summer of 1953 had opened the Stratford Shakespeare Festival in a circus tent. Guthrie had been keen to absorb as much Canadian talent as he could find, and many Toronto actors had auditioned for him and been accepted into the company. But Guthrie had also attracted a fair number of British actors, who had come for a summer season or two and decided to settle. A handful of these actors were now living in the city during the winter months, and naturally there was some indignation when they seemed to grab so many of the good roles on television.

Guthrie had left the Festival in 1955, and his place had been taken by the young and consummately English director Michael Langham. Langham's early years at Stratford had been difficult, we heard, because Guthrie had been loved as well as feared, and no one could possibly fill his shoes. But Langham had persevered and taught himself a great deal, and by the early 1960s was beginning to be recognised as a director of some genius who had an increasing command of the demands of Stratford's splendid but tricky thrust stage. As artistic director of the biggest, most professional theatre company in Canada – a company that had attracted the attention of distinguished critics from south of the border as well as Britain – he was in fact just becoming accepted as the tsar of the Canadian theatre. His name was mentioned in hushed tones by our Basil's group. Some had auditioned for him and found him arrogant and forbidding. But there was no doubt of his almost godly status.

The 1962 Stratford summer season was well over by the time I set foot in Canada, and in Toronto itself there was at that time only one theatre company mounting a full winter season of plays. This was the Crest Theatre on Mount Pleasant, between St. Clair and Eglinton. It had been founded some ten years earlier by Murray and Donald Davis, with their sister Barbara Chilcott, and was being run at that time by Murray Davis. Since my experience was entirely in live theatre, it was natural that besides sniffing around CBC's television and radio drama departments I would be keeping an eye out for the possibility of auditioning for the Crest. Some time late in October I saw a notice of auditions taking place there for a play by Jean Giraudoux called *The Enchanted*. I booked for an audition:

it was to be the first professional audition of my life. I don't remember whether I went to the library to read the play: probably not. But on the day appointed I took the subway up to St. Clair, and then the streetcar which slid east along St. Clair and then turned north onto Mount Pleasant.

The play was to be in the hands of an up-and-coming young director called Leon Major. He and Murray welcomed me pleasantly, and then sat side by side in the darkened auditorium. I remember nothing of the audition, but I will never forget what followed. When my stint was over, I left the theatre by the front doors and crossed over Mount Pleasant to wait at the streetcar stop for my journey back home. It was while I was there that I suddenly saw Murray emerging from the theatre, and then crossing the road right to where I was standing. I wondered whether he was taking the streetcar too. But no: he said, "Michael, we thought we would put you out of your misery right away. We would like you to take the part of The Ghost in the play. Will you do it?"

"I certainly will," I stuttered: "Thank you very much, sir."

"Good," said Murray. "Rehearsals start next Tuesday. See you then." We shook hands and he returned to the theatre.

I more or less danced my way back home. I don't ever remember being quite so elated as at that moment: I had been accepted for the first time into the theatre profession. The Ghost was a small role, but he had one important scene towards the end of the play, when the young ingenue appears to be falling in love with him. The ingenue, I later found out, was to be played by a young actress from Winnipeg, and freshly out of the very first intake of the recently founded National Theatre School. Her name was Martha Henry. The rest of the cast included Joseph Shaw and his wife Mary Savidge; Norman Welsh; Tudi Wiggins; Barbara Chilcott; and a young man called Henry Hovenkamp.

Though my role was small, it required me to join Actors' Equity, and I spent the rest of the week working through this process, as well as discussing with my other employers how I was going to continue to carry out my assignments for them. It would not be too difficult: given the small part I was playing, there would be many days when I would not be called in to rehearse at all.

I remember little of the opening days of rehearsal. We no doubt sat around and read the play together and talked about it in a rather bemused way: French drama was so very different from the plays we were used to. Anyway, I was concentrating intensely on the Ghost, determined to make it a starring role if I possibly could. I was not particularly helped by never having had an acting class in my life – I knew nothing of the actor's methods for 'creating a character'. But in my usual slapdash style I was confident I would be able to rely on native intelligence and ability.

It was around the third or fourth day that our director Leon Major stopped me in the hallway after lunch-break and said: "Michael, you've been to Oxford. What's this play all about?" It seems an innocuous enough question, but I cannot overstate what effect it had on me. First, of course, I had been assuming all along that Leon knew exactly what the play was about, and like the rest of the cast I had put myself trustingly into his hands, thinking only of my Ghost. Now here he was suggesting he didn't really know what we were all doing and where we were heading! But secondly, and more importantly, once I got over my surprise I started to think seriously and for the first time about the answer to his question. What *was* the play all about?

I'm not sure how much help I was able to be to Leon, but I will always be thankful to him, because his question set me thinking in a new way. How did the play fit together? What was the author trying to say? What were the relative importances of the different characters, and did they change and develop through the play? Was there some kind of a climax somewhere? Even when studying classic plays as part of my Oxford requirements, I had never looked at any of them from this practical, 'sawdusty' point of view. In other words, I began for the first time to think not as an actor or a scholar, but as a director.

In the end I doubt that either cast or audience ever quite knew what the play was trying to say, and there was a certain amount of cynicism about it backstage, with Joe Shaw's sardonic wit setting the tone. Reviewers were also confused, and there was a general feeling that the play should never have been selected. But we soldiered on. My Ghost was certainly no star, but I believe I was at least competent. And I much enjoyed making friends with my fellow-actors, many of whom I would continue to know and work with for years. Martha Henry's beauty and poise on stage was universally acknowledged.

By the time *The Enchanted* breathed its last puzzled breath, Christmas was almost upon us. The Glasscos were overwhelmingly generous and kind over the holiday season, bringing me into their homes as one of the family, and even giving me expensive gifts – something I was in no position to reciprocate. By this time too I had got to know other people. My Oxford friend Robin Grove-White had put me in touch with his Irish uncle, who it turned out was something of a literary presence in Toronto: his name was Kildare Dobbs and he had just published his autobiography, *Running To Paradise*. Kildare and his wife Mary McAlpine had had me more than once to their house on Duplex. Through my CBC contacts I had also met a young couple called Patrick and Joan Lyndon. Patrick was short, fair-haired and irremediably English, with a lugubriously long face and a mournfully comic wit to go with it. He had been a piano prodigy as a child, and had even given a solo concert at Wigmore Hall in London at the age of twelve. He had gone on to my own Oxford college, Worcester, where like me he read English, though tutored not by the brilliant Christopher Ricks but by his predecessor, the redoubtable Colonel Wilkinson. Patrick had emigrated to Canada eight or ten years earlier, and had first found work at a radio station in Cornwall. He had then taught for a while at Upper Canada College, but now worked in the magazine publishing business: he had not touched a piano since his teens. Joan was Canadian, dark-haired and attractive and with a subtle wry wit of her own. She had worked at the CBC as an editor before their marriage. They had recently started a young family, and had two young daughters.

Half a century later Patrick described being introduced to me at a Toronto party late in 1962 and clearly finding in me an intellectual soulmate. "I could not stop talking and listening to you," he said: "It was like meeting The Paraclete." Coming from Patrick with his ever-morose and world-weary view of life, this effusiveness was astonishing. "Joan felt the same way," he added. I am still not quite sure what was meant by these compliments (and had to turn to a dictionary to find that the Paraclete was nothing less than the Holy Ghost!). But there could be no doubt that I had managed to put a version of myself together at that time which gave a highly positive impression to others. Perhaps I also enjoyed being one of my kind: almost all my life – and especially at Oxford – I had been surrounded by supremely witty, intelligent and articulate English people, against whom I was, albeit unconsciously, measuring myself. We had all honed our social skills in conversation and debate over our young years, and had developed a good deal of assurance and even well-mannered cockiness – as well as a fair dose of self-regard. I had left all these scintillating young people behind in England, and found in Canada that I was able to interact with everyone I met with that same assurance, but without such competition. This would have been insufferable to Canadians, who it seemed were very much inclined to think little of themselves, if I hadn't also brought along that sensitivity known as 'charm'. I was very aware of how easy it was for Englishmen to throw their weight about when abroad, and was not disposed to do the same. In fact my genuine interest in other people, as well as a certain amount of (not entirely false) self-deprecation, made for a good social cocktail. I was beginning to feel at home.

CHAPTER TWO

A MAGIC DOOR OPENS

It was 1963, and my first Canadian winter was now in full spate. Antonio had long since climbed his ladder to affix my heavy wooden storm window three floors up, with its slot which I could open and close for air in my overheated room. I remember my astonishment at the sidewalks piled up with snow from the streets, and the black slush it turned into. But most of all I recall waiting wretchedly at unsheltered streetcar stops with the wind biting through my trouser legs at 4° above zero (minus 20° Celsius, but we were still using Fahrenheit then). I had not heard of long johns underwear at that time, and in fact have never worn a pair in my life, but I could have done with them in those early, straitened years. And how warm it was whenever you were inside, from private homes to banks or department stores! I was also intrigued at the way the large buildings downtown gushed clouds of white steam from their roofs. Cold was something I had been brought up with and was thoroughly used to – and loathed. But although outdoor temperatures in England never dropped to anything like those in Canada, the English in those days never really heated the interiors of their homes or public buildings. As a result, when you went outside your hands and feet were not really warm to begin with, and soon, with the flimsy gloves and boots we wore, became numb with both cold and damp. I was finding that in Canada you were always warm, if not stifling, indoors, and when you ventured out you stayed warm, inside your outdoor gear of fleece-lined jackets and cosy boots lined with fur or fake-fur. You also learned not to linger in the cold, but to dash from oasis to warm oasis. I often said, and it is still true, that I had been colder in England than ever in Canada.

Some time that winter, which saw the blowing up and eventual cooling down of the Cuban missile crisis, I took the Greyhound Bus down to New York, where my close Worcester friend John Weston was serving three months as a very junior Foreign Office staffer at the British Mission to the United Nations. My sister Jo was also there, as was my old schoolfriend Peter Cook, preparing for *Beyond The Fringe*'s transfer to Broadway. All these dear people I met during my few days in the terrifyingly cold city; it must have been February. I seem to remember John bringing me into a meeting of the General Assembly of the UN, and I certainly recall walking through the East Village with Peter and stopping inside the door of a small club to see and listen to a jazz pianist: his name was Thelonious Monk. I was awed by New York's almost superhuman energy, the sprouting of its skyscrapers, the thrusting of its traffic, the driving pace of people on its sidewalks.

Back in Toronto, I was hired as an extra in my first television drama – starring Christopher Newton, I remember (later to become the distinguished director of the Shaw Festival at Niagara-on-the-Lake), though I have no memory of the play: *Billy Liar,* perhaps. Later in the year I was a soldier extra in a campy black-leather production of *Antigone* directed by a young Peter Boretski, with Joseph Wiseman as Creon. These productions were both prepared down in the CBC's cavernous rehearsal building on Sumach Street. Their chief stars, it seemed to me, were their designers, because the fact that the shows were broadcast live meant that the set had to accommodate continuous action from scene to scene with almost no breaks. This was true of all CBC productions at that time – though for not much longer.

I completed my editing work for Grant Glassco early in the new year, receiving my last amazing pay-cheque for a couple of hundred dollars. And I continued to ferry back and forth from Professor Hoeniger's house delivering graded essays and carting away a fresh load. He seemed pleased with my work. But this had become my only source of income, and I was keen for a break and a less dreary occupation.

It was some time in March of 1963 that I was granted an audition with television producer David Gardner, who was casting for two short British plays, each of them starring the very fine Canadian comic actor Eric House. One of these plays was *A Resounding Tinkle* by the English playwright N.F. Simpson, whom I had met once briefly with Peter Cook, back in England. There are only three characters in this 'absurdist' play, but at one point they stop their madness to listen solemnly to a religious radio broadcast by a ninety-seven-year-old Father Gerontius. This was the role I auditioned for, and since it was very much in the British style I knew, I gave them my comic vocal old-man rendition, complete with mock-religious chanting. David responded warmly and offered me the part. I found out that he had asked the well-known Elmer Iseler Singers – already engaged to perform as a Salvation Army choir in the other play – to provide some choral responses for me. This was exciting. But what really surprised me was when he decided that Father Gerontius should appear not on radio as in the original script, but on the household's black-and-white television set. It was clear that at the age of twenty-five I didn't exactly look the part. But David assured me that the make-up people could do wonders, and I was able to hang onto my role.

One blue-sky Sunday in late March I remember from that year, when Bill and Jane took me out to the Glassco farm to join in the sugar maple festivities. It was a family gathering, and Bill's sister Gay was there with her husband John Evans and their children. It was my first introduction to this very Canadian occasion, which was carried out in traditional style, with the sap being collected from one tree at a time in the maple grove around us and poured into a large square tank, with a fire blazing beneath it. Plaid lumber jackets, toques, mufflers and gloves kept us warm, and we all tasted the newly-distilled nectar, our breath steaming in the cold, sunny air. I was astonished at how much sap was needed to produce how little syrup.

Diefenbaker's minority Conservative government fell that same month, and in the run-up to the General Election of April 8th I found myself accompanying Jane Glassco canvassing from door to door for her father Walter Gordon's re-election in the riding of Davenport. I watched the results at the Gordons' home, which that evening was filled with ecstatic Liberal supporters, including hockey player turned politician Red Kelly and future cabinet minister Mitchell Sharp. The Liberals won, though short of a majority. Walter Gordon regained his seat, and a few days later was appointed as Lester Pearson's Minister of Finance. I wondered at being so close to Canada's political centre of power so soon after arriving in the country.

Rehearsals for *A Resounding Tinkle* began later that month, and it was only then that I met the rest of the cast. Eric House, playing the hen-pecked Bro Paradocks, was short, dark and nervous, with the kind of sad face that well suited Simpson's deadpan humour.

Playing the hen-pecking Middie Paradocks was an even shorter actor, clearly English, shapely, with beautiful wide eyes and an infectious laugh. Her name was Helen Burns. The third character, though named Uncle Ted, was played (as the script calls for) by a woman dressed as a man. The part had been given to Patricia Collins: tall and leggy, attractive, thin-faced and blonde.

I suppose there are episodes in all our lives which we can point to as defining moments: a new way opens up, or a chance comment or unexpected encounter leads us on to some profound change. I had certainly had some lucky breaks in my first six months in Canada, and had been enormously helped by my influential friends. But on the set of *A Resounding Tinkle* I found myself in the midst of one such key moment. I became friends with Helen Burns.

Perhaps it began because we were both transposed from the country we still knew as home. Helen, who had spent several years hopping from one side of the Atlantic to the other, was apparently attracted to this reasonably bright young man who had so recently ventured over to Canada. Each day the little cast would go out for coffee or lunch at a restaurant nearby and have lively chats. But then one day, at the end of rehearsal, Helen asked whether I would like to join her that evening for an omelette at her apartment hotel on Jarvis. I was flattered and happy to accept.

I must have stumbled out of there some time between two and three in the morning, after six or seven hours of joyous talk and laughter from which I seemed unable to tear myself away. I was spellbound: a spell that has never been broken in the fifty and more years since that first close encounter. Helen was a consummate cook, a brilliant conversationalist, warm, uncannily intelligent and perceptive, charmingly wicked, enormously attractive and uproariously funny. All this I gathered that first evening. I was to get to know more, much more, of this extraordinary human being.

Helen evidently felt the same way about the magical fun we were having. Was there sexual attraction involved? Probably – on both sides. But it never occurred to me that I could have an affair with someone more than twenty years my senior. Besides, Helen was as far as I knew happily married. And by this time I had become very well aware of whom she was married to. Her husband was the bright star of Canada's Stratford: none other than its artistic director, Michael Langham.

From then on our work on *A Resounding Tinkle* was an unceasing delight. I became fascinated by the strange way Helen worked: by her mixture of imperious certainty and quick self-doubt. She was mysterious, unpredictable: her character was living a secret life, which we caught in odd glimpses. When she looked out of the window at the elephant that had been delivered to the house but which turned out to be the wrong size, she so clearly saw the elephant herself that we all saw it too. David Gardner was I think a little intimidated by her temperament, but he and all of us found her irresistibly funny. Eric House was funny too in his down-in-the-mouth way, but with far fewer flashes of unexpectedness. As for my own performance as Father Gerontius, it was buoyed up by Helen's pealing laughter in rehearsal, and I felt very much on home ground – even after three hours in the make-up studio being turned into a nonagenarian.

At some point when it was all over, and before Helen left town, we had a final dinner together. By this time she had told me that she thought that her Michael and I would get on well: it even turned out that before the war he had been to the same school in England, Radley College, that I had attended many years after him. She wanted to introduce us, and in fact issued me an invitation: why not come down to Stratford to stay with them at the beginning of July, when Michael would have finished re-staging

Cyrano de Bergerac and opened his *Troilus and Cressida*? I could see the plays while I was there. And Michael, his productions now staged, would be able to spend some time with us. It all sounded too good to be true, and from that time on I eagerly ticked off the days until my visit.

Meanwhile, other things were happening at Victoria College. I was invited to Northrop Frye's study one day to be shown a letter he had received, asking for his advice: the newly-founded Laurentian University in Sudbury was looking for someone to teach a course in their Summer School for six weeks, starting in the second half of July. Was I interested? If so he would put my name forward. Yes indeed, I thought and said: I was very much interested. Laurentian would pay my travel expenses and I think an accommodation allowance, as well as what seemed at the time a handsome fee. It was a chance to get out of the Toronto area and see another part of Canada. And it would keep my finances going a month or two longer.

A week or two later came more good news. Professor McLean, the head of Victoria's English Department, invited me on to his staff as an instructor for the coming academic year, to teach two courses. Would I consider it? This was a more difficult choice. I had decided firmly to myself that I was not going to become an academic; and besides, if I got too tied up with teaching I would not easily be able to take on acting assignments should they come along. At the same time the job would pay my way through the winter. I asked to think about it, and discussed it with Bill. And in the end I accepted. One encouragement was that I was asked to teach a new course which had been masterminded by Northrop Frye himself, and which exposed the students to a splendidly international selection of twentieth-century literature, including Golding's *Lord of the Flies*, Camus' *The Outsider*, Faulkner's *As I Lay*

Dying and Mauriac's *Nest of Vipers*. In 1963, in the University of Toronto's staid English Department yet, this was a remarkable innovation. And it meant I had some summer reading to get swiftly under my belt.

The July day finally came when I packed an overnight bag for Stratford and took the morning train down through the rolling agricultural land of Western Ontario under its summer haze. I was a mite nervous, but happy and excited to be seeing Helen again, and more or less confident that I would get on with her distinguished husband.

When I stepped off the train at Stratford station, Helen was there to meet me. We embraced, but I could tell at once that there was something wrong. Apparently the situation had changed: she had told me before that Michael was expecting to have time on his hands, having opened his two productions, since the third production of the Festival Theatre season, Shakespeare's little-known *Timon of Athens*, was to be directed by guest director Peter Coe. Getting Peter Coe to Stratford had been something of a coup: he had recently made his name with the first production of *Oliver!*, which had taken London by storm the previous year and was still playing in the West End. But yesterday Michael had received a call from Coe to say that *Oliver!* had just been picked up for Broadway, and that he would have to fly straight to New York to prepare the American production. So, very regretfully, he would not be available to come and direct *Timon* at Stratford. This had been a bombshell for poor Michael, exhausted from having just directed two productions back to back, because at this late stage there was no alternative: he would have to take over the play himself. Clearly Helen and Michael had had words, and Michael was not particularly pleased to have a young house guest he had never even met coming to stay just at this time. Helen said to me, "By all means come and stay, but I'm afraid we can only have you for a night or two because Michael will need every waking moment to work on the play."

Since the invitation had been only for a long weekend anyway, cutting it shorter was no great problem for me. We drove back to the Langham's stolid red-brick house on Trow Avenue, and Helen put together a salad lunch while we talked and talked and laughed and laughed, picking up seamlessly from our conversations of a few weeks earlier. I think we may have driven into town to do some shopping. But we were back well before five, when Michael was expected to return from the theatre. This was the meeting Helen had been so keen to organize, and I think she was as nervous as I, wanting it to go well.

Within a few minutes the front door opened, and in came Michael: slim, fair-haired, good-looking in an almost patrician way, and fashionably dressed. Helen introduced the two Michaels and we shook hands. Michael spoke immediately and all in one breath:

"Good to meet you have you read *Timon of Athens*?"

I said that I had read it once several years ago, but that I didn't really remember it at all.

"Here's a copy. Read it," he said, handing me the New Cambridge edition of the play. "I shall want a full report in twenty-four hours," he added with mock seriousness.

Twenty-four hours later, over a gin and tonic, Michael and I sat down in the living room, while Helen went off to the kitchen to prepare supper. I had stayed up late the night before to read the play, and had spent much of the day thinking and making notes.

Michael began by describing the production he had inherited at such short notice. Peter Coe had planned to create a modern-dress *Timon*. It was being designed by Stratford designer Brian Jackson and was set somewhere in the Levant in the 1920s, with the wealthy Timon to be played by John Colicos as a kind of Aristotle Onassis figure. Most remarkably, Coe had engaged the services of a rare musician to compose incidental music for the play: none other than Duke Ellington. Michael had spent the day with Brian, acquainting himself with the costume designs already prepared. He also went over the cast, making one or two changes. He as yet knew nothing of the music, but had talked with Duke on the phone, and arranged for him to come to Stratford in a few days.

We then began talking about the play. Michael, fresh from what was in fact his first close reading of it, was evidently unhappy at the obscurity, the opaqueness of much of that particular text, and aware of its unsatisfactory state, with obvious corruptions and some evidence of it having been a collaboration, perhaps with Thomas Middleton. He was afraid that the audience simply would not be able to follow some of the denser constructions, and the sometimes elaborate, almost metaphysical metaphors and images. We went through the first couple of scenes, analysing what people were actually saying to each other and trying to get to the nub of each moment. It was my first introduction to the Langham method: painstaking analysis followed by an astonishing way he had of transmuting the scene into a real life happening. He noted each character's every word and sentence, checked the notes for help in understanding odd usages and turns of phrase, and then went on to explore the nuance behind it all for signs of inner motives and intentions. More surprisingly for me, with my scholared reverence for the sacred text of the Bard, he occasionally wondered whether we could actually simplify some of those oblique constructions, to make the meaning more easily accessible to the modern ear. He was even ready to cut any word or phrase or line that he thought muddied the sense. I was shocked at the cavalier way he suggested these changes, but his intention was unassailable: he wanted the audience to understand what was being said so that they could follow the play without hindrance.

Clearly this approach was not one that could be taken with any Shakespeare text. No one would be happy with the re-writing of a loved and familiar play like *Hamlet* or *Othello*. But *Timon of Athens* was almost unknown and already an imperfect text: I seem to remember this was in fact its North American premiere as a professional production. Since no one except the occasional Shakespeare scholar knew the work, Michael felt confident that no one would be disturbed or even notice the re-writing.

The changes we contemplated of course interfered with the scansion of Shakespeare's iambic pentameters, and it was here I was able to help by working with him to arrange the simplified text so that it still retained its necessary five-beat rhythm. After my initial pull-back from such drastic alterations, I soon warmed to the job, and was able to put my academic familiarity with the language of the period at the service of the theatrical demands Michael was making. By the time Helen called us in to supper we had begun to evolve a way of working. We continued at it afterwards, until two or three in the morning.

So began a collaboration which I think surprised both of us. Michael, who had trained after school to become a solicitor, and who had then spent almost the whole period of the war itself as a POW, had never been to university, and was I think a little insecure in the world of academe. I was able to provide some scholarly basis for what he was wanting to do, and it was soon evident that Michael wished our work to continue. The idea of my staying with them only a couple of days was quietly scrapped, and evening after evening we worked through the text of the play from beginning to end, keeping ahead of his rehearsals when they began a day or two later. We re-wrote a great deal of it, and I suppose eliminated some of its subtleties. And all the while we were becoming familiar with a remarkable piece of theatre.

We reached a crux in the third act when the character Alcibiades is suddenly arraigned and banished for a murder of which there had been no previous mention: it's a famous *lacuna*. If you are editing such a play you can record the fact, puzzle over it and suggest alternative reasons for the corrupted text. But if you are directing the play you have to solve the problem dramatically. So, between Michael and myself a murder was arranged. Michael set a scene outside the opera house, with the audience emerging in evening dress. Alcibiades gets into an altercation with another gentleman. Swords come out, and the gentleman is run through, after which Alcibiades is arrested and marched away.

The scene needed a minimum of text, and I was able to concoct nine or ten lines of fake Shakespeare, which were eventually incorporated into the production. I was always gratified that not a single critic seemed to have spotted the impertinence.

The day came when 'the Duke' was due to arrive. He was no stranger to Stratford, having brought his orchestra more than once for concerts in the Festival Theatre, and had become very friendly with a female member of the Festival staff. But he had never written music for a Festival production before.

Duke flew into Toronto one afternoon, and a few hours later was delivered to the door of 19 Trow, where Michael and Helen welcomed him. I was introduced as Michael's assistant, and worked at being unobtrusive. Since the great man had arrived hungry, Helen whipped up one of her delectable omelettes, and we sat in the dining room to keep him company and watch him eat. And then, his supper over, we all walked over to the theatre, where Duke was to share some of the themes he had so far worked on. He sat at the clunky piano in the rehearsal room, with a select group of us sitting around as he played, in awe at the uniqueness of the occasion. Duke was strangely tentative, almost apologetic: "This is an idea I had for a kind of Gold theme. I don't know what you think, Michael…" I realized that he was in fact coping with a difficult situation, having worked on the play with Peter Coe and suddenly having to shift allegiance to a new director. But his charm and casual brilliance shone through, and Michael was of course captured, beginning to see how the period in which the play was set was going to be so surely stamped with Duke's authentic style.

In the end I was with the Langhams for nearly a week. I was kept well in the background the whole time, and not encouraged to attend rehearsals. There were moments when I had some workable idea for a scene and Michael took note of it, but it was clear that if he introduced it at next day's rehearsal it would be passed off as his own. Later he let me know that he would not feel able to acknowledge my help in the credits for the play in the printed program. None of this bothered me – I was so much honoured to be working alongside him, and learning infinitely from the experience. Helen was less easy about it. But she confided to me that over the years she had made major contributions to many of Michael's productions, and that none of her *aperçus* were ever attributed to her when Michael made use of them. That's how he was, she said.

Though many hours were spent battling *Timon*'s text, there were also many, many enchanting hours spent with Helen - and with Michael too at odd moments when he allowed himself away from his work. It was high summer and the days were steamy. Sometimes at nine or ten in the cool evenings they would decide to go for a drive. We would nose out into the farmlands around Stratford, balmy with summer scents and edged by moonlight. And all the time, there and everywhere, we would talk.

Helen had been born a Cockney girl, 'in the house of a violin-maker' in Soho's Golden Square – where oddly enough my father was to be working a decade later. Her mother was of Russian origin, and her father worked in the garment trade. They were extremely poor. But she had shown promise on the stage, and when she left school at fifteen had auditioned for RADA, which awarded her a scholarship. She used to talk of her time there, and the visits they had from some of the great writers of the day, like George Bernard Shaw and TS Eliot. Her brother was working in Germany, and one summer holiday Helen went out to stay with him. It was just as Hitler was coming to power: she told me she had even heard him speak. It was years before she was prepared to admit to me (or even to herself, perhaps) that she was of Jewish descent – Burns was originally Bernstein – and I can only imagine how nervous she was in Germany, where the persecution of Jewish people was just getting under way.

Helen's performances while at RADA attracted attention, and when she left she was immediately offered regular work in the repertory theatres then dotted all over Britain. She had an astonishing presence on stage, and offstage her sparkling personality and wit soon made her many friends and drew many wooers: I believe she had a brief affair with an Indian prince, and was also married for a short time. This whole rich past of hers fascinated me; my own upbringing seemed so drearily conventional by contrast. Though uneducated in a formal sense, she had the ability to absorb knowledge and ideas without effort, and was blessed with an exceptional ear for language. Though she must have grown up in a poor Cockney milieu, she had learned at RADA to 'speak proper', and had developed a refined middle-class English accent. She had also acquired a certain middle-class snobbery, directed not so much at the working class from which she came as at anyone with social pretensions. I believe she found my own background as interesting as I found hers: even though fiercely proud of her own achievements and status in life, she was very aware of the social advantages of the 'public school' experience through which her own Michael and I had come. And I had the added allure of an Oxford degree. One way or another, and for whatever reason, Helen and I became the closest of friends. But it was an obvious pleasure for her that Michael and I were also developing a personal rapport through the work we were doing, and this spilled out into the many hours we all spent together during those rhapsodic days.

Although I was asked to keep away from rehearsals of *Timon of Athens*, it was not long before I was given a ticket to *Troilus and Cressida*, and had my first heady experience of Stratford's thrust stage. Guthrie's first Festival stage, in the circus tent of 1953, had by 1956 been enclosed within a tent-like circular building, containing a noble auditorium of over 2,000 seats. In 1962 Michael and Tanya Moiseiwitch had re-designed her original stage to facilitate movement across it, and the somewhat feminine form of the original classical centrepiece with its pillars and balcony had been rebuilt as a much more masculine, almost Doric structure. On stage left and right of the central pillars, strong entrances now led down four or five steps to the centre of the stage, and so on to the 'tunnel' opposite, making diagonal movement across the stage a powerful feature.

This was the stage that met my eyes as I walked into Stratford's Festival Theatre for the first time. Like so many others before and after me I was bewitched by the splendour of the place: the rich, warm wooden platform of the stage, lit by a golden glow, with the quietly chattering audience clustering around it in a huge semi-circle, and filling the balcony. My first experience of a dynamic thrust stage; my first experience of this strange and complex Shakespeare play; my first experience of a huge and powerful cast of strong, assured actors, led by Peter Donat (as Troilus) with William Hutt, Tony van Bridge, Leo Ciceri, Powys Thomas, Frances Hyland, Douglas Rain and many others; and featuring as Cressida the beautiful and talented Martha Henry, with whom I had acted at the Crest the previous year. It was also my first experience of a Langham production, and I was swept away by the speed, the swirl, the power of the action on stage, the clarity of the language, and the way he had been able to choreograph shifting character relationships so that you not only heard but saw their changing shapes. I returned to watch the same magic a night or two later in the very different play *Cyrano de Bergerac*, with John Colicos in the title role. This was a re-mount of the previous year's production, which had starred Paul Scofield, and it was made clear to me by the Langhams that Scofield in the role had been superior to Colicos. But I was dazzled enough.

It was still well before the opening night of *Timon of Athens* that I had to leave Stratford to set out for Sudbury and my stint at Laurentian University. By this time our friendship was beginning to flower, and Helen and Michael insisted that the moment I return from Northern Ontario I was to come straight back to Stratford – to see *Timon* but also to spend more time with them. I was ecstatically ready to oblige.

CHAPTER THREE

BRANCHING OUT

Sudbury, a major railway hub, had also been Canada's principal nickel-mining town for many years, and the effluent from INCO's chimneys and its flaming slag-heaps had long ago turned the rocky surrounding hills into moon-country, with hardly a scrap of vegetation: the ground black, the trees stunted. My Canadian friends warned me that it was 'the asshole of the Earth', so I was expecting little when I arrived one Saturday on the train, a five-hour ride north from Toronto. After a day or two being put up by friends of friends, I found myself a room close to the downtown, in a strange castellated house belonging to a warm and friendly Franco-Ontarian family. This was to be my home for the next six weeks.

Laurentian University is now a significant cluster of buildings on the southern shore of Lake Ramsey. But in 1963 things were very different. The University had been founded only two or three years earlier, bringing together Catholic, Anglican and United Church initiatives. The Collège du Sacré-Coeur, in the heart of the town, had started out as the central temporary home of the new institution. The new lakeside site for the campus had only recently been cleared for construction, and meanwhile classrooms had to be housed in a multitude of different temporary locations in the somewhat dodgy area of downtown Sudbury.

And this is why, on my first day of teaching, I was surprised to find myself entering a little door off a commercial street and climbing a narrow set of stairs to a long, low-ceilinged room above a pool-hall. When my twenty-five students arrived, I was further taken aback to discover that several of them were nuns – arrayed in the full habit of those days.

Despite my friends' dark warnings, I grew to embrace Sudbury during the short time I was there. I enjoyed the teaching. The townspeople were friendly and gregarious, and I even found myself in tune with the northern industrial ruggedness of the landscape, which reminded me of my time soldiering in the north of England. Memories stand out: sailing on Lake Ramsey; driving down to the French River with a young Dutch couple and spending the day in canoes paddling through true Northern Ontario wilderness; lively conversations with a gloomy communist professor, who was coming to doubt whether Canada would ever fulfill its destiny as a socialist country; sitting in the vast men-only tavern and shaking salt into our beer; and playing the piano at the reception after a Catholic wedding of members of my landlord's family – where I saw their Catholic priest in that now almost forgotten role as the unquestioned and universally respected leader of his flock.

But the over-riding memory which I took away with me, and have never lost, is a surreal one: teaching *King Lear* to a bevy of religious sisters, while from the pool hall below floats up the profane sound of gently-clicking balls.

I received notes from at least two of the nuns just before the final exam, promising they would say special prayers for me if I gave them a good grade. Tempting offers indeed, but I managed to ignore them.

By the time I returned to Stratford towards the end of August *Timon of Athens* had opened to acclaim, and I went to see it the first moment I had. All the stitching and fixing hours I had spent with Michael were recalled as I heard our text springing to life. John Colicos's tendency to oratorio had been firmly reined in by his director. Douglas Rain's cynical Epimantus, portrayed as a seedy, rain-coated journalist, was typecasting for this brilliant, somehow heartless-seeming actor. Peter Donat's Alcibiades was nobly put-upon.

But beyond all this was my amazement at the inventiveness of Michael's direction. He had taken on the production at ridiculously short notice, already strung out by the work on his two previous plays. Michael was a director who was used to meticulous preparation, and this time there was no chance of that: it was perhaps this very suddenness that had set him free. He had also put his own stamp on the concept he had inherited, setting one scene in a Turkish bath-house – all towels and steam – and later creating (from our cooked-up scenario) a stunning stage picture as the rich elite of Athens emerged from the opera-house to witness Alcibiades' swordfight. And the Duke's penetrating, rhythmic score placed us from beginning to end in that 1920s milieu of wealth, cynicism and betrayal.

There was only one critic who was deeply disturbed by the merry way we had tampered with the play script, and that was Robertson Davies – a member of the Stratford Board of Governors, and at that time better known as an unexceptional playwright than the renowned novelist he was soon to become. Rob's rebuke to Michael came in one of those elegant handwritten letters for which he was famous. He felt that the audience's intelligence had been insulted by our ironing out the airy abstractions of Shakespeare's original text, and that they would have been perfectly able to cope. He may have been right. But the production's accessibility in the form we gave it was also undeniable.

The Langhams had now been joined by their bright and quick fourteen-year-old son Christopher, whose term at school had finished at the end of July, and also for a few days by their London friend, the extraordinary Hungarian Dr. Tibor Csato. Tibor was treasured by them both because he was credited with having saved Michael's life a few years earlier, by correctly diagnosing his strange and repeated episodes of drastic internal haemorrhaging as an allergy to aspirin and quinine. Tibor had long been deliriously in love with Helen, and though this never seems to have led to anything physical, Helen had a flirtatious way of keeping her admirers about her, like the first Queen Elizabeth. Perhaps I was just another one. Michael and Helen would tease me for years afterwards because I kept saying I was leaving tomorrow and then would postpone my departure to the next day – but it was Helen who kept me there. We would rarely retire to bed before two in the morning. If I said I was tired and wanted to sleep, she would offer an asparagus omelette, or an exotic set of chocolates, or a piece of music, or simply more scintillating stories and talk. I was lost – and I would sleep in and miss next day's morning train. I would then plan to leave in the afternoon, but she would say she had just bought a wonderful roast and that I shouldn't miss it. And so the days and the nights passed.

Being in the Langhams' ménage also exposed me to the heady world of Canadian and international celebrities who made the pilgrimage to Stratford during the summer. As part of their entourage at the theatre I had the opportunity to meet the former Governor-General Vincent Massey, and the current one, General Vanier. I met Helen Hayes, and Canada's most famous composer

Sir Ernest MacMillan, as well as Glenn Gould. And Jousuf Karsh 'of Ottawa' paid several visits to the Langham home with his birdlike wife Estrellita. We were fascinated by his ingratiating manner: I am sure he was interested in photographing Helen and Michael, but I don't believe he ever did. I also had the pleasure of meeting Canada's foremost German scholar, Barker Fairley, who was a great devotee of the Festival and had become a good friend and admirer of Michael. He was old enough to have known the Group of Seven painters (the only surviving photograph of all seven of them also features Barker), and his critiques of their work in the Canadian Forum in the 1920s had a lot to do with their recognition and celebrity. He was now becoming a painter in his own right, and I was to meet him in friendship many times again, over many years, until just before his death at the age of 98.

By the time that September approached and I simply had to leave in order to prepare for my teaching year in Toronto, my friendship with Michael and Helen was well cemented. We promised to keep in touch. And we did. In fact some time that fall I received a letter from Michael offering me a job at Stratford for the summer of 1964, as dramaturge for the Festival. No hesitation there: I was thrilled to accept. Meanwhile, there were eight months of teaching at Victoria College to be got through.

With the promise of a regular income for the next year, it was time to stretch my wings a little. I said goodbye to my kind landlord and landlady and their attic room on Madison, and moved across Bloor Street to a small second-floor apartment on Huron, only ten minutes' walk from Victoria College. I now had my own kitchen, and it was perhaps here, encouraged by Helen's peerless cooking, that I began in a rudimentary way to develop my lifelong pleasure in putting meals together.

Regular routines have a way of sliding out of the memory: of my many hours of classroom teaching that year at Victoria I recall almost nothing. What grab hold are the events and experiences that fall outside those repeated patterns of work.

Thus I remember making a growing number of good friends in the University faculty, among them the charming and clever Jack Robson — editor of the multitudinous works of John Stewart Mill — and his wife Ann; Paul Bouissac from France, who taught French and was far more interested in circuses; witty and warm Shakespeare scholar Brian Parker (born in Bunbury, Cheshire) and his equally scholarly and warm wife Dorothy from the United States; graduate students Stephen and Adrienne Clarkson; and philosopher Francis Sparshott.

Then I can recall, one grey November afternoon, sitting in the Senior Common Room when a colleague came in and told me that John Kennedy had just been shot and killed.

Towards the end of the year my Oxford pal Robin Grove-White wrote and said he was coming to Toronto with a friend, and could I put them up for a while? His friend, Paul McDowell, had been a member of the British band The Temperance Seven, and had also worked with Robin in a revue that went to the Edinburgh Fringe Festival. Their plan was to put together a revue in Toronto, and they suggested that I work and perform with them. A few weeks later they flew in, and so began many weeks of very cramped living, while Robin — with some help from his uncle Kildare Dobbs — began to establish himself in the city as a personality. Our evenings always had to include visits to bars, and it was not long before I realized that Robin was on his way to becoming a serious alcoholic. I still remember the panic in his eyes if as the evening approached its end he did not have a bottle of Scotch or a case of beer (or preferably both) to bring home with him. Sometimes, late at night, he would land up on the doorstep of his uncle or my friend Patrick

Lyndon – or anyone he could think of – to ask whether he could borrow alcohol of almost any sort. His great charm and wit got him through these importunings; his friends, even when they had been woken up, were nearly always prepared to oblige. Years later, long after he had returned to Britain, having sworn off drink and become a highly serious and influential citizen, Robin wrote: "Paul and I sponged off your generosity shamelessly, and friendship was tested, though I do remember lots of laughs fuelled by oceans of booze".

Yes. But I came to realize that my life was gradually being taken over by this somewhat dysfunctional duo, and that my own fondness for revue during my time at Oxford had not survived the move to Canada. Once again I found myself living with a foot in each of two very different worlds: the genteel academic calm of Victoria College's Senior Common Room, and the anarchic, jokey, plastered mania of life with Robin and Paul. They did put together a two-man act at Don Cullen's 'satirical' nightclub the Village Embassy, and eventually moved away to live off someone else. Robin went on to become, at least for a brief time, something of a Toronto television celebrity, working with Patrick Watson as both writer and performer in the TV weekly show *This Hour Has Seven Days*.

Looking for what was dishonourably referred to as 'a piece of skirt' was one of the pastimes that occupied us on our evening madnesses. I had a couple of short-lived affairs with attractive young women during these months, although, as before, I found myself unable to sustain my enthusiasm after the first or second sleeping together, and if one of them appeared to be falling in love with me, I bolted at once. When the poet Jay MacPherson asked me to accompany her to the Victoria College Ball at Casa Loma, I of course accepted, and we spent a pleasant and decorous evening together. Even then I was nervous that Jay might have had a shine for me, as the saying went. But I think she was as nervous as I was.

By December I had saved enough money to fly to England for Christmas, the first time I had returned since my emigration the year before. In the meantime my parents' situation had changed. Raymond, my father, having given up our hotel in Oxfordshire after many years of unsuccess, had turned back to pig farming – his early passion. When I left England he had just become manager of a pig farm in Northamptonshire, belonging to the eccentric socialist Ian Winterbottom, soon to become a Labour life peer. Father had made a fine job of this work, but his relationship with his employer had been less happy, and had reached the point when he felt he had to hand in his resignation. He advertised for a new position, and within a few weeks was hired as manager of a pig farm in Berkshire. They were sad to leave their little estate cottage in Northamptonshire, but simply delighted to be moving into their new home in the village of Inkpen, alongside the Berkshire Downs. It was a modernised and fully detached 18th century cottage, half red brick, half red hung-tile, and with a tile roof, set in its own spacious garden. By the time I arrived they had settled in comfortably. Dad's new job was going well, and he felt he had already made many improvements to his new herd. Tessa, my mother, had already produced good crops of flowers and vegetables in the garden, and was planning great things for the following spring. She had also joined the local Women's Institute, and as usual was looking like presidential material. They also now had their own car, a Morris Traveller, bought through Uncle Harold by my sister Jo, who had driven it up from Surrey while they were still in Northamptonshire. They were as happy as I had ever seen them. Jo flew in from Italy, and Christmas with the whole family was a jolly time – though I have little memory of it, apart from a photograph of Mother, Jo and sister Jenny outside in the frosty garden, modelling the night-dresses which our family friend Wilma Hessey had made as presents for each of them.

There was another reason for the trip back to the old country. For £10,000 Helen and Michael had recently bought a small house on Napier Road in Kensington – the first they had ever owned – and were due to move in on the first day of the New Year. Because Helen was unable to be in London until three or four days later (having accepted an acting role in Toronto on CBC-TV) they had asked me whether I could help Michael and son Christopher organise the place before Helen's arrival. Of course I was happy to do so, and felt even more part of the family as I carted furniture around, sorted books, put up pictures and plugged in lamps. I remember being amazed by Michael's lack of handyman skills: he could barely hammer in a nail. For Helen's homecoming, though, he knew exactly what to do, filling the house with rich bouquets of flowers. I glowed in the reflected warmth of their love for one another, and was as sad as when leaving my own family when the time came to return to Canada.

By the spring of 1964 I had earned enough money to realise a long-held dream: I bought a sports car. It was a demonstration-model MGB, green, shiny, black-seated, stick-geared and gorgeous. I think its price was $3,200, and of course I bought it with the aid of an obliging credit company. No one who was not brought up in Britain in the years after the war can imagine the lust with which boys and young men looked at the open sports cars of those days. There were still many of the pre-war chariots around in my childhood: Alvises, Lagondas, Aston Martins, Bentleys – these were the stuff of our dreams. But then the little post-war models came out: the new MGs, the Triumphs, the Morgans, the Sunbeam Alpines, and from Italy the Alfa Romeos. We all wanted one, and of course they were way beyond most of our pockets. Yet now, after eighteen months in Canada, I was able to park my very own beauty in the driveway of my apartment.

That same spring, early in April, I got marginally caught up in Toronto's supreme theatrical double event of that year. The original cast of *Beyond the Fringe* (Peter Cook, Alan Bennett, Jonathan Miller and Dudley Moore) had been brought from New York (where they had been replaced by a new cast), to play for a week or two at the cavernous and entirely unsuitable O'Keefe Centre. And at the same time and place Richard Burton was rehearsing *Hamlet* under the direction of John Gielgud. I saw something of my old school friend Peter Cook and his mates while they were there – I remember Jonathan Miller being irritated by the need to wear ties and jackets in smart restaurants and clubs, and describing the necktie as 'the codpiece of North America'. But somehow I also became friendly with some of the less starry members of Gielgud's company, and was able to sit in on his rehearsals. They were awed by Gielgud's reputation, but astonished by his loose direction: I remember the whole company arriving on stage for the first rehearsal of the final scene with its swordfight between Hamlet and Laertes, and Gielgud barking out to them: "Come on now, take your places: you're all actors, you know where to go". Somehow the confused and milling crowd found its way, but certainly with no help from its director. One of my friends in the cast, David Redfield, subsequently published a book about his experience.

Gielgud's idea for the look of the play was to take away the curse of traditional Shakespearean costume by having everyone dressed as they might appear on stage when performing in the last full run-through before the dress rehearsal. Much care was taken of course to ensure that each actor's apparently random choice of everyday clothes had some kind of appropriateness: Alfred Drake's Claudius in blue blazer and tie, Hume Cronyn's Polonius in a business suit, Burton's Hamlet in an undergraduate's open-necked shirt. My friends wangled me a ticket for the opening night, and I was able to see the idea played out, not unsuccessfully. But I remember little of it beyond Burton's booming voice and exaggerated diction. He was not an actor to inspire love or pity, and never quite seemed to give us the person behind the thick vocality of his words.

The excitement of Burton's presence in Toronto was much increased by the international interest in his blooming affair with Elizabeth Taylor, who was occasionally seen haunting the backstage of the theatre, or dining at the Royal York. But the excitement grew to boiling point one weekend when Burton and Taylor flew off to the US in a private plane and returned on Monday morning – married! That night Hume Cronyn threw a party for the newly-weds in the O'Keefe's rehearsal hall. Peter, still playing in *Beyond The Fringe*, was a friend and neighbour of Burton's in London, and was invited. He in turn invited me to go with him. And so it was that I found myself at the undisputed social event of the Toronto season, meeting and chatting with Richard, and even being introduced to the violet-eyed Elizabeth, diminutive in her gamine Cockney cap.

With the academic year over and some weeks before I was due to take up my duties at Stratford, I was anxious to put my MG through its paces, and decided to drive down to Washington DC to catch up with various Oxford pals, including poet-philosopher Keith Gunderson, now teaching at Princeton, my old Paris roommate Harrell Smith and his fiancée's family the Fales, and also Worcester friend Lloyd Weinreb, now a Law Clerk at the Supreme

Court. After a couple of convivial nights at Princeton with Keith and his wife Donna, I drove on to Washington. Lloyd took me on a tour of the Court (not then in session), and through the Fales I was able to visit the Capitol, and even to sit in on a meeting of the Senate, presided over by Edward Kennedy.

Washington was still suffering from the shock of JFK's assassination, and its mood was jumpy and uncertain. It was also dealing with the surging Civil Rights movement. The March on Washington ("I have a dream…") had taken place only seven or eight months earlier. Malcolm X had met with Martin Luther King at the Capitol less than a month before. And during these tense spring days Lyndon Johnson was working his phones tirelessly to put together the votes needed to support Kennedy's Civil Rights Act, which passed into law three months later. The schism between the segregationist South and the liberal majority was a palpable source of tension in the capital, and I still remember Southerner Mrs Fales' bitter, frightened face as she talked darkly about the 'niggras' taking over.

I then drove on south to Charlottesville, Virginia, where I met up and stayed with the brother of Harrell. It was there I had my first fascinated sight of Jeffersonian America, at Monticello and the University of Virginia. Finally turning homeward, I took advice and headed back north along the nearly completed and amazingly beautiful Blue Ridge Parkway.

After the long, grey and bitter winter of Toronto, an abiding memory of the whole trip was the warmth and the sunshine of a southern spring, and the apple and peach blossom along the Potomac.

I was also struck by the difference between Washington and New York. New York was the living, writhing embodiment of America's freedom: free enterprise unfettered. Washington on the other hand, in its public buildings and monuments, uttered the familiar paradigms of America's formal aspirations to freedom, cut proudly in silent marble. "Fourscore years ago…"

But I also took away with me a strong and heartening sense of the United States of America at its moral best. The country was caught up in a struggle between good and evil, and though nothing was certain it did look as though the good of 'justice for all' would triumph at least for the moment – partly as a result of Kennedy's sacrificial murder. There was an epic quality in all of this. I have often wondered since how the lobby-frenzied world of present-day American politics, deeply fragmented and dominated by the money of corporations and billionaires, would have dealt with the situation of the 1960s. Not well, I think.

CHAPTER FOUR

A SUMMER AT STRATFORD

The year 1964 marked the fourth centenary of Shakespeare's birth, and Laurence Olivier, then artistic director at the Chichester Festival, had invited Michael Langham to bring his Canadian Stratford company over to Britain to perform in the recently-built Chichester Theatre as part of the festivities. Michael had decided to send his celebrated production of *Love's Labor's Lost* and Jean Gascon's *Le Bourgeois Gentilhomme*, later to appear in the summer season. Then, after its *succés d'estime* the previous year, he added *Timon of Athens* to the roster.

 I had paid a short visit to Stratford at the end of March to be with Michael for the restaging of *Timon*. I was also happy to catch the revival of Michael's signature production of *Love's Labor's Lost*. I can still remember waving off the bus as the company left excitedly for the airport, and wishing I could be with them. Our Stratford had not been seen in Britain since Michael's production of *Henry V* had appeared at the Edinburgh Festival in 1956, when Michael's inspired idea of inviting francophone actors from Montreal's Théâtre du Nouveau Monde to play the French king and court had been greeted with huge applause. And Christopher Plummer's performance as Henry was Britain's first introduction to the work of that extraordinary actor, then less than thirty years old. So anticipation was now high on both sides of the Atlantic.

The Festival company was warmly received in Chichester, and returned buoyed up by enthusiastic notices from London's premier critics. *Love's Labor's Lost* was acclaimed for its wit, its choreographic skill, and its superb use of the thrust stage. *Le Bourgeois Gentilhomme*, though it had its admirers, was maybe too French, too decorous in Jean Gascon's version with Gabriel Charpentier's harpsichorded score, to appeal to general English taste. But of the three productions, it was *Timon of Athens* which had created the biggest stir. For one thing the play was hardly known in England, having received very few productions if any in the twentieth century. And then again it was found to be superbly dramatic, with remarkable performances by John Colicos as Timon, Douglas Rain as Apemantus and Peter Donat as Alcibiades. Above all, Duke Ellington's score held the whole sometimes awkward and unwieldy play moodily together. It was also entirely accessible to the audience. Of course I liked to think that our long hours spent on the text the previous summer had paid off – and I was happy that as in Canada, none of the critics had mentioned the impertinent introduction of pseudo-Shakespearean lines in the third act.

My summer contract coincided with the return of the company. I had rented an apartment on the edge of town for the summer, and settled into it soon after returning from the States. I was also allotted an office next to Michael's, where I was greeted on the first day with a whole pile of scripts which had been accumulating, sent by hopeful playwrights over the previous year or two, or even longer. Stratford had never hired a dramaturge before: the title was almost unknown in English-speaking theatre, and I used to say afterwards that much of my summer job was taken up with explaining the word to puzzled visitors. My main task as I understood it was to serve as a literary resource for the artistic director, and I soon had my hands full, dealing with a backlog of unsolicited manuscripts. Canadian plays were at this time a rare commodity, with very few outlets available to them throughout Canada. Producing a Canadian play was still a risky undertaking, and was seen commercially by many theatres as a kiss of death. Stratford had produced two or three Canadian plays since Michael's arrival, but there was little enthusiasm for them, and no small-stage outlet where they could be presented at modest cost. I read many of these plays with care, and tried to provide the author with a useful critique. But I was unable to give them much encouragement about the possibility of a Stratford production, at least in the immediate future.

Stratford was in fact still wrestling with its mission. It began in 1953 as a summer festival devoted to presenting high quality Shakespeare productions to a North American audience on its unique thrust stage – and including a nod to the Greeks in 1954 with Guthrie's production of *Oedipus the King,* repeated in 1955. Shakespeare was still its principal theatrical activity. But it had also used and more recently purchased the Avon Theatre in the centre of Stratford – a fine old proscenium stage seating an audience of eleven hundred – and here as early as the Guthrie days it had supplemented its Shakespearean fare with Gilbert and Sullivan operettas. With the inclusion of both singers and a pit orchestra in the summer season it had made sense to add a more pervasive musical dimension to the Festival, and by the time I arrived on the season there had already been several years of concerts rounding out the repertoire, featuring solo artists and the Festival Orchestra, as well as music theatre productions, including *The Soldier's Tale* and

Turn of the Screw. Major classical artists such as Claudio Arrau, Glenn Gould, Maureen Forrester, Peter Pears and Benjamin Britten had performed, as well as jazz artists like Duke Ellington, Count Basie and Billie Holiday. Louis Applebaum, who had been the Festival's music director since the beginning, had recently been succeeded by the triumvirate of Glenn Gould, Leonard Rose and Oscar Shumsky.

It was not surprising that with all this cultural activity, strongly subsidised by federal and provincial funds, Canadian artists would mutter about the lack of support for Canadian theatre creations at Stratford. On the other hand it was giving work to scores of actors and musicians, as well as to designers, prop-makers, publicists and administrators. While Michael's own interest and genius lay in the interpretation of Shakespeare and other masterpieces of the English repertory, he was sensitive to the perceived Britishness of the Festival, and anxious to recognise Canadian creative talent when he saw it. The need for 'Canadian content' was a continued subject for discussion.

Meanwhile he had been dealing with another question: could the powerful thrust stage of the Festival Theatre be adapted to the presentation of proscenium-stage classics, like the works of Sheridan, Goldsmith and Wycherley? For this year of 1964 he had decided to experiment, and Wycherley's *The Country Wife* had been announced for the season, along with *Richard II* (to be directed by Stuart Burge), and his own production of *King Lear*. The Avon season was to feature *Yeomen of the Guard* (directed by Bill Ball from San Francisco) and The *Marriage of Figaro* (under the direction of Jean Gascon).

With the return of Michael and his company from Chichester, the work of the summer began. The Festival at that time kicked off at the beginning of June with three productions opening in the

Festival Theatre on successive nights: a huge challenge for actors and especially for production people. *Le Bourgeois Gentilhomme* was already in production, having played in Chichester, and so had just a handful of further rehearsals scheduled. But *Richard II* and *King Lear* were starting from scratch, with six weeks of rehearsal time to share between them. Once the three premieres had opened, work would begin on the fourth play of the season (*The Country Wife*), which would premiere some six weeks later, in the middle of July.

It wasn't long before Michael began talking to me about *King Lear*, and it was soon clear that he was intending me to work with him in the same way that we had developed during the preparation of *Timon*. But whereas before I had always been in the background, this time I was officially on the staff, and was able to function as an assistant to the director, sitting with him at rehearsals, taking notes, and spending the evenings discussing the next day's program of scenes.

I soon realized what an extraordinary life experience this was going to be. In the first place I was fortunate enough to have studied *Lear* extensively at Oxford, and already knew it better than any other Shakespeare play. And then I was beginning work on it in the service of a director who knew the Stratford stage better than anyone alive. But there was more than this. I had already experienced Michael's approach to Shakespeare with *Timon*, and had begun to witness the way in which he moved the text onto the stage, the way in which he travelled purposefully from a detailed study and understanding of the words into a compelling vision for dramatic stage action. And most thrilling of all, I was sharing in a personal experience that was unique to Michael himself.

Michael had travelled to France as a second lieutenant with the Gordon Highlanders in the ill-fated British Expeditionary Force, and was captured in May 1940 on the retreat to Dunkirk: the third

British officer to be captured in the war. He was taken to a lock-up behind the lines in France, from which he managed briefly to escape. He was soon moved from there to a prisoner-of-war camp in Germany, and then to other camps. He attempted two more times to escape, but each time was recaptured almost immediately. After his third break-out he was transferred to a maximum-security prison, from which there was no possibility of escape for the remainder of the five full years he was in captivity. It was then that he began to direct stage productions with the prisoners – much to the approval of the camp commandant, who preferred to see his prisoners involved with *Kultur* rather than planning escapes. (Michael used to recount how he was putting together a production of *The Rivals*, but was having difficulty with costuming it when the camp commandant heard of the problem, and arranged for costumes to be lent by the Frankfurt Opera!)

But there was one play chosen as the subject of a continuing workshop, a play that was thought to be beyond their resources to produce, but which they felt to be supremely worth studying and discussing. The play was *King Lear*. A small group of prisoners got together once or twice a week to read and discuss the play, led not by Michael but by a former harbour-master from Haifa, whom Michael described as the wisest man he had ever known. This, he used to say, was his university. And the wise harbour-master served both as his mentor, and in some ways as the father that he had never known: his father had died in India soon after Michael was born.

Michael's years as a prisoner of war, from the age of twenty to twenty-five, a time when the luckier among us are blossoming into full maturity with the world before us, marked him in many ways, and among other things he left captivity a fervent socialist, anxious to build a new and juster world. The play of *King Lear,* looked at from inside a harsh prison camp and by men deprived of so many comforts and necessities, enduring so much humiliation and frustration and living without the solace of family or female company, offered a view of humankind which was deeply scarred, alone, cruel and dark. But the foolish majesty of the King, his wretched abuse at the hands of Goneril and Regan, the sweet, unbearable directness of Cordelia, the smiling evil of Edmund, the sadism of Cornwall as he has Gloucester's eyes gouged out, the staunch loyalty of Kent and Edgar: all this, *mutatis mutandis*, was the stuff of their daily experience. And holding together this whole grim tapestry was the soaring magnificence and intricate subtlety of Shakespeare's language and poetry – giving form to the epic story, and joy and hope to its prisoner-students. (Poetry was a precious commodity in prison camps. I learned from a Finnish poet many years later that if you were able to recite a poem by heart in the concentration camps, it earned you a cigarette.)

This was Michael's story, recounted to me over glasses of wine as we bent over the text of the play. And this was the story that he conveyed more briefly to his cast on the first day of rehearsal. From then on, each one of us involved felt a special air of excitement and privilege to be joining him in this undertaking. Now, nearly twenty years after the war had ended, he had finally felt emotionally ready to embark on his very first production of the play – as though it had needed so long in the womb of time to begin delivery.

My duties as dramaturge slowly accumulated as the weeks went by. Besides my dealing with scripts, Michael wanted me to cope with a fair amount of his correspondence for which he had no time – and even once for an article on the thrust stage, which I wrote and which appeared in the British newspaper *The Observer* under his name. He also expected me to be supervising the schedules of the training staff that Michael had gathered together to assist the younger members of the company with their development. Trish

Arnold was the movement teacher, and Kristin Linklater coached voice and speech. Senior members of the company, when available, gave master classes in acting. I was also asked to run a workshop with the apprentices. The classes were well attended, and of great value, though there was always the problem of finding enough time to go into depth with anything creative: the actors were enormously busy during rehearsal periods, and desperately wanted to enjoy their leisure time when at last the final production had opened. But even then many of them had to continue with understudy rehearsals for a further two weeks, leading up to an understudy run-through of the play, occasionally supplemented by some of the principal actors giving of their time. When we finally had a few scattered hours to devote to a workshop, we worked on a handful of scenes from Gogol's *The Government Inspector*.

I was also responsible for meeting dignitaries and taking them on a tour of the theatre (my prize catch was Dame Judith Anderson). And I served as Michael's liaison with Barney Jackson, the leader of the Shakespeare Seminars, which had been established by Michael in 1960 and run in collaboration with McMaster University. These were still ahead of us, taking place in August, and bringing some highly-distinguished Shakespearean scholars to the Festival, including Alfred Harbage, Derek Traversi, Robert Speaight, Jan Kott and John Crowe.

Stuart Burge called on me to do some research for him on *Richard II*, a play I enjoyed and had written on while at Oxford. But my over-riding priority was *King Lear*. I spent as much time as I could in rehearsal and many evenings with Michael at his home, working on the text line by line, and discussing the next day's scenes. I also attended production meetings with composer Louis Applebaum and designer Leslie Hurry.

Leslie was one of the more eccentric characters to work at the

Stratford Festival. Now in his late fifties, tall and bowed, with a mass of lanky white hair, red face, a huge imperious nose and jutting chin, he was a ceaseless smoker, and being an asthmatic had the cough to go with it. He lived in a remote English cottage in Clare, Suffolk, which he often talked of lovingly, and was very much the innocent abroad in North America (he never ventured into the United States; like many artists he had been a devout communist in the thirties and was sure that he would be denied entry).

Everything about the modern world confused and terrified Leslie. On his first arrival at Toronto airport there had been some mix-up and no car was waiting for him, so he had to telephone Stratford, a hundred miles away. Somehow he found the number, and a coin-box telephone. He told us later that he had some Canadian money with him, but had no idea of the names of the coins or their value. So when the operator asked him to insert ninety-five cents, he asked:

"How do I do that?"

"It's simple," replied the operator: "just put three quarters and two dimes into the slot."

"I've got some coins here," replied Leslie in a rising panic, "but I don't know what they are." He fumbled through the change in his hand. "I have some with a moose on the back, and one with a ship, and some with a beaver. I really don't know..."

"That's fine," said the operator, unfazed. "Just put in three moose, one ship, and two beavers."

And that is how Leslie got through to the Festival and signalled his arrival on Canadian soil.

Leslie had made his name in the 'thirties as a painter, but during the war moved into the theatre, designing the ballets of *Hamlet* and *Swan Lake* for Robert Helpmann at Sadler's Wells. Guthrie then picked him to design his production of *Hamlet* at Stratford-on-

Avon, where he went on to design *Medea, Cymbeline* and *King Lear*. His costume sketches were themselves works of art, and in his unique, instantly recognisable style, with large carefully drawn heads (which, as Michael used to say, all looked like Leslie himself) and then a blaze of almost Klimt-like costume, finishing in a diminishing mermaidish sweep towards the feet, which often never materialised at all. He was perhaps the first Stratford designer to extend his painting skills to the actual painting of the fabric on the finished costume, and would spend hours in the costume room, cigarette hanging from his lips, smoking out the sewing ladies but amazing them with the vigour and colour of his designs.

For their production of *Lear*, Michael and Leslie had decided on a primitive, almost Anglo-Saxon look, setting the play very much in the early British pagan world Shakespeare had conceived for it. This called for much imaginative work on the part of the designer, and Leslie with his bent for almost fairy-tale fantasy, sometimes on the edge of camp but never succumbing, was in his element. The props were of bone, or wood, or stone, or iron; the swords great two-handers; the cloaks and tunics of fur and rough sacking-like fabric. Leslie, together with composer Louis Applebaum who supplied a score full of horns and sounding brass, was creating a world complete.

Into this world stepped Michael's cast of characters, led by John Colicos as Lear, temperamental, edgy and loud like the king himself: Hughie Webster as the Fool; Mervyn (Butch) Blake a handsome, credulous old Gloucester; Douglas Rain as Edgar; and the peerless Tony van Bridge as the loyal Kent. And the women! Diana Maddox and Frances Hyland as Goneril and Regan, and Martha Henry as Cordelia. A true cry of players.

There is no way in which I can recreate at this distance the mounting excitement of our work on *King Lear* as one rehearsal followed another, and as our evening sessions continued without cease. There was no question of tampering with the *Lear* text the way we had played fast and loose with *Timon*. But I continued to be astonished how ready Michael was to cut a line or two here, a speech there, or to transfer a speech to a different character, or to reverse lines to add to the momentum of a scene-end. And I watched in studious wonder as he made use of the fast-flowing thrust stage to move from one scene to the next with not a moment's tedium, always shifting the focus point. I also marked and learned from the way in which Michael ensured that all sides of this wrap-around audience were able to share the moment, continually moving in the auditorium from one side to the other to check that no one was being left out.

Above all I watched how he choreographed scenes between two, or three, or four characters, so that their movements signified their changing psychological relationships. Speaking a line to another person while looking away from that person makes the import of the line very different. Coming up close and looking intently into another's eyes can signify threat as well as intimacy. Walking away while talking to someone makes the eventual turn back all the more significant. The thrust stage insists on large movement to ensure that all parts of the audience can share. But the way in which these movements are arranged can add astonishingly to the audience's perception of what is going on between the characters. This was Michael's supreme skill.

I remember one day in particular, when Michael was rehearsing with Lear and the Fool, in the scene where the Fool is taunting the King with his foolishness in not seeing the evil of his daughters and the goodness of Cordelia:

"I marvel what kin thou and thy daughters are: they'll have me whipped for speaking true, and thou'lt have me whipped for lying."

Michael had set the scene with Lear seated at one side of the stage, and the Fool dancing around him. Every so often Lear would respond to one of the Fool's barbed observations by cracking a whip in his direction, the Fool jumping quickly out of range. All of a sudden Michael stopped the rehearsal.

"John, Hughie," he said, "I'm sorry but it's just not working. I've got an idea. John, get up for a minute please, and Hughie, you sit where John was sitting. You see, John, it should be you and not the Fool who ranges around the stage. He is the confident one. It is you who are being goaded and trying to avoid the stings."

They played the scene again, and suddenly it fell into place. The Fool was no longer jumping away but was a sitting target, and Lear's fury with him could easily have led to a whipping. The fact that Lear threatened the Fool with his whip but fell short of actually striking him was a clearly visible sign that part of him accepted the truth of the Fool's barbs. The change was palpable. Of course John's amour-propre had to be a little appeased, since his royal status was being undermined. But this was the whole point of the re-staging, and he soon recognised it. The Fool at that moment was King.

A few weeks into rehearsals, Helen arrived from London, and life at 19 Trow gained a fresh zest. Helen was gradually incorporated into our discussions of the play, and added new thoughts, new insights. Occasionally she attended rehearsals and her responses afterwards were listened to keenly by Michael, always sensitive to her unique sensibilities, her extraordinary ear and awareness of language and character.

My own relationship with the actors was smooth and happy, and I prided myself that my accustomed charm was working its magic. It took me some while to realise that their warmth and friendliness with me was at least partly a result of their perception that I was close with the boss: it would be highly impolitic for them not to be friendly with someone so obviously in Michael's favour. No doubt this closeness was resented behind the scenes, but I was not aware of it, and my presence at rehearsals seemed to be accepted as long as I kept my head down, and deferred visibly to our director.

With Helen's presence, though, the acceptance was not so easy. I soon understood that some actors, especially the senior among them, felt that Helen's presence somehow got in the way of their personal relationship with their director.

One night this blew up. Michael – and I suppose myself – had been invited to a late-night party at the home of John Colicos. Helen had arrived in Stratford by this time, and was no doubt invited too, but decided not to go. So Michael and I walked over, to find that most of the company was there and drinking hard, as we all tended to do in those days. John and Michael certainly tossed back the whisky, and at some point John got aggressive and turned his anger on Michael, accusing him of allowing Helen to dominate him in the direction of the play, and saying that Helen was always interfering. Michael reacted angrily, going up to John and saying: "You have just insulted my wife, and I feel like striking you for this." He hesitated, and then went on: "In fact I will strike you!" And he slapped John across the side of his face. John lunged savagely towards Michael, whereupon the whole company, working like a well-rehearsed crowd in a dramatic scene, held the two antagonists at bay, and eventually calmed them down to a point where John apologised, and Michael accepted the apology. We left soon after, and before long were back at Trow Avenue, waking up Helen and recounting the whole drama to her in excited detail. She could not help but be amused at being the Helen of this miniature Trojan War.

But the incident pointed up something that Helen had long confided to me. In her early years with Michael she was enjoying a blossoming acting career in England, which she said she had put aside to accompany Michael to Stratford in 1956, with the understanding that she would be able to continue playing lead roles in Michael's new theatre. What she was not prepared for was the resentment towards her from the rest of the company. If she was given a lead role, they felt, it was not because of her talent but simply because she was the artistic director's wife. Sensitive to this, Michael tended to allot her minor roles: Jessica in *The Merchant of Venice* rather than Portia, one of the lesser *Merry Wives of Windsor*, and so on. This had become increasingly a source of friction between them, not made easier by the evident hostility to Helen from some more vocal members of the Stratford company, including I believe both John Colicos and Douglas Rain.

Finally, in this year of 1964, Michael had responded to Helen's increasing frustration and discontent by casting her in the title role of Margery in his production of *The Country Wife*. The male lead of the play was Jack Horner, played by – John Colicos. And Margery was married to Pinchwife – played by Douglas Rain. Though Helen was thrilled to be finally appearing in a leading part, you can imagine how uneasy she was to be playing with actors who she felt, with some justification, resented her. But this challenge was still ahead of us.

Michael's relationship with his Lear survived the quarrel, and the production continued to develop as the summer progressed. From all these rehearsals one stands out in my memory.

It was the day of the first dress rehearsal, and excitement was high as scene after scene unfolded, with Leslie's costumes seen for the first time and splendidly reinforcing the rude barbarism of the play. Michael was enjoying himself immensely, giving me notes one after another in quick succession, when suddenly, into the midst of our harsh Anglo-Saxon world walked production manager Jack Hutt in his blue blazer and tie. "What on earth is going on?" asked

THE BEST FOOLING

Michael, angrily, as Jack continued onto centre stage, came up to Kent and whispered in his ear. Tony van Bridge gave a shout of horror and ran off. It was only then that Jack looked out to Michael in the auditorium. "I'm sorry, Michael. But we just received a message that Tony's house is on fire." Immediately the whole company ran out, and the dress rehearsal dissolved. Everyone's first thought was to rush away to lend a hand, and townspeople talked for days afterwards of the spectacle of Ancient Britons on their bikes furiously pedalling along the lake to the site of the blaze. Michael and I followed soon in his car, and were relieved to see Tony and his wife Betty sitting in his garden surrounded by piles of furniture and belongings that had been retrieved, with Tony, still in costume, holding and stroking his beloved dog and cats, which had been safely rescued. Smoke continued to billow from the house behind him.

With the three first plays successfully opened, and *Lear* triumphing, rehearsals began for *The Country Wife*, with Michael having to launch immediately into its direction. He was tireless, and happy to be working on it with designer Desmond Heeley, who had designed for the play some extravagant Restoration clothes (he would never call them costumes) and a splendid diagonally chequered 'tile' floor covering the whole top surface of the stage, combining with neo-classical arches to transform the uncompromisingly Greco-Elizabethan stage into a 17th century world.

Helen always approached her roles with huge diffidence, but this time more than ever. There was so much at stake. I soon discovered that in the evenings after rehearsal she would want to sit down with me and go over her part. In fact it wasn't long before I found myself in the role of personal coach to Helen, dissecting every word and every scene, with Michael's approval – and even gratitude, because with his hands full working on the production he was unable to devote to her the attention she demanded and needed.

When *The Country Wife* opened in late July, Helen scored a great personal triumph as both actress and comedienne. Her timing, her splendid mixture of innocence and guile, took the audience and the critics by storm. The reception of her performance was a vindication of Michael's casting her in the lead, and little was said at Stratford after that about her taking advantage of being the artistic director's wife. Helen would say later that my assistance had made her success possible. I knew better. But I also knew I had helped to build up her confidence in the face of the hostility she sensed – or imagined – in the company. She happily enjoyed her triumph: yes, she was a star.

My final task of the summer was to work with Barney Jackson on his Shakespeare seminars, which attracted a loyal bunch of theatre-goers keen to enjoy the combination of theatre-going with lectures from Shakespeare scholars and also meetings and discussions with the actors of the company. Much of the pleasure for them lay in the socialising, and it was by and large a happy time for the members of the company involved, with the heavy load of the season's work behind them and only the performances to continue through into the fall – with a final few weeks of school matinees to finish off the season.

Only one memory of those seminars stands out for me. I was called upon among other things to moderate a discussion in which a group of company actors sat up on stage at the Avon, each of them talking about the plays from his or her own standpoint, and then answering questions from the floor. All went well until Robert Speaight got up to ask a question. Now Speaight was a man of some eminence, having worked in the British theatre as both director and actor (he was the first Becket in *Murder In The*

Cathedral), and being also the author of a number of books. He was clearly someone who enjoyed – and felt he was entitled to – the limelight, and having to sit in an audience while others ran the show was apparently not easy for him. So when he got up, it was not to ask a question but to begin a lecture. I forget now what we were all talking about, but it was clear that he did not intend to stop. I exchanged glances with my colleagues on the stage as the minutes ticked by, and after saying "Thank you" fruitlessly a few times, I finally got up and cut him off, saying "Thank you, Mr Speaight. It's good to have heard all that, straight from the horse's mouth. Now does anyone else have a question?" Speaight sat down and spoke no more.

As we were heading back to the hotel after the session, I asked the eccentric and wayward Oxford scholar John Crowe whether I had gone too far.

"When Speaight came up to Oxford after the Great War," he began in his highly cultured and heavily stressed English speech, "within a few weeks, by universal acclamation, he was dubbed the University Bore. He remained undisputed in that position until his third year, when his younger brother came up to Oxford. Within a few weeks his brother was acclaimed University Bore, and Speaight was demoted to Second Bore."

My enchanted summer season at Stratford was drawing to an end. Enchanted, because for all the hard work there were also many happy evenings and days off. I spent a good part of them with Helen and Michael, and our friendship became tighter. But I also enjoyed good times with members of the company – particularly in the bar with Eric ('Nick') House from *A Resounding Tinkle* (and now appearing in *The Country Wife* as Sir Jasper Fidget) and with Hughie Webster, all of us smoking and often drinking heavily. I also teamed up with the young and handsome Leon Pownall (whom we all felt was a Prince Hal in the making) and his beautiful wife Sharon: I would pack them into my MG and head off down the straight road to the beach at Lake Huron, frequently hitting over 100 mph on the way. Sharon sat beside me, with Leon up behind, hair blown back in the slipstream, feet on the bench seat – no safety belts mandated in those days.

Southwestern Ontario in summer was a hot, scented, sexy place, and the Festival was awash with liaisons of all kinds. Members of the company eyed one another in the bar after the work of the day, drinking much more than they should, and chatting one another up before often enough sidling off for a night together: perhaps the start of a romance. The theatre, after all, is a place and a trade which treasures emotional openness, and where public morals tend to be set aside. And still I kept myself aloof.

Michael and Helen were, I suppose, filling the place of parents and family for me, and I was supremely comfortable in their presence, not yet needing to explore my sexuality. Even when we were not working on the plays we basked in the language of Shakespeare and in the stories of the theatre. It was rare that a conversation did not include some riotously funny tale of theatrical disaster – some of these already transmitted to them from an earlier generation by Tony Guthrie. They had their own fun with Shakespeare's words too, accumulating names which shot out of the text, like the music-hall star Miss Lily Tincture (*Two Gentlemen of Verona*: "pinched the lily-tincture of her face...") or the German cobbler Hans Apt (from *Hamlet*: "thoughts black, hands apt, drugs fit and time agreeing") And when we were sharing a moment of special peace and contentment, out from Helen – or from Michael – would come Andrew Aguecheek's childlike comment from *Twelfth Night*: "This is the best fooling, when all is done."

There was a special topic to engage us. After nine years at the helm of Stratford, Michael had asked for and been granted a sabbatical year, starting in January 1965. Their plan was to travel to Greece, and to take their son Chris out of school so that he could be with them. And the idea that grew more and more powerfully among us during that summer was that we would club together to buy a house on a Greek island. I think it was I who found and bought Ernle Bradford's travel guide to the Greek islands, and Helen and I pored through it, exploring one island after another, until their names rang like golden coins showered down from Olympus into the Aegean: Santorini, Delphos, Hydra, Aegina, Sifnos, Lesbos…

I would dearly like to have joined them on their journey the following year, and I think they would have been glad to have me along. But I had already made up my mind that once my contract was completed at Stratford in September I would immediately fly back to Europe. In fact I had already decided to spend a few weeks in Greece during the fall, before returning via Italy (where I would see my sister Jo) to England for Christmas with the family. I was sure I would have no funds to return to the Mediterranean after this long jaunt. So we discussed the idea that I would serve as a scout. Through London contacts of Helen's we had the names of agents who might help us to find a house. I would get in touch with them when I arrived in Athens, and I would case a few joints, sharing my discoveries with them by post as I went. They would then check out the possibilities when their own Greek adventure began a few months later. And so it was decided.

Looking back, I believe that my extended trip back to Europe was also something of a test of my desire to commit my future to Canada. I had now been in the country for just two years, and in that time an exciting world had opened up for me in the Canadian theatre, in television and in academe. I had made many friends, and begun to establish the beginnings of a reputation, though perhaps in too many directions. And I had been immensely lucky, finding myself at the heart of the country's most prestigious playhouse, and becoming a close friend and colleague of its brilliant leader and his family. On the other hand, my connection with the Langhams was in some ways a continuation of my English experience. Though Michael had spent six months or more of each year in Canada since 1955, he then returned to Britain and continued to direct in the old country. He was still the consummate Englishman in his manner and clothes, and though he made efforts to soften his English accent – he would sometimes pronounce 'France' to rhyme with 'pants' – no one would have ever taken him for a Canadian. Helen, who had spent even less time in Canada and who had been resentful at her career going off course because of Stratford and its demands on her husband, was even less committed to life in the new country, and was capable of spouting off some fairly arrogant comments about the parochial place she found herself in. When feeling defensive she even allowed her accent to become more English and plummy than it already was. (I used to say that whatever anyone said about Helen, good or bad, was true. She could be snobbish, difficult, sarcastic and cutting, angry, self-pitying and jealous; true. She could also be generous, kind, highly sensitive to the plight of others and inordinately, brilliantly funny. True as well. Custom, in other words, could not stale her infinite variety.)

Helen was swift to pounce on any suggestion that Canada might be a better place for me to hang my hat than her beloved Great Britain. And as a good Cockney girl, she loved London more than anywhere in the world. But I still had a hard time imagining myself returning to Britain and starting once again to find my place; I felt I might be back in the same dither that had finally propelled me to the New World in 1962. This was the test I was giving myself. My decision to spend time in Greece was perhaps the hankering for a beaker full of the warm south – and not just Greece's warmth but her ancient culture, and the dry beauty of her landscape. Was I also subconsciously putting myself finally in the way of sexual experience at last? Perhaps.

My plans for Europe were substantially helped by a new commission. While still at Stratford I had been approached by CBC's Schools Television Department and asked whether I would host a series of six half-hour programs on poetry for schools, conceived and written by the Department's Head, Bruce Attridge, and to be directed by Perry Rosemond. (One of the cameramen was John McGreevy, who was later to become a distinguished documentary film-maker, and a lifelong friend.) It was a fine project, and I think we even won some kind of prize in the USA. The series was shot in late August and early September, and was to give me a solid basis of funds with which to venture over the water.

Some time in mid-September, then, I closed up my office and apartment in Stratford and returned to Toronto. I continued to sub-let my Toronto apartment, and was kindly allowed to park my sweet MG in the driveway of the Lyndons. I said goodbye to them, to the Glasscos and to various other Toronto friends. And then I was off.

CHAPTER FIVE

SHALL I STAY?

I had not set foot in Greece since my visit as a schoolboy in 1955, and romantically chose to arrive by ship, taking the boat which left from Bari in Italy, sailing overnight to drop anchor in Corfu in the early morning, and then setting sail once again and travelling along the ancient Corinth Canal (first attempted in ancient times, but not cut successfully until 1893) to the Piraeus, from where I got my first matchless sight of the Parthenon five miles away atop the Acropolis. Once disembarked I took the underground to the centre of Athens and made my way to the same modest hotel, the Estia Emporon, where we had stayed on a school trip ten years before.

I settled into a small room, and the next day went in search of the agent whose name Helen had given me: I think his name was Nikos. Nikos was a tall and elegant man in his forties. He spoke English, and received me with great charm, having already heard something of my mission. He took me off for a coffee, and I remember being fascinated by the way he would occasionally stop in mid-walk, fingering his worry beads, continuing on his way after perhaps thirty seconds. When I knew him a little better, I asked him why he did this. He seemed to be in no way conscious of the habit. "Perhaps I was thinking," he said at last. I have since imitated the stopping-and-thinking habit, and can vouch for its value.

Nikos introduced me to a fellow agent, a woman, who wanted to show me a property on the island of Hydra, a short boat ride from Athens. Some days later I took the ferry to the island, with the plan to stay one night there while she introduced me to the house. It was modern and pleasant enough but with no view of the sea, and surrounded by other houses. Hydra was close enough to Athens to be crowded already with new housing and tourism. I didn't think it would suit our dream, but I made polite noises as we toured the place from bottom to top.

The house was unfurnished, but in the main room I noticed a chair, a small table holding a typewriter, and in the rollers of the typewriter a half-written page. A rough pile of typed sheets sat beside the typewriter. I asked about this, and she said that there was a writer living next door who had a young family he needed to get away from in order to work, and he had asked whether he could make use of the house while it was empty. He was working, she said, on his second novel. I asked who the writer was, and she told me it was David Cornwell, better known by his nom de plume John Le Carré. He had recently, she said, had a success with his first book, *The Spy Who Came In From the Cold*: had I heard of it? Yes indeed, I said, looking again curiously at the pile of sheets on the table. The top page bore the title *The Looking-glass War*. "Would you like to meet him?" she asked, and within a few minutes she had knocked at his door, and we were invited to drinks that evening. I remember little of the occasion other than his red hair, charm and intelligence. From his fairly recent Foreign Office days he seemed to be acquainted with the name of my friend John Weston. And he was of course, like me, an Oxford man: always something of a bond.

I returned to Athens the next day, having let the agent know that I liked her house, but that it was not quite what we were looking for. Besides it was only available for rent, and we wished to make a purchase. I went back to Nikos, and within a day or two he invited me round to meet a friend of his, a poet, who needed money and was wanting to sell his family home on the island of Sifnos. His name was Georgios Likos.

We were introduced, and I soon discovered that Georgios did not speak English, and that our only common language was French. This was not a great problem, and from then on I called him Georges, and thought of him as plain English George.

George, yes, was a poet, who had been described, Nikos told me, as Greece's answer to TS Eliot. He wrote long, discursive, religious and philosophical poems. He was talkative, extremely well read in several languages, and highly emotional. We went off for a coffee and an *ouzo*, and over the next hour I heard his story.

He came, he said, from the island of Sifnos, where his family had been feudal lords of the isle since before it was part of the Ottoman Empire. They had a house at the top of the island, where in their past days of glory they had entertained the King of Greece. It was a wonderful house, he said, and he would like to live there. But a terrible thing had happened. George had got married soon after the war, he said, to a beautiful Athenian girl of unimpeachable breeding. They had a grand Orthodox marriage, as was to be expected for the only child of the Likos family who ruled Sifnos. The whole island celebrated.

George and his new wife went to live in Athens, but would return every year for religious feasts and family gatherings. But as the years went by, he and his wife became more and more estranged. They had no children. She resented him spending time on his poetry, and once took one of his manuscripts and threw it in the fire. At another point he left the house in a fit of rage and despair and went to see a film. She followed him to the cinema, found him sitting in the audience, and broke an earthenware pot over his head. Eventually and unsurprisingly the marriage broke up, and they were divorced.

This turn of events was more or less accepted in Athens, but such a thing was unheard of and totally unacceptable on the still almost mediaeval and highly religious island of Sifnos. His parents were outraged, but felt compelled to keep the divorce a secret. They disowned him, and absolutely refused to allow him to set foot on the island. All this had happened seven years before. In the intervening time first his father, then his mother, had died, and now George was their sole heir. But his finances were in a bad state, and he had decided that he must sell the family home in order to keep afloat. He showed me a photograph of it, and I knew at once it was the kind of place we were looking for. I asked the price, and he said 'Ten thousand dollars'. It was arranged that three or four days later we would take the boat from the Piraeus to Sifnos, stay the night in a hotel, and in the morning visit the house. So began an adventure which still, fifty years later, is vivid and fresh.

I bought a return ticket to Sifnos at a shipping agent, and on the day appointed I met George on the dock at the Piraeus. The boat, carrying small freight, chickens, a couple of goats and a few passengers, left in the late afternoon, and called in at one or two islands along the way. As we chugged into the gathering dark of the Aegean we talked and talked. He told me he had always wanted to be a ship's captain, but his father had not allowed it. He still felt more at home on a boat than anywhere. But as we sailed on towards Sifnos I began to notice George's increasing apprehension. It was seven years since he had last visited the island of his birth, and though excited, he was fearful of the reception he would find. I felt honoured to be with him as he made this return to his ancient home. It was a calm, warm night under moonlight and stars, and the sea shimmered with points of light as it stretched away towards the moon.

It was now after midnight, and while still ten miles out George called me over to the prow of the boat. "Smell it," he said, shaking. "Smell the heather." I smelt the breeze, and yes, there it was, the scent of his island's wild heather wafting towards us through the darkness. "Seven years since I smelled that scent. It's heaven for me."

Around one in the morning we docked in the little port of Kamares, gathered our bags, stepped ashore and started walking along the quay and up towards the town. There were still men about, and as we climbed the cobbled street, we heard someone cry out "Georgios! Georgios!" A youngish man ran out into the street and knelt down in front of George. "Georgios! It's you!" he cried. He grabbed hold of George's hand and kissed it, and made the sign of the cross. The other men came up and crowded round, and he shook their hands and kissed one or two of them on both cheeks. He talked for a few minutes with them, but then told them he had to get to bed. "Come to the old *taverna* tomorrow night," he said, "and we will have a drink together."

He said his farewells and we continued up the hill to the tiny four-room hotel that he had booked for us: it was the only hotel on the island, and had been built during his absence. They were expecting our late arrival and showed us each to our rooms, and I went to sleep in a haze of rich new memories, wrestling with the epic story I was being privileged to see unroll. The Disappointed Captain, the Moon, the Heather over the Water, the ecstatic cry of "Georgios!" as the Sailor came Home from the Sea, the Prodigal

Son returned, Odysseus finally set foot once again on Ithaca.

We were up early, had a coffee and a bread roll and a glass of water at a nearby café, and then climbed up towards the centre of the island. We reached a flat stretch of land at the top, like a dusty common, and he pointed out the low profile of his house at the far edge of it. There were tears in his eyes. Then, as we started walking towards the house, an elderly woman came running across the common from our left, crying "Georgios! Georgios! They told me you were here!" She was weeping, and when she reached us she embraced George and kissed him on his cheeks. George introduced her to me as Katina, but Katina took no notice of me. She was busy reaching into a bag to bring out a massive old key, some seven or eight inches long. "I have the key," she said. "I have kept it ever since your mother died. We have been taking care of the house. Two years ago there was some damage to the roof and it was leaking. So we fixed it. And we paid for it to be fixed. If you could pay us back that would be good. Oh, Georgios, Georgios!" And she embraced him again.

The woman was his mother's old housekeeper, perhaps even a nanny in far-off days. Her rush of words was translated for me by George as we continued up to the house, followed by Katina – worried lest George would find fault with her upkeep. The great rusty key turned in the lock of an iron-studded door, and we stepped into an inside courtyard. George straightaway burst into tears, and kept moaning as he showed me the rooms which opened out from the courtyard on three sides. It had been built perhaps in the early nineteenth century, the walls of stone, the doors and windows in faded dark wood, elegantly carved. Two of its sides looked over houses and cliff; the third opened on to the sea far below us. In the spacious main salon George pointed out faded photographs of the King's visit to the house before the war, of his grandfather, father, mother and aunts. He showed me the very primitive kitchen and bathroom, and then the bedrooms – including his own. I was beginning to wander round the place by myself, considering its possibilities as our dream house, and knowing how Michael and Helen would respond to its age and simplicity, when George came up to me, his eyes streaming. He grabbed my shoulder and said, *"Michel! Michel! Je m'excuse! Mais c'est pas à vendre! C'est pas à vendre!"* It's not for sale! It's not for sale!

Poor George, overcome with the emotion of his return, simply could not bear to consider the disloyalty, the treachery even, of parting with his family's home, the home of his childhood and so long unseen. It was *The Cherry Orchard* revisited: the heirs unable to endure selling the old house, tremulous family retainer in the background, financial disaster looming. A whole world slipping away.

Since the whole purpose of our voyage and visit was to consider purchasing the house, George's sudden reversal rather set me back. But as I looked around again, I realized more and more that this was not a house Helen or Michael would buy. It was built like a fortress on the crest of the hill. It looked not outwards but inwards. And above all it was far away from the blessed blue Mediterranean we had set our hearts on. In a way, George's change of mind let me off a hook: I could continue to please George by admiring the house, while knowing it was unavailable.

Katina had brought invoices with her, and I saw George going over them cursorily and then handing her a wad of bank notes. And so we left, drawing the heavy outer door closed again and turning its ancient key.

We took some kind of lunch in the local *taverna*, and then in the afternoon George hired a taxi to take us to a small church along the coast. Perhaps it was the church where he had been married.

He showed me round, and then knelt in front of one of the icons for many minutes. We returned a long way round, and finally back to the area near his home in the early evening. At seven o'clock we made our way back to the *taverna*. George went ahead of me. The place was jammed tight with men of all sizes, shapes and ages, and as he entered they stood up as one and in unison let out a great cry of "Georgios!" George shouted a greeting back and then with an extravagant wave of his hand he shouted in Greek to the owner behind the bar: "Drinks all round!"

I stood back as they came forward and shook his hand, some embracing, some kissing. We were finally led to a table where there were seats placed for us, among old family retainers. We were served our own drinks, and later a meal. There were no women in sight. Some hours later, George handed the innkeeper another roll of notes and we took the road back down the hill, collecting our knapsacks at the hotel as we passed. Ten or twenty of the men followed us to the quayside, and stood there until the boat came. Half an hour later they waved us off as we left the dock and headed back over the wine-dark sea into the darkness, bound once again for the Piraeus.

Besides chasing houses rather ineffectively in and around Athens I also made friends. A young French couple with a Volkswagen Beetle drove me with them to the beach one day. Another time I talked with an elderly Indian gentleman staying in my hotel who turned out to have been a close friend of Gandhi, and lived in the ashram that Gandhi had founded. Once I was introduced to Patrick Leigh-Fermor on the street, and we chatted briefly: I knew he was a war hero, but nothing else about him. But somewhere, somehow, and not long before my boat was due to take me back to Italy, I also met the most beautiful girl I had ever seen. She was American. She had hair the colour of hay, blue-grey eyes, a classic nose, a lovely generous mouth and the most swan-like neck. Her whole body was golden brown from the Greek sun. She was a goddess. She was also highly intelligent and funny. Let us call her Joanna.

I cannot remember how we met: perhaps at a restaurant in the Plaka, or even on the beach that day with the French couple. We met again for coffee, and went to a party or two together. I found Joanna breathtakingly attractive, and by the way she behaved to me it seemed she felt drawn towards me too.

One night three or four days before my departure I took her out to dinner at a little restaurant round from the hotel. After a happy meal, made happier by a bottle of piney *retsina*, we decided to walk to the Akropolis, and strolled off happily entwined. It was the night of a full moon, and in those days, on such a night as this, the gates were open to visitors who wanted to see the Parthenon in the moonlight. The charge was minimal – in fact I am not sure it wasn't free. And when we got there we were the only people to have chosen that clear November night to make a visit.

I defy anyone to name a place more beautiful, more sensual and yet more elemental and august than the temple of the Parthenon by moonlight. We revelled in its light and darkness, the shadows of the great pillars streaking the paving stones of the temple floor. Hugging and embracing and kissing, we drank in the views over Athens, and of the Aegean Sea in the far distance, and the night sky. And all of a sudden Joanna began dancing away from me, twirling in the moonlight. I followed her lead and began dancing too. We took the whole temple for our dance-floor, running, wheeling, turning, flying, our hearts pounding, and laughing in the sheer joy and wonder of it all.

Later, much later, we went back to her tiny apartment, and slept together. For the first time I was at ease after we made love and stayed the night with her, sharing coffee in the morning before I took off back to my hotel. We made plans to meet in Rome the following week.

I took the boat back through the Corinth Canal to Bari, and from there the train to Rome to stay with my sister Jo, whom I had last seen in New York two years earlier. In the meantime she had returned to Rome and was working once again for the Food and Agriculture Organisation of the UN. Her other news was that she was engaged, and in fact living with her husband to be, whose name was Geppino. He was a traveller for a pharmaceutical company, and also a fairly senior member of the Italian Communist Party. He was short and dark, somewhat older than my sister, charming and intelligent. He had been married before and had two young children, now in their early teens. We had a happy get-together, followed by dinner at Jo's favourite restaurant in Trastevere. I told them of my romance in Athens, and that I expected Joanna to join me within a week or two.

But within a day or two something happened to blight my budding affair with this most beautiful girl. I found that I had developed gonorrhea. In some discomfort and knowing it had to be treated, I had to share the news with Jo and Geppino. Geppino's medical connections made things easy. He walked along with me to the nearest hospital, and within a short while I had been treated with my first shot of antibiotic, with more to follow.

Since Joanna didn't know where she would be staying in Rome, I had given her my sister's telephone number. A few days later, when she arrived in Rome and phoned me, I had to tell her what had transpired. It was a difficult call, and we were both in tears. But I told her that I felt we could not meet again.

I have wondered since whether my cutting off the relationship in this way was a piece of prudish nonsense. On the other hand, since I had slept with no one else there was no doubt that I had caught the dreaded pox from Joanna. This meant that I was not the first person to have slept with her. I would have been naive to think anything else, but she seemed to have shared her favours around rather carelessly, and this I found hard to accept. Above all I was responding to my cruel disappointment. For the first time ever, I had found myself wholly engaged with a woman. We had shared one of the most emotionally and aesthetically profound moments of my life in the moonlit Parthenon. And then, after all that, and after my newly-found ease with a woman, I found myself diseased.

After a week or two with my sister, and now whole again, I took the train back to the Channel and crossed to England, to spend another Christmas at home with the family.

The New Year brought a new excitement: Jo had announced to the rest of the family what had up to now been a secret between us: that she was getting married. Geppino would be coming over to England in the first days of January. The two of them would then fly to Glasgow for a day for a civil marriage ceremony. They would then return to London and come to a high-class restaurant off the King's Road, where Father in his suit and Mother in her finery would meet Geppino — for the first time — and we would sit down to what I suppose would be called a wedding breakfast. These arrangements made Mother — and Father even more — distinctly uncomfortable. Mother would no doubt have liked to see Jo getting married in a traditional church wedding, bridal gown, bridesmaids and all. But she knew Jo well enough not to expect such a thing. Father was deeply unhappy and even suspicious of the wedding arrangements. Why Scotland? Was this an authentic marriage? Geppino was already married, and divorce was more or less unknown in Italy: was he divorced? — In which case would marriage to Dad's beloved eldest daughter make him a bigamist?

Dad would also no doubt have preferred to see her marry an Englishman.

But there was nothing the poor fellow could do about all this: Jo was thirty years old, and knew her own mind. Perhaps Geppino's marriage had not been dissolved, and perhaps – unlike England – Scotland didn't care. Anyway the arrangements went ahead. Father, Mother and Jen took the train down to London, where we all met the Happy Couple back from Scotland and enjoyed a delectable dinner – for which Father insisted on paying.

A day or two later Geppino and Jo came down to Inkpen to spend a few days 'getting to know the in-laws'. I remember us taking Geppino for a car-ride around beautiful Berkshire, and how he looked at the prosperous farms and fat cattle through communist eyes, as a bourgeois front for rural exploitation. Perhaps he remembered approvingly how Stalin had handled the kulaks.

It was not long before the family split up again. Jo flew back to Italy with Geppino and Jenny, who by this time had come down from Oxford and was teaching at a boy's prep school (a job she loved and seriously thought of staying with), soon took off for the beginning of her term-time.

That left me. I had loved my time in Europe, and in Greece I had had two elating experiences that would stay with me for life. I seriously debated the possibility of returning permanently from Canada. But the more I looked at, the less sense it made. I had no stronger possibilities of a suitable job and a career in England than I had in 1962. Canada had been good to me. Could I do the same things in London that I had done already in Canada? I doubted it.

I caught up with the Langhams on Napier Road in mid-January, staying with them for a few days and giving them a full report on my house-hunting efforts. They were soon to be leaving for Athens, and promised to write regularly.

It was while I was staying with them that Helen played for me the record of a new young singing group that was starting to become popular in the UK. I hadn't heard of them before, but Helen thought they were marvellous. They were called The Beatles.

That was also the month that Winston Churchill lay on his deathbed. I remember seeing the red light lit on Big Ben tower, and even visiting the House of Commons to hear a debate, heavily overshadowed by his imminent demise. He died the day I flew back to Toronto.

CHAPTER SIX

HOME AGAIN

Within two weeks of my return, Canada broke out its new Maple Leaf flag, amid some disgruntlement but a good deal more rejoicing. Somehow the sense of renewal it brought had its effect on me too, as I began to pick up the threads of my Canadian life.

I was not at all sure what I was heading back into. The year of 1964 had seen momentous experiences for me, both in the theatre and out of it, and I could hardly expect the richness of it all to continue. I still found myself reluctant to settle down to a single-minded career; if there was any one occupation I hungered for, it was still to be a writer. What kind of writer? I was not sure, except that I had no wish to compose advertising copy: I suppose I wanted to be a 'serious artist' – a novelist or a playwright.

Meanwhile I had to earn enough money to sustain me. Help soon came from an unexpected source: before I had been back in Canada more than a week, having found somewhere to live and retrieved my MG from under the snow, I had got back in touch with Robin Grove-White, and no doubt gone out with him for a drink or two – or more. But it was through that apparent layabout, surprisingly, that I landed my first new job. He called me one day to say that he had become friendly with Jeremy Brown, the Entertainment Editor of the *Toronto Telegram* ('the *Tely*'), which was a fairly lowbrow but lively and decent newspaper. Jeremy might be prepared to offer me something at the paper: would I be interested? I was, and the next day we travelled down to the *Telegram*'s smart new building on Front Street West, and into Jeremy Brown's office.

Jeremy was a big, smiling man, with a stutter and an easy blush. He was amazingly respectful of me – Robin had obviously set me up. I brought him my curriculum vitae, which was still sparse but had some useful recent qualifications for him to consider. He looked through it, and after some talk and laughs asked me whether I would like to become book critic for his newspaper. I asked him more about the job, and he told me he would need three columns a week, which would normally appear on Mondays, Wednesdays and Saturdays, but might sometimes be pre-empted in favour of more urgent news. They would amount to approximately 800 words each. I could choose which books to review from the review copies he passed on to me. And for each column he would pay me $25. We made a deal, and I walked out of there with eight or ten books under my arm, having made an undertaking to start producing copy by the following week.

I had always told myself that as someone working on the creative side of professional theatre I would never accept a job as a drama critic. But being a reviewer of books was somehow different, since I was not yet the writer I hoped one day to become. It was also something I could do in my spare time – unlike the work of the drama critic, who must attend opening nights and deliver his immediate judgments to appear in the paper the next morning. Time would have to be spent reading, but this was something I did anyway. As long as I hit my deadlines – which in those days meant of course delivering my typewritten copy by hand to the office on Front Street – I was free to do other things as well. BAWTREE ON BOOKS, alongside a smudgy mug shot of me, started to appear within two or three weeks. I was proud to see it there. I had a byline!

Soon after my start as a journalist I was approached by CBC's Bruce Attridge to host a second series for them, this time introducing schoolchildren to the structure and work of the United Nations, in four half-hour episodes. This was a topic after my own heart, and with a sister working in one of the UN's agencies I even, quite unreasonably, felt qualified. Perry Rosemond was once again the director, and it was a pleasant gig. – A couple of years later I am sure my English accent would have disqualified me.

A month or so later another opportunity came up, when the Crest Theatre announced auditions for their spring show: Joan Littlewood's *Oh! What A Lovely War*. The original Stratford East production had taken London by storm in 1962, and was brought to Broadway in 1964. This was to be the Canadian premiere. It was to be directed by Kevin Palmer, who had stage-managed for Littlewood in London and knew the piece backwards.

I auditioned, and to my delight was hired. I was even happier to learn that my good friend Eric House was to play the leading role of the Sergeant-Major.

As many will know, *Oh! What A Lovely War* tells the story of the First World War, from the June 1914 assassination of Archduke Frederick in Sarajevo to the Battle of the Somme in 1916. But it begins as a pierrot show on the pier in a seaside town in the happy pre-war days, with the whole cast in clown costume. Then, as events unfold, the cast play all the different characters – the Kaiser, General Haig, field officers or private soldiers – but remain in their clown suits, simply putting on a helmet, or army cap and Sam Browne belt, or a bowler hat, tiara, or nurse's headgear. The brilliantly ironic effect is to make the whole war a kind of cruel farce, every character in it a victim of the clown show of Europe's politics. This bitter irony is supported – maybe even engendered – by the cheerful/ironic/sentimental songs of the first World War, developed in the music-halls and carried out to the Front: *It's A Long, Long Trail A-winding, Tipperary, Oh We Don't Want To Lose You, Keep the Home Fires Burning* – and of course *Oh! It's A Lovely War*.

Like the rest of the cast, I played many parts, and I suppose I had been chosen for my singing as much as for being able to act with a variety of British accents, while my experience of musical revue, with its quick changes of character and costume, came in extremely handy. It was a happy rehearsal period: the comedy made us laugh, the horrors of war moved us deeply, and the songs raised the spirits as singing always does. Kevin was determined that our production should be a mirror image of the original, only reluctantly allowing his actors any leeway – except for Nick House, who was born for his role. The Crest had even rented the original clown costumes from Stratford East, and we enjoyed finding the names of the first cast sewn into the inside of our collars: Victor Spinetti, Barbara Windsor, Brian Murphy... As in all plays involving a group of soldiers we developed a powerful camaraderie and great commitment to the show, which opened to fine reviews some time in April. It played for three weeks, and drew such good crowds that we begged Murray Davis to extend the run – we could hardly bear the idea of the world we had created coming to an end. But for reasons I forget now it couldn't be done, and we sadly parted as the last night came and went.

All through the rehearsal and performance period of *Oh! What A Lovely War*, I continued to hammer out book reviews for the *Telegram*. It was a useful experience in two ways. First, any essays I had written up to this point had been for school and university, and composed to impress my teachers. Now I was expected to write for the Common Man: someone who was not an academic, and had to be spoken to without condescension and without too sophisticated a vocabulary, and yet with intelligence, brevity and even wit. Secondly, I had to meet a multitude of deadlines – three a week; there was no time to dawdle, and I had to make decisions quickly and firmly. All this was I think now a useful preparation for my subsequent work in the theatre, with its need for program notes, articles and summaries, and with time always an enemy. Among the books I reviewed I remember John Lennon's *In His Own Write*, Manchester's *The Making of A President* (Lyndon Johnson's 1964 election), and a book of essays on Canada by Edmund Wilson, which I trashed, attracting an angry letter from the man himself.

My job extended to writing obituaries of literary people, and I remember sitting in the offices till late researching and typing up a summary of Somerset Maugham's career and contribution, when he was taken ill and not expected to live. I stumbled out at midnight with the column done. In the event he recovered and lived another eighteen months.

I was also sent one weekend up to Orillia to cover the first conferring of the Stephen Leacock Award for Humour. I sped up north in my MG and enjoyed a couple of days of expense-account living beside Lake Couchiching, watching *Telegram* writer Greg Clark receiving the award and turning in a reasonably humorous column when I got back to Toronto.

A few weeks later I was approached by a commercial TV station and agreed to do an occasional book report for them, adding to my television experience and marginally to my income. BAWTREE ON BOOKS in fact did something to establish me in the city as a minor celebrity – if that is not too pretentious a word.

Soon after I joined his staff, Jeremy took me in to be introduced to the *Tely*'s legendary chief editor, Doug MacFarlane. He was too rarefied a figure for us to become friends. But I did get to know some of my fellow journalists on the paper. There was Ron Evans, the enthusiastic and hornrimmed-spectacled drama critic; McKenzie Porter, the moustachioed, very English and very conservative old buzzfungus, who wrote columns full of shock and horror at what the world was coming to. And there was DuBarry Campau, married to *Time Magazine's* Toronto stringer Serrell Hillman and one of Toronto's genuine eccentrics, with her bright red and obvious wig and her jewellery and gipsy costumes. And then there was Jeremy himself. I became lifelong friends with him and his family.

Those first months of 1965 were, in fact, the first time I felt I was becoming part of Toronto's 'scene'. Much of this could be attributed to my good friend Robin, whose wit and boozy charm opened many doors. Through him I became a regular at the Sunday brunches of the writer Charles 'Chuck' Israel and his hospitable and often somewhat tipsy wife Verna. They lived in a handsome house on the side of one of Toronto's ravines, and would invite television friends like Paul Almond, writers like Barry Callaghan, Kildare Dobbs and Robert Fulford and young pups like Robin and myself. We would also go frequently to the home of Hugo and Louise MacPherson on the edge of Wellesley Park. Hugo was still teaching then, but was shortly to become a rather unhappy Commissioner of the National Film Board. He was highly sophisticated and a connoisseur of the arts, and his guests tended to include artists like Harold Town and Jack Nichols.

I also continued to see Bill and Jane Glassco, who had suffered a heart-breaking loss the previous year when their firstborn son Benjamin, while being babysat by Bill's mother Willa, crawled his way through a hedge and drowned in the family swimming pool. Bill was still pursuing his academic career, but was clearly unhappy. He made it clear how much he envied the more exciting life that I was living, and I used to urge him to drop everything in favour of the theatre. It was to be another two or three years before he took the brave step, giving up his teaching and founding the Tarragon Theatre. His personal income made this possible, but he was always very Scots about it, and never flaunted his wealth.

It was this year, too, that I took up with an actress (as she would have called herself then) who was somewhat older than myself, and very sexually experienced. Her maturity eased my concern at being 'needed'. She had a way of treating our sleeping together as casual and a bit of a lark, and we lived together for a few weeks in very amiable harmony. Our affair came abruptly to an end, though, when I discovered that I had contracted venereal disease again. It seemed that my liaisons with women were destined to end in disaster.

It must have been in the late spring of that year that I was offered two different jobs within the space of one week, attracting me in two entirely different directions.

The first came through Bruce Attridge, who had been the producer of the two schools' television series I had hosted for the CBC. He invited me down to his office for a meeting and told me about a new university which was opening up that fall in Burnaby, British Columbia, to be named after the nineteenth-century explorer Simon Fraser. He showed me sketches and photographs of the striking new campus now being constructed following the designs of Canada's best-known architect, Arthur Erickson. He showed me brochures and lots of printed material, from the BC Government – and from the Chancellor they had appointed to oversee the rapid erection of the campus, Gordon Shrum. Bruce then told me that he had just been appointed Chairman of a 'department' to be called the Centre for Communications and the Arts. The Centre was to be a component of the Faculty of Education, which was being conceived on a wholly new and experimental principle by a Dr Archie MacKinnon, an education specialist recently appointed as Dean of Education at the new University. The other components were to be Behavioural Sciences, Social and Philosophical Studies and Physical Education. The binding principle of the Centre was to be the emerging study area of Communications, as the lens through which the arts were to be viewed and practised: this was the time, of course, when Marshall McLuhan, the guru of communications theory, was the reigning intellectual among those who sought to be new and innovative.

Bruce was now actively searching for artists to head the different arts areas. The young Canadian composer R. Murray Schafer had accepted the position of Resident in Music. Would I be interested in becoming his Resident in Theatre? The starting salary would be $5,000 a year. I expressed great interest, and promised to get back to him within a few days. I needed time to think. The appointment would involve a major displacement, transferring myself across the country to British Columbia, about which I knew very little. I took some of the material with me, and began talking over the idea with friends like Robin, Patrick and Joan Lyndon, Charles Israel and Kildare Dobbs.

It was while I was mulling over the offer that I got a telephone call from my old Victoria College colleague, Paul Bouissac. While teaching French at the college, Paul in his spare time had been pursuing his first love: the circus. He had now miraculously put together a circus company, which would be touring Ontario this summer. He had elephants, lions with their lion-tamer, performing dogs and circus horses. But he still had to fill one important position: would I join his company as the circus clown?

THE BEST FOOLING

I asked Paul what on earth he was thinking of to make me such an offer. I had no training, no experience as a clown. He told me that he had seen me in my clown costume in *Oh! What A Lovely War*, and that that was when the idea came to him: I was, he felt, a natural. How about it? He would pay me, if I remember, $200 a week.

If ever there was a moment and a place when "two roads diverged in a yellow wood", this was it. On the one hand a highly-respectable and well-paid position at a university, calling on my newly-won theatrical experience and knowledge, and with apparently a great deal of creative leeway: and on the other, a highly doubtful but overwhelmingly attractive launch into the unknown, promising a gipsy, bohemian existence among the special tribe of circus people, and certainly exposing me to the possibility of popular success but also of dismal failure. Which would be the road not taken?

It says something for my adventurousness that I considered my possible career as a clown quite seriously. But it says something for my conventionalism – or maybe my good sense – that I reluctantly told Paul I did not think his offer was right for me just at this time. (In the event, Paul's circus tour was a disaster, and when they ran totally out of funds and food for their livestock somewhere in northern Ontario, they had to cancel further performances and shoot the lions. As I used to say afterwards, telling this with a sigh, there was no knowing what would have happened to the clowns.)

Mind you, the Simon Fraser position also called for a spirit of adventure. It involved a move of nearly 3,000 miles, to work at an institution that had not yet opened its doors, under conditions that no one could predict, in a province where I knew no one, with colleagues I had not yet met – apart from Bruce. I was also a little dubious about Bruce's ability to steer a ship through these uncharted waters. He was a gentle, kindly and rather tentative soul, and I guessed that he was expecting rather more sweetness and light than might be at hand in such a project.

My friends were unanimous in encouraging me to go west, and I relished the thought of taking my little MG on the road. Joan Lyndon, Mary McAlpine and Jeremy Brown's wife Brenna were all from British Columbia, and assured me that their friends would be on hand to welcome me when I arrived. This was encouraging. But I was also leaving a city which had been good to me, and in which I was beginning to be known and even appreciated. I particularly thought of Stratford, and of the Langhams. I had been receiving beautiful letters from Helen and Michael about their experiences in Greece, and was extremely keen for their return to Canada so that we could continue our friendship. But I could expect no further work from Stratford during Michael's 1965 sabbatical, and after that – who knew?

I would also have to sign off from the *Telegram* where I had been making a minor name for myself. I doubted whether I would have the leisure to look for similar work in Vancouver: perhaps anyway I had done my time in that department. By accepting the position I would also be saying goodbye to my slowly-emerging career as an actor on stage and television: there would be little chance to hit the boards while I was running a theatre program for students, and it would be as a director rather than actor that I would be functioning. I had not directed any play since I had produced *The Beggar's Opera* with marionettes at school ten years before. I was nervous at my abilities in this direction.

And so the to and fro went on, as April turned into May. At the end of that month, I called up Bruce, and accepted his offer. I would need to report for duty at Simon Fraser in the last week of August.

Bruce then put me in touch with Murray Schafer, and we got together for lunch at the Balkan Restaurant on Elm Avenue. Meeting Murray, I soon knew that I was in the presence of a rare personality: highly intelligent, witty and rebellious. That day he was also charming. We had evidently both taken our jobs in a spirit of 'why not?', both attracted to the idea of being in at the beginning of a new institution, both interested in education, both passionate about the arts. He, much more than I, was committed to everything that was new in the arts, having walked out of the University of Toronto's music school in disgust at the stupidity of the system. He wanted a job where he would have time for the overriding mission of his life, which was to compose music. Some years earlier he had interviewed Ezra Pound, edited the music that Pound had written for an opera, and written a book about Pound's music. He had also recently published a pamphlet entitled *The Composer in the Classroom*, based on his experiences working musically with schoolchildren. I soon realized that this new colleague of mine would be pushing me into new paths, and that my conventional and even stuffy theatre experience was about to get shaken up.

I remember both of us being wary of that strange creature we were going to be part of: a Centre for Communications and the Arts. In trying to imagine a form for it, Murray mentioned the German Bauhaus School, conceived by Walter Gropius after the Great War to break away from the old arts academies and rethink the training of young artists; going back to basic principles of design, bringing together artists of different fields under the umbrella of architecture, reassociating the arts and crafts, giving freedom to teachers and encouraging new ways of teaching and original experimentation – and all this under the banner of an ideal socialism. It was the first time I knew of the Bauhaus in more than name, and determined to do some more reading before leaving for the West. In our case it seemed that the combining principle was to be not architecture but communications, for which Marshall McLuhan was clearly the guiding light. Murray also knew a great deal more than I did about McLuhan, and had devoured his seminal book *The Gutenberg Galaxy*, published three years earlier. I walked out of that first meeting of ours stimulated and challenged. The Bauhaus was to become a continuing target of study for me, and its combining of the arts (first dreamed of by Wagner the previous century) became a dictating idea from that moment on. When in later life I became associated with new music theatre work, it was to Murray that I owed the first inspiration.

As I recall that first conversation now, I realise how amazing it was – and fortuitous for me – that both he and I were hired as the result of the decision of just one man. No advertising for the job. No list of candidates. No selection process. No formal interview. Neither of us had doctorates. How different it would all be today.

It was no more than a few months into 1965 that I heard from my mother that Dad's job in Inkpen was coming to an end: the farm owner's brother had been away in Africa but had now returned and was to take over the pigs. In fact this was opportune, because for the last year or more Dad had been suffering from breathlessness when he was mucking out the pens. He had been to the doctors and they had diagnosed emphysema, his lungs affected especially by the ammonia in the pigs' urine. He had been happy returning to pig-farming, his first love, but it was clear that this way of making a living had run its course for him.

At this point, sister Jo brought up once again the idea that our parents should move to Italy. Mother had already fallen hopelessly in love with the country on her now annual visits, bringing back hand-painted Italian ceramics and all sorts of other memorabilia, and speaking of her times there so happily that Father had felt almost threatened. Several times he had summarily rejected the idea that he might accompany her on one of her visits, even if Jo paid for their travel. Too expensive, too much to do at home, none of the right clothes, won't let Jo pay: 'perfectly happy with England, thank you very much'. But the imminent loss of his pig manager's job, his health problem, and his realisation that he had the slenderest financial resources finally got him to agree to a two-week charter flight to Rome, for which he laid out funds for a white suit and a Panama hat.

Within two days of his arrival, and after a couple of bucolic visits out into the incomparable Italian countryside, with stops for a delicious and absurdly cheap lunch in a rustic *trattoria* or two, Father suddenly announced over the wine: "I think I could live here". From that moment on, they spent their holiday touring Umbria and Tuscany in the search for a possible home. Jo continued the hunt after they left, and eventually bought an old abandoned farmhouse, set among olives and vines a few kilometers from Montevarchi. It sat on the eastern edge of the Chianti, and faced a spectacular view of the Pratomagno, the range of hills east of the river Arno. She paid I think £2000, of which I put up one third. She also set about renovating the house, with a plan that would eventually provide a bathroom, a new kitchen and central heating. The ground floor, originally designed for livestock, would become the living room and dining room.

Though sad to leave Inkpen, Mother was ecstatic about the move, and in October of that year they stored some of their books and paintings and furniture with their oldest friend Wilma Hessey, then – with Wilma's expert help – packed their most precious transportable belongings into and on top of their now ageing Morris Traveller, and set off for Italy. Father had never driven on the 'wrong' side of the road before, but somehow he managed through France and Switzerland, and we have a fine photograph of them unpacking the car soon after their arrival. Among the boxes can be seen the grandmother clock bought from Mrs Kanoozel in Devon in 1942, a large copper bowl (rescued from an ancient copper, God knows when) for storing firewood, and a copper warming pan. Not what you might call necessities, but 'decencies' at least.

The house was called 'Muricce', but they decided to rename it. The house up the lane was called 'Casa del Monte' (House of the Mountain), so for their new home they chose 'Casa del Bosco' (House of the Woods).

As with all alterations, there was some hope that things would be completed by the time the 'Aged Ps' came to occupy the house. No such good luck: the health authorities had decided that before anything else was done the roof would have to be raised a metre, and this major piece of construction was still in process when they arrived. In the first weeks and even months they were able to live in only one room upstairs, with a Primus stove, a paraffin heater, and beds and bedding from Jo. At first there was no electricity, and water only from a single tap downstairs. You have perhaps learned enough about our parents that they accepted these conditions without complaint, and even with excitement. It was one of Tuscany's coldest winters, and they endured temperatures in their one room, which were sometimes little above freezing. Not only that, but Father had bought himself *Teach Yourself Italian* before he left England, and began sitting down for several hours a day to learn the language. They were now fifty-seven years old.

The previous year my younger sister Jenny had accepted a position as an *Instruttore* teaching English at the University of Florence. This meant that she was able to ride her newly-acquired

Vespa to Montevarchi most weekends to keep the parents company. And of course Jo was regularly making the three-hour car journey from Rome to bring goodies from FAO's commissariat and to talk with the contractors.

The hope was that if Father could become at least conversant with Italian, he might be able to pick up a little money teaching English. It seemed a remote chance. But within a few months Jenny saw a notice from the British Institute in Florence, advertising for an English teacher. Dad donned his one suit and drove into Florence to be interviewed for the position. His credentials were minimal: he had left school at sixteen and had no subsequent academic qualifications of any kind. All he could claim was an abiding knowledge of and love for the English language, and a preparedness to work hard and conscientiously.

To the astonishment and delight of the whole family, he landed the job. It may be appropriate here to note that after nearly forty years working in many different situations, he had finally found his vocation. He taught for the next eight years, and his classes were always oversubscribed, because the news soon went round that if you got into Il Professore Bawtree's class you were certain to pass. With his age and natural air of authority he also soon became the *doyen* of the teaching body. He even led them out on strike to get holiday pay, a fight which, under his determined and principled leadership, of course they won. I would never in many moons have imagined Father as a leader of labour unrest. But there it was.

CHAPTER SEVEN

GONE WEST

Some time in the middle of August, I gathered my things and myself together, resigned from the *Telegram*, said goodbye to many good friends, and set off west along the TransCanada Highway. It was to be a trip I would make several times again, though I never quite got over the surprise of driving for a day and a half and finding I was still in the same province. After the rocky outcrops of Northern Ontario and the slow skirting of Lake Superior's northern shore, Manitoba and Saskatchewan passed swiftly by, giving me my first views of tumbleweed, and of the vast prairie sky with different weather systems at each point of the compass. On, on into Alberta, and that first incredulous glimpse of the Rocky Mountains ambling along the western horizon as far as the eye could see. I pulled in for the night at the Voyageur Inn in Banff, now finding myself totally encircled by towering peaks, and not suspecting for a moment that many years later I would be calling this place my home. On, on, down the Kicking Horse Pass into British Columbia, through the Rogers Pass, past Revelstoke and then finally down, down, on a seemingly endless slope toward the Pacific. My move westward had given me for the first time some sense of the size and grandeur of my newly-adopted country.

Through friends of my Toronto friends I was put up at the house of a middle-aged poet, the mother of a small boy and lately separated from her sculptor husband. But through other contacts I was soon able to sub-lease a second-floor furnished apartment in a fine house on the ocean side of Point Grey Road. From my open windows I could smell the salt air and hear the lapping tide, watch the sunset, and see the logging rafts being tugged up English Bay to Granville Island, with the big cargo ships lining up further out, waiting their turn to dock and be laboriously unloaded: container ships still lay in the future. Across the Bay at night were the lights of West Vancouver, or the distant wail of foghorns when the sea mists rolled in. It was good to be so solidly rooted on the ocean shore.

I remember little of my first drive up to the campus of Simon Fraser; so much was to be taken in. Bruce welcomed me in his new office, and introduced me to various colleagues, including his Vice Chairman; the group psychologist, Tom Mallinson (specialising in 'interpersonal communication'); our Dean, Archie MacKinnon; the Academic Planner and chairman of the English Department, Ron Baker; and the Resident in Visual Arts, Iain Baxter. Later I was to meet the formidable Chancellor Gordon Shrum, and the less formidable but personable President, Patrick McTaggart-Cowan, trained as a meteorologist and soon to be nicknamed McFog. Murray Schafer was also around, and before long I was invited to his home for dinner and to meet his wife, the exceptional singer Phyllis Mailing.

I was taken to 'my' theatre, which was still being completed, and still missing its 400 seats: I was assured they would be ready soon. On the floor beneath sat the offices for the new Residents, and a meeting-room.

Back outside, I marvelled like all new arrivals at Arthur Erickson's Lhasa-like takeover of the top of Burnaby Mountain, with its huge glass-covered quadrangle and its cascade of steps up to a wide terrace, where the office building on its concrete stilts slashed the sky above. Looking out from the terrace we could see Mount Baker in Washington State, ninety miles to the south, and on the north side the waters of Indian Arm snaking off into the forest and mountains.

It was not possible to take all this in without a lift of the heart. Everything was to be invented fresh, with a new and brave cluster of buildings to house it all. Old modes of thinking were to be discarded. The talk was all of the world we were about to make: a new place of learning, new kinds of teaching, new ways of thinking about the arts, new colleagues. 'Creativity' was one of the watchwords.

It goes without saying that I wondered whether I was ready for the task. I was a lumpen traditionalist, comfortable with the language and craft of Shakespeare, soaked in the canon of English literature, and with the gentle manners of a thousand-year-old culture. What had all that 'stuff' to do with the elemental world in which I now found myself?

I had not just 'relocated': I had finally moved from the old world to the new – a shift far more profound than my shipping out over the Atlantic three years earlier. In Toronto and Stratford I had found a market for my English education and knowledge of things: eastern Canada was an extension of old Europe. But here on the top of our mountain I stood as though in an abstract painting. We were a brilliant blob of raw colour between the mountains and the sea.

Shrum's central idea for his university's instruction was that in each course a master teacher would lecture to a large body of students twice a week and that each master teacher would have working alongside him or her a group of five or six junior faculty and graduate students who would function as 'tutors', and would conduct weekly tutorials, for which the class would be broken up into smaller groups.

I soon found that as the 'Residents' in theatre and music, Murray Schafer and I were to be the master teachers in the fields of music and theatre. I was to be seconded to the English Department to lecture in the first-year drama course: Drama 103. I was in fact, as I found to my surprise and nervousness, the 'master teacher' in drama.

There were no credit courses set up in Theatre, and theatrical activity was going to be entirely extra-curricular, bringing together students from all disciplines who were interested in being involved. In an educational world now dominated by the need to parcel out knowledge into 'credits' towards a degree, it might seem strange that back in the mid-sixties I was embracing the idea of a non-curricular theatre at the university. 'Non-credit' suggested to some a lack of seriousness, but on the contrary, I was entirely in agreement with the plan. After all, my own experience at Oxford was exactly the same. There was no theatre degree program at Oxford: theatrical activity at both college and university level was run entirely by students, and attracted actors, directors and theatre technicians from every field of study from physics to classics – many of whom went on to distinguished theatrical careers. I liked to say, not entirely jokingly, that our theatre work was not non-curricular but 'supra-curricular': far too important to be constrained within the curriculum.

Another distinguishing feature of Shrum's plan for the university was the setting up of a trimester system. There were three trimesters in Simon Fraser's academic year, and students were able to enroll for each semester separately. Faculty would teach two semesters in every three, but could also teach three semesters and then spend the next two away. This flexibility was much appreciated by many students and professors. Its disadvantage was the lack of continuity from one term to the next: you never knew who might be returning and who not. And within non-curricular activities it was particularly difficult to build a 'culture', when the participants were continually changing. It was a system that had been developed with icy logic from the money-based idea that post-secondary education could be accumulated in discrete units, like pennies in a jar.

Feeling somewhat lonely, I put up signs over the campus inviting students interested in theatre to come to the theatre lobby the next Monday evening. I wondered what I would do if no one showed up, but to my relief twenty or more came by, and we were able to discuss plans. It was my thought that we should produce one play each term, and this seemed to go down well. I took names and asked about the theatre experiences of each of them, and was pleased to find that several had credentials in community and even professional theatre. Among those who attended was one Tom Kerr, who had enrolled at Simon Fraser as a mature student, having already had some professional experience as a director – he had even assisted Tyrone Guthrie. So it was not long before I hit upon the idea of him directing our first production, enabling me to concentrate on the logistics of producing Simon Fraser's very first play, in a theatre which, when our rehearsals started, still had no seating, no staff, no infrastructure of any kind. He was only too glad to oblige, and suggested Robert Bolt's *A Man For All Seasons*, which had had successful runs in London and on Broadway a few years earlier. And so it was decided: we would hold auditions the following week.

In retrospect, I believe that my relief at being able to pass the job on to Tom came partly from my lack of self-confidence as a director in my own right. From my work with Langham I knew what to do: I simply had never done it alone. Such lack of self-assurance was in fact to tinge my work in the theatre for several years: my often original ideas of what could be done, and my eloquence in articulating them, often persuaded people to come along for the ride. But it took a long time for my self-belief and tenacity to match my imagination and rhetoric.

For now, though, all was well, and I set about equipping our theatre as best I could: harrying the architect and builders for seats and lights, and for the completion of the painting of the auditorium; arranging - I forget how - for the design and building of a set and costumes for the play; persuading my boss Bruce Attridge that a theatre simply could not be run without a technical director – and managing to source the funds to hire Jan Visscher for the role. His talents, we were to find, were varied and invaluable.

Through my connections with the English Department I met two new faculty members (of course we were all new), who were to become special friends. John Mills was born a Cockney, and had bummed around Canada for many years – running a laundry in Montreal, working on the DEW line in the Arctic – before deciding to enroll as a mature student in English at the University of British Columbia; he was also writing a novel. Jerry Zaslove was American, and had come north to Canada after studying Comparative Literature, most recently at the University of Washington. Both John and Jerry had been hired as junior members of the English Department, and through them I soon met Professor Ralph Maud, whose special interest was Dylan Thomas, but who was also enthusiastic and knowledgeable about Charles Olson and the other Black Mountain poets.

Meanwhile, the University's form and functions were stumblingly taking shape around us. Like the rest of our colleagues, my new friends and I had been drawn to the idea of becoming part of a newly-created organism – one that we could help to grow. We were after all living in the middle of the sixties: Western society was heading into a crisis, brought on by the death of Kennedy, civil rights strife, the Vietnam War, and a widening generational divide. The assumptions that had directed Western culture were now being heavily questioned or even being thrust violently aside. Universities were unique – outside the heavily-disciplined armed forces – in bringing young people together in mass groupings, and were rapidly becoming the focus for confrontation with the forces of order and stability. The excitement of all this was the chance, and the desire, to make all things new. The risk was instability and even violence as the opposing forces clashed.

In this welter of excitement and fear, Simon Fraser, the newborn child, was ripe for kidnapping. It had been conceived and brought to birth in the astonishingly short time of two years, by the Province's populist Social Credit government, which saw it as a powerful and propaganda-rich step forward in its buccaneering leadership – along with the Bank of British Columbia and the extension of the Pacific Great Eastern Railway, soon to become British Columbia Railway. Simon Fraser's Board of Governors was made up of eight businessmen, who were chosen no doubt for their business acumen but also for their closeness to Government circles, certainly not for any expertise in the formation or running of a university. They were happy to leave academic decisions to their chairman Gordon Shrum and his appointees. Little did they guess at the problems they would soon be dealing with.

The faculty assembled by Shrum and his Deans came from Canada, Great Britain and the United States, each of them bringing a separate set of experiences and expectations, and each with a different idea of what might constitute the ideal university. Some came up the west coast from the University of California at Berkeley, a focus of opposition to the US bombing campaign in Vietnam and home of the Free Speech Movement, which had responded the previous year with massive protests to the administration's ban on political activities on the campus. This group, already hardened political activists, had jumped at the chance of creating a people's university free of administrative tampering, free of encrusted tradition, free of authoritarian rule – and in a country free of America's militarism. Others flew in from more traditional universities in Canada and Britain, and were most concerned that the new university should not be seen as a Mickey Mouse place but that it should establish and maintain the high standards of scholarship they brought from their previous institutions. My new friends John and Jerry were different again. John was an adventurer, with an old-fashioned Labourite hatred and mocking envy of the 'upper classes' and a tendency to joke about the things that moved him the most. Jerry was the purest theoretical anarchist I had ever met, with a warm smile and a fine mind, though with an abiding difficulty in expressing himself clearly, a new thought bumping into almost every sentence before it was completed. He also had that engaging gift of assuming that you knew what he was talking about. Confused as we might be, no one wanted to disappoint him.

Though the three of us were very different, we were all vocal and, you could say, anti-establishment. We became known before long as 'the Young Turks'. As John reminisced half a century later: "What we contributed was a feeling of *festivitas*: here we were, young and vigorous and full of ideas, and there they were – the wiser heads prevailing, the retro academics dressed in suits, the authority figures. You were one of *les jeunes*, and a noticeable member of it."

Under acute pressure of time, the University needed not only to start teaching the two or three thousand students who descended on (or rather ascended to) our mountain campus that September, but also to create its constitutional structure. This began with the election of a Senate, which would be the arbiter for every element of the University's life apart from its budget. For some reason, I was asked if I would stand for the first Senate elections. I agreed, and soon found myself a charter member of that supposedly august body.

The Senate had scores of elemental decisions to make, from determining the grading system that Simon Fraser would adopt to deciding whether or not a Code of Conduct would be created for the guidance of students – especially in the first student residence, which had just been completed. Then there were policies to be agreed on with regard to credit transfers from other universities, and the entrance qualifications to be set for mature students. We had to decide on matters of attendance and plagiarism, and the penalties to be meted out to offenders.

We were in fact assembling the building blocks of a new society, and were faced in every vote with a personal conflict between preferring to duplicate the methods and policies with which we were familiar from our own experience in other places, and wanting to invent new ways of doing things. It was fascinating to watch, with each vote, how clearly the new Senators divided off into conservatives and progressives, with the usual bunch of waverers in between. I used to say afterwards that it was the only body I had ever been part of where I felt I had to brush up on my Plato, Hume or John Stuart Mill before each meeting. I was, perhaps you could say, a moderate progressive: but, seen as their representative by the bolshier elements of faculty, I was often taken aside by more fervently radical types outside the Senate and firmly instructed how to vote on thornier issues.

It was natural that with all this power over every aspect of the new University's life, the Senate would become one of the first targets of controversy and eventually wrath. Faculty progressives – and of course the newly formed Students' Union – proposed forcefully that the Senate should include at least one student representative. They also campaigned to demand, in the interests of transparency, that Senate meetings be open. These were early days for such flagrantly democratic proposals, and the President came out strongly against them. At the next meeting I was a little embarrassed when my friends John and Jerry turned up and took seats against the wall to assert their right to witness the proceedings. After muttered consultations around the Chair, the Senate's secretary approached them and awkwardly requested "the absence of their presence", a phrase which gave them great delight as they consented to retire. They had made their point.

We all rely on past experience to give us a zone of assurance from which we can tentatively explore the new; that is what growing up is all about. But at Simon Fraser, which had sprung full grown from the forehead of BC's Premier 'Wacky' Bennett, there was no past experience, no zone of stability. It was a while before we realised that this effort to 'make all things new' was creating great psychological stress, as we found ourselves caught between the comfort of the familiar we had brought with us and the fear of untrodden ways. At Simon Fraser in that first year of 1965 the pressure was intense, with no institutional systems to hold on to, no respect of authority yet forged or earned, no ways of doing anything yet established – from the penalising of student misdemeanours to the ordering of stationery. Lines of authority had yet to be laid down, and every attempt to draw them was aggressively questioned. Those in senior positions, who had arrived proud and self-confident, now found their every decision analysed and often enough scorned and rejected. Paranoia was soon in the air, and hostilities hardened.

One by one, faculty members began to drop (the next two or three years saw one fatal heart attack, a death from leukemia and two suicides). One of the first casualties was our own Bruce Attridge, whose previously mild heart condition swiftly worsened. Six weeks after term began he went on medical leave – never to return. His place as Director of the Centre for Communications and the Arts was taken by our most senior academic and Vice Chairman, the group psychologist Professor Tom Mallinson. Things soon took on a surreal turn as he applied the methods of an encounter group to our staff meetings. One genial opener I still remember:

"Let's all sit down, and take a good look at the kinds of things we see ourselves as doing."

Tom's professional lack of 'affect' drove me wild:

"Tom, we're opening in four weeks and there are still no seats in the theatre!"

"I see."

"And the lights are not being delivered till next week!"

"I see. Look, take a seat. Would you like a coffee?"

"Tom, I am getting really, really angry!"

"I see."

Tom's experience of the passion that can be unleashed by artistic conviction was extremely limited, and we Residents stirred uneasily under his genial but ineffective leadership.

Meanwhile, my lecture assignment with the English Department was to give me my first chance to approach the teaching of theatre in a new way, following Simon Fraser's ceaseless injunctions to break with traditional methods. Traditional drama courses in English departments in those days (and maybe still) were in fact simply studies of dramatic literature, with the class moving steadily from one set text to the next over the course of a term. There were texts already set for our course (Pinter, Miller, Tennessee Williams and so on), but, fresh from my experience in the professional theatre, and inspired by my recent introduction to the work of the Bauhaus, I decided to leave the discussion of the texts to my tutors, and to use my lectures instead to introduce my students to the basic principles of theatre. In that first term, I gave my lectures in a large lecture auditorium, but from the second term onwards I was able to teach in 'my' theatre, with its wide stage, its curtain and its lights and seating: I was able to use these resources to expose the students to the properties of light and darkness, to the element of surprise in the rolling back of the curtain, to the techniques of building interest and excitement. We viewed the whole spectrum of dramatic effect, from minimal to maximal, culminating in melodrama. In discussing character I opened the curtain one time to reveal eight chairs, all of different sizes, colours and degrees of comfort, from an old armchair in rusty velvet, through an elegant dining-room seat, to the stackable unit in blue plastic which was readily available around the new campus. This gave rise to the whole question of what makes a chair, and of differences and similarities: we hovered, in fact, close to the Platonic essence of 'chair'. We were also able to observe the 'character' of each chair, and from there to consider the word 'character' as applied to people.

At this distance I cannot guess or remember how effective all this was. I know that the head of the English Department had his serious doubts. But as in every other field of activity, there was great reluctance to criticise anyone who was doing something new and different. I was allowed to persevere. And for the first time in my life I developed some ease in speaking more or less extempore to large assemblies of people.

As can be seen, it is difficult to launch into my experience of that first year at Simon Fraser without finding myself sliding away into the complex story of the University itself, in which for four years I was so heavily engaged. Sufficient to say that somehow we soldiered through that first term. *A Man for All Seasons* was a respectable first showing for our fledgling theatre program, with some fine playing by Blain Fairman as Thomas More, by the rotund Owen Foran as Wolsey, and by a young Norman Browning as Cromwell. The whole shaky institution breathed a collective sigh of relief to have survived, and we soon fled away down the mountain for the Christmas season. We would come back to find, of course, that nothing had become easier. Nor, as 1966 came up over the horizon, did I have any idea that this coming year would be pivotal in my own life.

CHAPTER EIGHT

RUSSIAN INTERLUDE

The second semester began straightforwardly enough. I put up my welcome signs and once again was glad to be able to muster a fair group, among them some new recruits, with others from the previous term's activities. I had also been busy tossing around ideas for my own first production, and in my talks with Jerry Zaslove had fastened on Gogol's *The Government Inspector*. Gogol held particular fascination for Jerry: he had already published a paper on that uniquely strange Russian writer, and was able to introduce me to the entirely Russian concept of *poshlost*, translated in many different ways, among them 'banality', 'complacent mediocrity' and 'self-satisfied vulgarity'. The rascally Mayor and his upward-aspiring wife and simpering daughter, with all the council members of this remote and squalid little town, are all imbued with *poshlost*, and when they hear with horror that a Government Inspector is going to descend on them incognito, they assume the next visitor to the town – a characterless little clerk running away from his creditors – to be the Inspector in disguise.

Simon Fraser's mountain-top grandeur, thrown into place by a

Social Credit government led by a former hardware store owner, somehow resonated with Gogol's play, and made it a happy choice for me – and of course for Jerry, who came eagerly to early rehearsals with a mission to convey the precise quality of *poshlost* to more or less mystified young students. This was the first full-scale play I had ever directed, and I soon came to relish the comedy of it, finding in fact that I had some skill in making things both pointed and funny.

It was three or four weeks into the term when late one evening I received a call from Michael Langham. He was in Winnipeg with the Stratford company, having just directed and opened a new play called *Nicholas Romanoff*, starring William Hutt and Frances Hyland as the Tsar and Tsarina. The play had been commissioned by Stratford from a young American writer named William Kinsolving, and Michael had made an arrangement to preview it at the Manitoba Theatre Centre before opening it at Stratford's Avon Theatre for twelve performances during the coming season. So far, so good. But Michael was calling me in great distress, saying that the play lacked drama of any kind, and had turned out to be a crashing bore. Would I please come immediately to Winnipeg, see the play, and then meet with Kinsolving and give him some ideas for improving it before its Stratford run the following July?

I was doubtful what I could do but was happy to try and oblige, and a few days later I took off to Winnipeg for the weekend, arriving at the perfect time to savour the full brutality of February on the Prairies. I met with Michael, who handed me a script and then went into detail about his view of the play's shortcomings. Kinsolving, Michael felt, had not succeeded in lifting the action off the page of history. Every scene was like a re-enacted tableau, accurate and lifeless. So he felt. After sharing a drink and a snack I went to the theatre and sat through the play, trying both to appreciate it and to take notes. A tall order. The play had received the full Stratford treatment in its production values, with gorgeous costumes by Leslie Hurry (who had travelled with the company, and whose opinion of Winnipeg's climate was unprintable) and powerful music by Louis Applebaum. Michael's staging of the piece was as skillful as one would expect, but there was no question that the play lacked life and forward movement.

When it was over, Michael and I battled back to the hotel through wind and snow and over several whiskies analysed the problems. Next morning I met Kinsolving for breakfast. He did not entirely appreciate this stranger foisted on him by Michael as a kind of play-doctor, but he took it well, and went away with a bunch of notes. He was asked to come up with his revisions in four or five weeks. I returned to British Columbia, and went on with my production.

Towards the end of March, and well after *The Government Inspector* had opened and closed a pleasurable four-day run, I heard once again from Michael. He had just received the revised script, and told me that whereas the original had severe problems, this new version was 'totally unplayable'. He sounded very shaken, and seemed to be imagining a disastrous failure at the Avon in July. He told me he was sending it to me by courier, and asked me to do whatever it took to re-write the play. He also told me he had talked with Kinsolving, who had little choice but to accept Michael's view of his work, and of what needed to be done. I had a free hand.

The new script arrived, and in my spare time I toiled over it, trying to see how I could massage it into some sort of shape along the lines that Michael and I had discussed. But the more I worked, the harder it seemed to become. After a week or two, I stepped back from it, and tried to imagine what I would do if I was writing a play about the final years of the Romanovs, but starting from scratch. What Kinsolving's play lacked, I felt, was a point of view. I imagined some kind of narrator, through whose eyes the story could be seen. The problem was that there were two ways of viewing the decline and fall of the dynasty and the rise of the Bolsheviks. So I imagined two narrators, one a Romanov and the other a Bolshevik, battling for control of the play, their fight reflecting the struggle between the autocratic Romanovs and the people of Russia.

I had agreed that I would fly to Stratford the moment my term was over in early April, and I set out braced for Michael's disappointment when I told him I simply couldn't see my way to rewriting Kinsolving's play. I assumed he would swiftly get in touch with some more experienced playwright and give him the job.

Arriving in Stratford, I told him of my difficulties with the script, and said I could only imagine starting over from the beginning and writing a new kind of play. He wanted to know more, and I told him some of my thoughts. "That's great," he said. "So why don't you write it?"

"What do you mean?"

"I mean I'll commission you to write a new play," said Michael.

"But that's impossible," I said. "There are only six weeks before the first rehearsal. It can't be done. Besides, I've never written a play in my life!"

"Look," he said, "You have one of the finest theatre companies in North America to write for. You have a wonderful designer, who has already designed many of the clothes, and can design more as needed. You have the finest theatre composer you could wish for. You have a director who is not half bad. And look, half the tickets have already been sold. What playwright could turn down such an opportunity?"

The idea was absurd, but Michael was insistent. I was moved by his faith in my ability to do the job, and I reasoned to myself that if the result was a dismal failure it would have to be Michael who would take the blame: how could he possibly have expected that a totally inexperienced writer could produce a play in six weeks? After another hour of discussion, and several more whiskies and cigarettes, I said I would give it a go.

To make things tighter still, I had to return to Vancouver for a couple of weeks to plan my absence for the summer semester before settling back in Stratford to write in earnest. Michael would then put me up at his house on Trow Avenue (Helen was still in England), and I would be able to take over the dining room. A typewriter would be provided from the Festival, as well as anything else I needed.

Back at Simon Fraser I got permission to be away for the summer, and set about finding a replacement Theatre Resident. I don't remember how it happened, but I recommended the appointment of an actor I had met in the Stratford company in 1964. His name was John Juliani. I had also recently signed a lease for an apartment on Wall Street in Burnaby, facing the Second Narrows. I was able to sublet this apartment to Juliani for the summer.

Meanwhile I was spending every available moment in the Vancouver City Library reading all the books I could lay my hands on that dealt with the 1912-1918 period in Russia. I was particularly interested in the Romanov family, and before long came across Tsar Nicholas' brother, Grand Duke Michael Alexandrovich, who had fallen in love with a divorcée named Natalie (Natasha) Brusova and married her, and as a result had been exiled from Russia by his brother and was living in London until war broke out in 1914, when Nicholas summoned him back to help defend the Motherland. I even discovered that when Nicholas abdicated in 1917, he did so in favour of his brother Michael, and for forty-eight hours Michael was technically Tsar. Hence my title, *The Last of the Tsars*. Here perhaps was my Romanov narrator – someone extremely close to the royal family but alienated from it through following his heart. For the Bolshevik narrator I decided to create a character whom I called Samoilov, which was in fact the name of a party member mentioned by Trotsky, and one of those passionate believers who used to travel through the land at this time, evading the Tsar's secret police (the Okhrana) and spreading the message of revolution. I was also happy to have access to the diaries and correspondence of the Tsar and Tsarina, who used to write to one another in English. Much of their dialogue was to be taken straight out of these sources.

My return to Ontario was imminent, and a few days before my departure I started writing: by the time I left for the East I had completed twenty pages of text. My friend John Mills drove me in my MG to the airport – he would be looking after the car in my absence.

When I had settled into the plane I looked for the thin plastic briefcase in which my precious pages lay, and to my horror I was unable to find them. I then remembered that I had put them on to the roof of my car when leaving. They must have fallen off into the street.

This was what you might call a setback, and when I arrived in Stratford many hours later, I had to tell Michael the classic good-news-bad-news story: I had made a really good start on the play and written twenty pages – BUT I had lost them on the journey. Michael was aghast. I cheered him up by telling him that on the plane I had already started re-writing, and that because the first draft was so recent I felt I could recreate the missing pages in a day or two. Which I did. (Two weeks later a parcel arrived, which turned out to contain my missing brief case. The postman had found it in the bushes near where my car had been parked, and enterprisingly had somehow tracked me to Simon Fraser, where a kind secretary had forwarded it on.)

The next day, as Michael left for the theatre, I began settling into what became a regular routine in his dining room, pounding away on the Festival's old Remington, and slowly covering page after page of blue paper. When Michael returned from work that first day I had already recreated the missing pages.

From then on I was able at five o'clock each afternoon to report another few pages completed, and Michael would pop next door for a drink with Executive Producer John Hayes while I soldiered on for another hour or so. Within ten days I had completed the first of my two acts, and for the first time I shared with Michael what I had done. He seemed happy and said that he had some ideas, but I should just keep going. It was now just less than three weeks to the first rehearsal.

At some point Michael confided to me that he had not told his Board that he was dropping the Kinsolving play, because he felt they might not be able to cope. He had thus taken entirely on himself the responsibility for inviting me to write a replacement play. When Floyd Chalmers, then Board president, discovered in late May what was going on, he was extremely angry, as Michael predicted he would be. But, as Michael had also calculated, it was by then too late to do anything about it. Michael's shouldering of the full responsibility for the change of play was courageous, but of course depended entirely on his faith in me. His calm confidence was inspiring: he had somehow persuaded himself that I would be able to complete the commission. I was less sure.

Meanwhile he was having to face a potentially much more difficult situation with the acting company. Actors had been contracted to play characters in a play that had now been discarded, and were having to wait to find out what the new play would offer them, either in the same character or in another. Bill Hutt's leadership of the company during those strange weeks was critical. After all, it was Bill himself who had to suffer the biggest change: it was already clear that the leading role in my play would be not Tsar Nicholas but his brother Grand Duke Michael, and Langham had already confided this to Bill. Bill would have to give up the throne. But there was still no completed script for him or anyone to read. Only faith in Langham kept things on a more or less even keel, while I kept sweating away at 19 Trow Avenue.

Then, halfway through the second act, with countless strands of action weaving along in my text, I got stuck. For a whole day I couldn't produce a word. "How's it going?" asked Michael when he returned from the theatre at the end of the day. "Nothing," I replied miserably. "I just can't get anything to work." Michael didn't flinch for a second. "Don't worry," he said, smiling and relaxed as ever. "These things happen. You'll be fine tomorrow." And he left me to agonise for another hour or so before dinner.

The next day the same thing happened, and once again Michael was calm and confident, popping next door and leaving me alone for the last tortured and unproductive hour of the day. I tried everything – walks by the river, hot baths, phone calls to friends, Agatha Christie, double Scotches. Nothing helped. For the third day my page was a blank, and only Michael's imperturbable faith kept me from taking the first train out. But then that night, some time between sleep and wake, an amazing thing happened: three pages of text suddenly sprang complete into my mind, pulling the play's various strands together and breaking the deadlock. I rose early and had the pages written out by breakfast.

Within another week the second and final act was complete,

leaving about five days to work on a second draft. We read the play together, and Michael's advice and suggestions were invaluable: I was far too close to it to know what I had written. During one or two of those final evenings I walked over to the Avon Theatre and stood there alone on the darkened stage, reading my script aloud to test its rhythms. On the first day of rehearsal the cast had the first act in their hands. By the afternoon of the next day they were able to read through the play to the end. Their reaction was mostly positive, although Frances Hyland, who played the Tsarina in the earlier play, was not happy with her new incarnation in mine, thinking she came across as a nasty piece of work. She gracefully withdrew from the role, which was taken on greedily by Amelia Hall.

William Kinsolving's lawyers naturally demanded to see my text, concerned that I might have lifted sections from the previous work. But it really was a new play, a fact that they soon readily acknowledged: "We don't own the Russian Revolution," they admitted. Kinsolving was disappointed and hurt by the turn of events, and I felt badly about this, even though Stratford fulfilled its financial obligations to him. I wondered whether he assumed I had used my position as play doctor to pronounce the patient dead and then to muscle in on replacing him. As I hope is clear, this was not the case.

The Last of the Tsars, as I titled it, featured some of the same characters as Kinsolving's play: the Tsar and Tsarina, Rasputin, and other members of the Court, as well as Kerensky, the first prime minister following the March revolution. But I had also introduced four new major characters. Besides Grand Duke Michael (William Hutt) and the Bolshevik Samoilov (Tony van Bridge), there was Grand Duke Michael's English servant, Johnson (Barry MacGregor), whom he had brought back with him to Russia. And there was Natalie Sergeevna Brusova ('Natasha'), the divorcée whom Michael had married against the strict injunctions of his brother. The Montreal actor Kim Yaroshevskaya was brought in to play Natasha, and Joel Kenyon replaced William Hutt as the Tsar (this was my suggestion – he had worked with me in *Oh! What A Lovely War*, and looked amazingly like Nicholas the Second).

We were also blessed by the fact that my play was to be played in repertory with the opera *Don Giovanni*, and that the entire opera chorus was available to us to fill out the stage. We were thus able to marshal a fine crowd to stand in for 'the Russian people', and to make use of their powerful voices for the singing of the Russian national anthem – to be eventually supplanted by *The Red Flag*.

I had learned in my reading that Grand Duke Michael had been captured by the Bolsheviks after the revolution and taken to the distant province of Perm, where in 1919 he was living in a barn, still looked after by the faithful Johnson. From this situation I developed the idea of presenting the whole story of the collapse of the Tsardom, the Great War and the revolution as a flashback, narrated by Grand Duke Michael as a supremely gracious host welcoming the audience and sharing his story, while its characters – the Tsar and Tsarina, Rasputin and the rest – appeared as he talked, and played their scenes while he watched or took part in them. The Russian soldiers guarding him also took on the roles of soldiers in the Great War. And Samoilov, who first appears as a loyal Bolshevik coming to sneer at a captive Romanov, later wrestles with Michael for control of the play's events. In the end, with the approach of the White Russian army towards his prison in Perm, Grand Duke Michael was taken out and shot. I was planning for this to be the final scene of the play, as we returned to the 'real time' of Michael's imprisonment in 1919.

All this involved a good deal of play-within-a-play theatricality, and I must have been seriously influenced both by Pirandello and also by my recent involvement in *Oh! What A Lovely War*. Playing with time and space in this way put pressure on our audience – but also on the characters of the play, whose occasional confusion I allowed as part of the action. Holding this space-time magic together as a kind of presiding deity was the character of Natasha, who with her seductive femininity and intuitive wisdom had no problems with the coming and going of it all. "Events are objects," she says at one point, "You can throw them around." There was no doubt in my mind of the person I had taken as my model for Natasha. It was none other than Michael's wife Helen, who had first cast her spell on me three years earlier, and still remained a powerful force in my life.

The change of play placed huge pressure not only on the cast, who had to rehearse a new play from scratch, but also on the design department and the wardrobe, with Leslie Hurry having to design and supervise the building of costumes for the new characters. He also had to design a new stage set. He covered the whole back of the stage with a drably-painted gauze, behind which stretched a massive double-headed eagle of Russia, set over a red cross and surrounded by icons. This 'iconostasis' was for the most part invisible, but shone through the gauze at times in the action when the Romanov dynasty had its brief shining moments. The stage itself was as bare as the barn it portrayed, with just one large hexagonal rostrum that could be moved around, and two hexagonal stools. Palace chairs were occasionally brought in by flunkeys for the court scenes, and canvas army chairs were introduced for officers in the field. Otherwise changes of scene and time were achieved with lighting and sound.

Having lived through the searing pressure of producing the play script, I found the rehearsal period to be comparatively plain sailing, and remember little of it. I would attend rehearsals and take notes, and every evening would confer with Michael, adding a line or two here, a mini-scene there, shifting sentences and even scenes around, and changing the odd word. Actors would also feel free to make suggestions, many of which I was able to incorporate. My own memory of that time was warm and positive: I felt there was a genuine shared excitement in pulling off this risky venture. I was not of course exposed to the customary actors' gossip behind the scenes. Just as well. I was continually buoyed up by Michael's faith in me: he wrote a note to me during that rehearsal period, which I still have: "I cannot tell you how profoundly I admire what you're doing – and the very responsive inner world of your work." Oh joy!

The play opened to a full house on July 12th, 1966. There was sustained applause at the end, and the Festival administration clearly felt, with some relief, that Michael's gamble had paid off. The critics were less certain: "Audience Likes 'Tsar', But Critics Divided", ran one column a few days later, after several reviewers had had their say. The *Toronto Telegram's* Ron Evans – my former colleague – began with "Today I exult. Stratford has found a brilliant new playwright". The *Globe and Mail's* Herbert Whittaker sat on his customary fence, while the Toronto Star's Nathan Cohen, whose dismissive columns were legendary, described the evening as a "fiasco" and "bad theatrical hokum."

I still have in my possession faded photocopies of newspaper and magazine reviews, which continued to accumulate during the twelve performances of the play over the next six weeks, coming in not only from local Ontario towns but from Montreal, Chicago, Boston and New York: it was a novel experience to find my name suddenly bandied about. In general these later notices were kind to our production, and not only because many of them knew the circumstances in which it had been created. The Pirandello-ish playing around with theatrical reality intrigued some, but confused or annoyed others. The influence of *Oh! What A Lovely War* was spotted (the *Saturday Review's* notice was headed 'Oh What A Lovely Tsar'!), and there was a general feeling (shared by both Langham and myself) that if it were to be remounted we would undertake some fairly substantial revisions. But as the performances progressed and the actors settled into their roles it was clear that most audiences were captured and moved. Much of this was due to the inspired playing of Amelia Hall as the valiant and tenacious Tsarina, and to the power of the playing by Stratford's other stalwarts: Bill Hutt's urbanity, Tony van Bridge's fervour, Joel Kenyon's vacuous sweetness of personality as the Tsar, Powys Thomas' manic Rasputin. How lucky I was to have these splendid actors to bring my first play to life.

More stimulating for me than the newspaper notices were the handful of letters I received from friends and acquaintances. The literary and drama critic Clifford Leech, who had recently moved to Toronto from England, mentioned some need for 'tightening up'. But he went on to say, "The play gave me only delight and an experience I would not have missed"; the actors "were outstandingly served by the words you gave them". He later wrote the introduction for the printed text (Clarke, Irwin 1972), and described it as "the most sensitively written Canadian play I have ever seen."

Somehow Ralph Maud, the Dylan Thomas scholar and my colleague from Simon Fraser, also found his way east and took in a performance. I still have and treasure the letter he wrote afterwards and left for me, which starts:

Bless you for the wonderful performance I have just seen at the Avon Theatre... I could not resist tears many times... it did plough into me like putty - me the putty."

Most happily for me, Ralph seemed to have understood and appreciated the role of Natasha in the play:

I think you know what you did with that wife Natalie – of course you do, since the play is constructed round her. I'm trying to tell you what you did <u>to me</u> with that pretty pretty wife. And do you know it's what I've been hearing in my inmost ear for the last two weeks - the last two weeks especially. For I was trying to tell my students (and myself) about it through Whitman and the others both semesters. That statement of Whitman's 'There will never be any more perfection than there is now'. And you had the same thing going in your mind all that same time. The play brought it out... There wasn't a weak performance and there wasn't a dull second, and I am very grateful for the experience. You are a moralist...

All best to you (to put it mildly)
Mildly,
Ralph

Many years later I was discussing the whole 'Russian play' adventure with Michael's colleague and neighbour John Hayes, and happened to mention how Michael's calm had got me through, especially during that bleak time when he would come back from the theatre to hear that once again I had not written a word the whole day. 'He was quite unshaken," I said, "and perfectly confident that I would win through." "Confident!" exclaimed John: "What are you saying? He would burst into my house and say "God, John! Give me a double Scotch! He hasn't written a damn word all day! We've got a disaster on our hands!"

So there you are. Who says that good directors are bad actors?

CHAPTER NINE

SEA CHANGES

Towards the end of that month, thoroughly washed out in mind and spirit, I flew to Rome to see my parents in Tuscany, who were still exulting in their new Italian home, and to spend time in the capital with my dear sister Jo.

During my stay in Rome Jo had to take off on business for two or three days, leaving me with her car, and alone in her apartment just off the Piazza Navona. And it was during this time in that momentous year that I went out one sultry summer evening into the Piazza to sit and sip a Sambuca in one of the cafes, to take in the astonishing beauty of that ineffable lozenge-shaped square with its three fountains, and to enjoy the easy enjoyment of Italians at their leisure – eating their pasta or *osso buco* at long tables, or strolling lazily between the fountains, talking, shouting, laughing. As I watched, I saw two or three young men strolling among them, one sitting on the edge of the great central fountain by Bernini: the 'Fountain of the Four Rivers'. And gradually I realised that these young men were on the lookout for partners – male partners.

It may have been the hot summer night. It may have been the sustained and self-denying efforts I had been making for the previous three months. It may have been the new self-esteem that my play's reception had given me. But for whatever reason I found myself getting up, and slowly walking into the crowd. And soon I found myself talking in my broken Italian to the attractive young man — nineteen or twenty perhaps — who sat at the fountain's rim, and whose name I remember was Luigi. Soon I sat myself awkwardly beside him. And I was no longer Michael B., the budding playwright featuring in headlines across a far continent, but simply '*Michele*', otherwise anonymous, alone in a foreign land. My long years of denial, that self-imposed sentence, seemed for a moment to falter. I was looking out through the doors of the prison. And for the first time I allowed myself to contemplate the idea of being free.

I was afraid, and after a few minutes got up and muttered something like *'forse a domani'* – 'maybe tomorrow'. And I took off, back to the apartment. It was not late: perhaps ten or eleven. I undressed and lay down.

I did not sleep that night. It was as though an express train flying through the night at a hundred miles an hour had suddenly started cranking into reverse. A screaming of brakes, a clanging of iron rails, a juddering of wheels, my whole body thrown about like a boulder, smashing into the bed. A battering of pleasure and pain. The word 'yes!' ripped out of me. I was twenty-eight years old, and had just taken a first hesitant step on the difficult journey to become a whole person. That step was both terrifying me and thrilling me beyond measure.

I often look back almost with amusement to that fateful moment in the Piazza Navona, as I think how easy such a move had been for so many people so much younger than I; but also with sadness for those bound as I had been by the rigid social pressures of their upbringing, and like me unable for so long to stand up to the imagined shame and embarrassment involved in stumbling out of the closet.

I returned to Canada in time to see the final performance of *The Last of the Tsars* at Stratford. Beside me in the theatre was Helen, who by this time knew the full story of her embodiment in Natasha. Naturally – being Helen! – she felt she could have played the role much better. But she did tell me how deeply moved she was by such a powerful demonstration of my love and admiration for her. My loving friendship with both her and with Michael had been even more thoroughly cemented by the events of that extraordinary summer. We were family.

So then it was back to the maelstrom of Simon Fraser University as it entered its second year. In my long absence, my summer replacement, John Juliani, had established a firm grip on our theatre activity. He had mounted an apparently powerful set of short plays, two by de Ghelderode and two by Arrabal. But this was not just a one-off: John had been promoting the productions as the first of a series, to be performed under the title 'The Savage God Theatre Company'. The free spirit of our tender young university had been interpreted by John, with his Catholic upbringing and his training under the nuns of Loyola College in Montreal, as an opportunity to open up the dark side of the psyche. The name of his venture was apparently borrowed from a comment of Yeats after he had seen a performance of Jarry's *Ubu Roi*, and was taken to signify nothing less than literary and theatrical revolution.

John was an attractive and charismatic, if worryingly saturnine, figure, and his espousal of the 'Savage God' had won him devotees among our theatre students, many of whom responded to the sense of danger those words conveyed: to the excitement of the monstrous and the unsayable.

I had also been nurturing revolutionary new ideas in my first year, and they had continued to germinate even during my hectic days at Stratford. But they were leading me in a very different direction from John's.

Among my bundle of photocopies of *The Last of the Tsars* reviews I find the report of an interview I had given to Bruce Lawson of Toronto's *Globe and Mail*, a day or two after our opening. Its banner headline was agreeably eye-catching: 'After a trial by fire, Michael Bawtree arises as a phoenix playwright'. The article reported on the strange way my play had come into being, and my thoughts as I looked back on the whole process. The conversation had then moved to the play itself:

"His play, he protests, is not political," wrote Lawson, and went on to quote me as saying: 'I find it very difficult to fight under slogans. I'm very sceptical about mottos. Almost any organisation starts to build its own substitute for human relations – it might use the term 'comrade' – because it realises it has to substitute some sense of family for the family it is destroying. It's the same for all, not just the Communists.'

"To Bawtree, the character of Natalie – wife of the Tsar's brother –is a key to the play and to Bawtree's own attitude," the piece went on. " 'She represents the human values of love and compassion... She embodies those virtues I find dear,' he said: 'Natalie is the spirit of the structure and technique, accepting completely the moment: the acceptance of being... She is anarchic by being able to forget all time. Up to a point, I'm embracing anarchy.' "

So I was embracing anarchy 'up to a point', was I? In fact I had been quite heavily submerged in the principles of political and philosophical anarchy during my two terms at Simon Fraser. My mentor was my friend Jerry Zaslove. Through him I had taken out subscriptions to two anarchist magazines, and had begun to explore for the first time in my life the complex relationship between society and the individual, and the way in which individual needs and desires in Western culture were subsumed within the demands of a fictive 'society', under a heavily-empowered leadership. Naturally, given my experience of the theatre, I began following this up with a study of the way in which theatre production was organised, and felt strongly enough to pen an essay about it for my own consumption:

"In England," I wrote some time that year, "it was not until 1890 that the first director undertook the *mise-en-scène* of a play with no other function in the group than to direct. I cannot help juxtaposing twentieth century's 'director's theatre' against Europe's twentieth century dictatorships, filling the gap between the fall of fully-fledged competitive enterprise and the rise of decentralised participatory government. The gap is proving tediously, not to say murderously, long."

I went on to expand on the theme:

"The justification for the dictatorial powers of a theatre director is the need for homogeneity in an artwork, the need to maintain artistic 'standards'. Only by entrusting the work of the theatre group to the control of one man, it is assumed, will a uniform product, an interlocking and mutually interdependent assembly of parts, a just proportion, be satisfactorily achieved. It has not yet struck home that these artistic values, these requirements for an artwork, are themselves a product of the same society that produces and glorifies directors. We demand 'standards' which only artistic dictatorships can provide. And playwrights (including myself) produce theatrical material that can only be presented by recourse to dictatorial means – works demanding those same standards of homogeneity and proportion.

"It may be that theatre cannot do without this overall direction: that the temporary society of a theatre company in the preparation of a work, is either a dictatorship or it is not workable at all. But to someone who mouths every day a simple faith in the capacity of men to govern themselves, an unquestioned acceptance of the need for theatrical dictatorship is intolerable. What we fight for in the large society must surely be attainable – more easily attainable – in miniature. If participatory government in theatre cannot achieve homogeneity and just proportion, it may be because these are the demands of an un-multiple society: participatory government in theatre may create an end product conforming to its own standards, perhaps conforming to none. At least it has an excellent chance of being faithful to life – to a more abundant life."

This concern over the fact that the 'perfection' of a collaborative work of art (like drama, opera, orchestral music or ballet) requires dictatorial means, had become stronger and stronger within me, and as I returned to Simon Fraser I decided not to embark on the directing of another 'major production', but instead to see if I could interest our theatre students in setting up a workshop to develop a play together. Before the term began it was natural to consult with my friends Zaslove and Mills, and I found them eager to assist. For John this looked like a happily socialist enterprise. For Jerry, it was a chance to test the limits of non-leadership – in fact, of anarchy. We all three of us had also noticed that the University, though still restless, had begun to settle down. The administration had shaken off the worst excesses of its inefficiency, and the nervous climate was notably cooler. In the Communications Centre we had arrived at a moment of equilibrium. It had to be snatched.

My belief was that a theatre workshop, formed to create a theatre production through the collaboration of all participants, was in fact ideally suited to the situation of an inclusive university theatre. What it demanded of its members was not merely acting skill but the experiences and ideas of different backgrounds, lives and studies. The voluntary and extra-curricular nature of the theatre program meant that the students would come from all departments and faculties of the university. They would not be 'drama students', but a cross-section of people interested in making theatre, and bringing to it the experiences and interests of their own work – political science, chemistry, philosophy, biology, history, literature.

Acting during this process thus became a secondary or complementary activity. This, I felt, was at least a part of what acting should be – a response to life rather than a substitute for it. The university student was perhaps better equipped than many professional actors for the demands of such an experiment. With little *amour propre,* with no experience of the slave position of the actor in most theatrical activity, he could readily grasp the opportunity to participate. Neither theatrical talent nor even intellectual sophistication as students would be of as much benefit to them as the capacity to respond to situations as a whole thinking-feeling person. This, in any case, was what I felt to be the ideal educational situation – not only in theatre but in all studies. Too much education treated people as students rather than students as people. What we did in our theatre workshop might not only provide a model for theatre creation, but a model for creation, a model for communal activity in general.

In my talks with John and Jerry I was particularly concerned as to whether we needed a ready-made topic to develop, or whether that as well could be trusted to group decision. I felt that in the early stages there might well be a need for attractive ideas, and that I should at least be in a position to propose alternatives.

John made a generous suggestion. For some time he had been

interested in a labour dispute that had taken place just after the First World War in Washington State, some five hours' drive south of Vancouver in a small lumbering town called Centralia.

On Armistice Day, 1919, a predominantly American Legion parade, marching through the town, had attacked the local Union Hall of the more or less communist Industrial Workers of the World – the IWW, known familiarly as 'the Wobblies'. The Wobblies had fired on the parade, but it was not clearly established whether they had fired in self-defence following an attack on the Hall, or whether the attack was launched in response to their firing on the parade: it was significant that at the last moment the parade route had been changed in order to go by the Union Hall. In any case, four Legionnaires had been killed. The Wobblies, a dozen of them, had been rounded up and taken to the town jail. That night, at seven o'clock, the lights in the town had gone out, and passing cars had their headlights smashed by people patrolling the streets. In the blackout a group of townsmen had descended on the jail, thrust aside the single police guard, and removed the leader of the Wobblies. He was taken to a car and driven, followed by a convoy of other cars, to a bridge outside the town, over the River Skookumchuk. On the way the Wobbly was castrated in the back seat of the car. When the convoy arrived at the bridge, the Wobbly was taken out and lynched. He was hanged three times with different lengths of rope, apparently a usual procedure in lynchings; and then the lights of the automobiles were turned on to him and he was shot to pieces. His name was Wesley Everest.

For the killing of the American Legionnaires the surviving Wobblies were given sentences ranging up to 42 years. No one was ever found to stand trial for the castration and murder of Everest.

For some time, Mills told, he had considered writing a play on the Centralia incident. He now suggested – or did I ask first? – that it might be appropriate for the collaborative project in mind. I was enthusiastic. My liberalism already saw the kind of interpretation that could be given to the story – an orthodox example of the evils of capitalism, of the sufferings and injustices meted out to the working class by proprietary interests. It had appeared that little or no work had been written on the subject. Dos Passos had given a semi-fictionalised account of it in his book *1919*. It had figured in one or two histories of the Wobbly movement. And from time to time articles had been penned on it in journals and generally left-wing periodicals. Mills gave me one of them, which had appeared in the *North West Review*. It was obvious that we would have to do a considerable amount of our own research. The close proximity of Centralia to us in Vancouver would also enable us to survey the scene at first hand, and to interview older Centralians for their memories and opinions. It was difficult to imagine a more suitable theme. John offered to be a member of the group, and to join in the work of writing. When the semester opened, and three or four thousand students assembled on campus, the way was clear for us to begin.

I describe the Centralia workshop's inception here only within the context of my developing vision of an 'un-led' theatre. During the fall of that year I worked hard during our Monday and Friday evenings to foster a genuinely participatory process, throwing decision-making back to the group rather than taking the easier and quicker route of deciding on my own – and watching myself closely for signs of covert manipulation or faked democracy. I was often aware of how keenly the group hungered for leadership, and what a strain it was to deny it to them.

We had originally planned to mount our production in November, but within a few weeks we realised we would need a lot more time: by the time we broke up for the Christmas vacation we had generated a bunch of scenes transcribed and edited from our improvisations, while two or three of the students, who had taken on roles as 'writers', and acted as a sort of brains trust for the group, had sketched out other sections. Discussions with this group led to my first clean break with the participatory model: I grudgingly undertook – with their grudging acquiescence – to pull together the bits and pieces we had compiled, and to come up with a working script in time for the opening of the following term in January.

We had also discussed the limits of our process, and had agreed – with some dissent – that from now on the production would unfold in the regular way, with a set script and a director. It was even agreed that regular auditions would be held, and that they would be open to all students, whether or not they had participated in the workshop up to that point. My belief in 'un-led' theatre had evidently reached its limits. It was to be some years before I would try it out again.

Meanwhile, we arranged for students during the Christmas break to make the five-hour journey down to Washington State to take photographs, to explore the newspaper archives, and to interview any inhabitants old enough to remember the events of 1919. Their discoveries surprised us all. In the centre of the town was a war memorial featuring the statue of a doughboy and listing the four Legionnaires who had been shot; they were described as having died 'in uniform, in the service of their country'. Citizens were asked about the memorial. One thought it related to the Great War; another told of 'mad snipers' who had shot at the Armistice Day parade. The bridge on which Everest had been lynched had come to be called Hangman's Bridge, but it had been pulled down and replaced several years before. The records of the *Centralia Daily Hub* and the *Daily Chronicle* were missing their editions dealing with the incident, and in the State Archives at Olympia the newspaper editions for that week had also been removed. None of our expeditions could find anyone who would talk about 1919. The young ones frankly didn't know; their elders would turn away. It seemed that the town had closed its eyes and ears to the night of November 11th, 1919.

One other momentous event in my life that year must be recorded.

I had not forgotten my tumultuous experience in Rome a few weeks earlier: from it I had learned – for the first time, amazingly – that there were places where men on the search for male partners could be found. Late one night in early September I was driving my snazzy MGB around the streets of Vancouver's English Bay, which I had discovered to be a 'cruisy' area, and where I was hoping, I suppose, to meet and even pick up a willing but also attractive partner. Those who have done their share of cruising, male or female, will know the wretched compulsiveness of this kind of search. Around and around you go, deciding again and again to give up and go home, but then finding yourself making just one more turn around the block, and then one more, and then one more, as the night deepens. It's both thrilling and exhausting: in fact, a mug's game.

As I went round once again past the bandstand that stood on a sweep of grass on the edge of the Bay, I saw a figure flitting through the trees. I parked. The figure, a young man, approached my car nervously, darted away again, paused and returned. I rolled down my window. "Hi," I said. "Hi," he said. I was as nervous as he. "Do you want to come for a coffee?" I asked, opening the passenger door. "I don't know. Maybe," he said, looking at me, and then looking round again into the dark behind him.

Eventually, more and more nervous, he climbed into the car. "Where shall we go?" I asked.

"I don't know... P'raps the White Spot up on 4th. Do you know it?" So there we went.

Astonishingly, I had just met the person who was to share my life for the next forty years and more. His name was Colin Bernhardt.

As we sat in the car at the White Spot drive-in, drinking our coffees and perhaps even devouring a couple of mayonnaise-laced hamburgers, I heard something more of Colin's past. He was twenty-four years old and had been in Vancouver only two or three months, having left his wife and child in Edmonton. He was working as an orderly at Vancouver General Hospital. But it was and had always been his dream to be an actor. He had taken part in workshops in Calgary where had been born, and, when he and his wife had lived for a time in Montreal, he had attended classes at the National Theatre School with the distinguished voice teacher Eleanor Stuart.

I asked him whether he had completed grade school. No, he had reached only Grade Ten. His schooling had been very much disrupted by a terrible road accident when he was fifteen. Both his parents had been killed instantly, and Colin, who was in the back seat of the car, had suffered grievous injuries and was in a coma: in fact they held back his parents' funeral for four days in the expectation that Colin would be buried with them. But Colin did not die. After a week he recovered consciousness. He had terrible injuries to leg, arm and skull, and was in hospital for six months.

I was to hear much more of Colin's traumatic life story over the weeks, months and years that followed, but even on that first night I was bowled over by his charm, his beauty, his intense vulnerability and his passion. He also came across as someone damaged and confused, and easily taken advantage of. It struck me that what Colin needed was a chance to set his sights once again on the theatre. And for this he needed training.

Colin's educational qualifications did not make it possible for him to come to Simon Fraser, but it so happened that over the previous year I had made friends with an actor named Anthony Holland, who had just started a theatre-training program at Vancouver City College. I asked Colin whether he would be interested in applying to Anthony's program. Colin's eyes shone. Yes, he would be thrilled, if it was possible.

I called up Anthony the next day. His program had already been going a week, but he agreed to see Colin, and within another day or two had accepted him. I paid for his first fees. The College would also enable Colin to bring his schooling up to Grade 12.

So began our relationship. Colin remained jumpy and unpredictable. He was still suffering deep pangs of guilt over his separation from his wife and son, which had been brought on largely as a result of the behaviour of his mother-in-law, who insisted on living with the young couple, and would refer to Colin as 'the cripple.' It was several weeks before I saw him smile for the first time: a radiant moment, and the first of thousands of smiles and roars of laughter over the years.

Colin was enormously happy to be at the College, and with my help he decided to move out of the apartment on English Bay, which he was sharing with a gay couple, and into his own place, a ground floor apartment almost opposite Vancouver City Hall on 12th Avenue West. We saw each other two or three times a week, and slowly I began to earn his trust.

When the holiday season arrived, though, there was a hitch. I would have loved to spend Christmas with Colin, who would be especially lonely away from his son. But I had to tell him I could not do so, because I had long ago committed myself to joining the

Langhams for Christmas, and in an exotic spot: La Jolla, California. This came about because Michael had been approached earlier in the year to get involved in a plan to create a new theatre on the sea-cliffs near San Diego. The driving force behind the project was John L. Stewart of the University of California at San Diego, and it was he who had engaged Michael, as well as the distinguished architect Bert Goldberg, designer of the famous Marina City complex in Chicago. Gregory Peck was also on his team, as well as two wealthy San Diego business men, one of them being Robert O Peterson, the millionaire founder of California's Jack-in-the-Box Restaurants. Stewart invited Michael to come to La Jolla over the Christmas season to take part in a brainstorming session, and, when Michael told him he would need to spend Christmas with his wife and son, Peterson offered them all a luxurious apartment in a new building on the promontory of La Jolla village. Michael also wanted me involved in the project as a consultant on how the relationship between UCSD and a professional theatre might work. So he invited me to join them, and to share their apartment over Christmas. Naturally I had accepted.

This was 1966, and the airy fantasy of the whole idea was very much in keeping with the *Zeitgeist* of the time. UCSD, founded only a few years earlier, was still at the stage when insistent visionaries were listened to, and John Stewart was a dreamer who was insistent and who dreamed no small dreams. He had evidently persuaded his backers to support him, and money seemed to be in plentiful supply.

Only a few moments survive the erosions of memory. I can dimly recall a two-day retreat in the Borrego desert at the Casa del Zorro resort. And I remember standing in the midst of wasteland on the cliffs overlooking the Pacific, together with Michael, Bert Goldberg and Bob Peterson, while John Stewart marked out his proposed site for the theatre. I recall the balmy climate, and the opulent stores of La Jolla village. And I especially remember being invited to lunch with Michael and Helen at Bob Peterson's dream-like home on Point Loma, above San Diego harbour. It was fortified around by a high, solid wall, and could be entered only by pushing a bell at the gate, speaking on the intercom, and then waiting for a manservant to come and open up. Inside the palisade lay an elegant garden in the Japanese style, bringing you in down a path which (to confound demons) zigzagged across a goldfish pond to the front door of the house. The interior was equally 'designed' and luxurious, with the living room looking expansively down over the blue waters of the harbour. But there were battleships tied up in the distance, and every few minutes a fighter plane would roar in noisily to the landing strip at the Naval Air Station across the water. This was 1966, yes, and the Vietnam War was moving into full swing. The contrast was eerily memorable. I remember nothing of the lunch.

But above all else from this strange trip, I recall New Year's Eve. Gregory Peck had invited Michael and his family up to Los Angeles to see out the year at his house in Hollywood. The invitation had been extended to me, and that afternoon a chauffeured limousine arrived to pick us up and drive us up the coast to LA, where Peck had arranged for us to be put up in a garden bungalow at the Beverly Hills Hotel. After we had settled in and had a drink or two – and maybe some supper – a car arrived to take us to the Pecks. If fantasy had taken hold in La Jolla, here it rose to a whole new level. How often would I or anyone else get to spend New Year's Eve with Gregory Peck and his wife Véronique, where the guests included Anthony Quinn, Tony Curtis, Michel Legrand and Groucho Marx? Michael and Helen were entertained by the Pecks, and Chris and I were left to circulate rather awkwardly. Out of all of the luminaries, it was only Groucho who engaged with us; he and the future comedian Chris had a lively exchange.

Two days later I was back in Vancouver, arriving after dark. I made my way at once to Colin's apartment. There were lights on, but when I knocked at the front door, no one came. I was sure Colin was there, and guessed that he was making a statement about my having abandoned him over the holiday. Getting a little desperate, I found a ladder in the front yard, took it around to Colin's side window, climbed up and started knocking on the glass. Sure enough Colin was in, and he eventually told me not to be an idiot, and that he would open the door. He used to tease me for years afterwards about my attempt at a romantic break-in.

It was only a couple of months later that we decided to set up home together. We each gave up our own places and found an apartment in a newish building on 14th Avenue, a block or two east of Granville. Our shared life had well and truly begun.

Nothing came of the La Jolla venture. The tumultuous years of the late sixties, with the Vietnam War raging and universities erupting all over the continent, were not the best setting for such grandiose schemes. It was not until 1983 that La Jolla Playhouse (originally founded in 1947 by Gregory Peck, Dorothy McGuire and Mel Ferrer, and having closed its doors in 1964) was born again under the direction of Canadian-American director Des McAnuff, in a purpose-built theatre on the UCSD campus. So John Stewart's dream did eventually become a reality.

Before term began again in January, I made a decision that surprised me: I realised that I did not want to direct our play myself. The reason was in fact a physical one: back in November I had made a lightning weekend trip across the continent to New York (to meet with Michael on the La Jolla venture) and had returned mightily sick with what turned out to be mononucleosis. My doctor had treated the symptoms of this – above all a raging sore throat. But the illness had left me wretchedly weak and listless. I felt quite unprepared to muster the physical energy required to direct.

There were only two people around with enough experience to take over. John Juliani had been my colleague and fellow Resident in Theatre for eight months now. John had rather more experience as a director than I had myself. But he had begun work in the late fall on two one-act plays of Arthur Kopit, and these were scheduled for production towards the end of January as part of his 'Savage God' series. I discussed the problem with him, but he could not abandon his own production at this stage. He promised to join us and help in any way he could when Kopit was over.

The other person I felt I might turn to was Paul Bettis. I had brought Paul on to the theatre staff during the previous term. A brilliant, Oxford-educated young man, whom I had got to know in Vancouver during my first year, he had attended many of the workshop meetings and was very familiar with the project. I now asked him whether he would take on the direction. He was somewhat overwhelmed, especially since there was as yet no script. But he gamely agreed, and took up right away the responsibility for casting for a list of roles which I gave him.

I was now free to cobble together a script, making as much use as I could of the three sections that had been sent to me by members of our writers' group. The story line, as I found myself developing it, mirrored the actual process of our workshop, beginning with a narration of the incident in our workshop setting, and proceeding through the kind of debate featured in our fall meetings, and our improvisations of the various scenes leading up to the confrontation of the Legionnaires and the Wobblies. At the same time the action slowly led towards a dramatic contretemps between the Director who wanted to stay true to the authenticity of our portrayal, and the Stage Manager with the theatre's technology at his command, who insisted that we squeeze the maximum dramatic power out of the incident, if necessary exaggerating or distorting the historical facts in order to shock and overpower the audience. Each party had its adherents, and finally the Stage Manager engineered a coup d'état – taking over the third act, which I had not yet written out, but which was to consist of the Armistice Day procession, the shooting of the Legionnaires and the imprisonment of the Wobblies, and finishing up with the castrating and lynching of Everest. (Comparisons can obviously be made with my so recently-written Stratford play *The Last of the Tsars,* in which two characters wrestle for control of the action, and of the historical material with which it deals.)

Paul completed the job of casting, but found that we were one or two actors short for the large company we required. To solve the problem I got the idea of asking Anthony Holland whether any of his students from Vancouver City College might join us for our production. Thus it was that to my secret delight my new friend Colin became a member of the *Centralia* group, as also did his fellow student Len George, son of Chief Dan George of the Tsleil-Waututh Nation. Paul was insistent that if I did not direct I would at least play the role of Director. I accepted. Meanwhile, we both felt that the ideal person to play the Stage Manager was John Juliani, with his saturnine good looks and commanding manner. John was agreeable, though he would not be able to join us until a week or two before the production, which was set for the beginning of March.

So was set in motion a strange happening indeed: the dramatic version of a parallel real-life situation. Over the course of the year in which we had both been on the staff at Simon Fraser, John and

I had gone our separate ways. John had brought his 'Savage God' series into being, leading his group of actors with a powerful, charismatic zeal, and gaining their loyalty and devotion, as he worked on plays that crossed over conventional bounds and into the psychology of cruelty. I on the other hand had repudiated the whole idea of leadership in the theatre, attempting to create a genuinely democratic process, without knowing quite where it would lead. I too had my loyal group of collaborators. John and I had never crossed swords, but it was clear we were on very different paths, and I certainly felt uncomfortable with his style and methods, as no doubt he was with mine. We were now about to play out these differences in the *Centralia* play.

Perhaps it was as well that we had a theatrical vehicle available to us in which to embody two rival philosophies. In putting together the playscript I had in fact engineered 'John's' take-over. I created the gentle humanist 'Director' overwhelmed by the insistence of violent melodrama; 'John' was the charismatic Leader impatient with the niceties of human behaviour, and ready to embrace the violence. Comparisons with Hitler's fascist takeover of Germany in the 1930s were not lost to us, and indeed were part of the message of our play.

To design costumes for the production I approached a young woman I had heard about, newly arrived in the city from England. Her name was Susan Benson, and this was her first opportunity to design a production in Canada. We were to become lifelong friends and colleagues, and for Susan it was the start of a stellar career as a designer in Canadian theatre.

The spring of 1967 was entirely taken up with the preparation of what we were now calling *The Centralia Incident*, under Paul's competent though sometimes menacing direction: he would move around wielding a stick, and once – to his own surprise and remorse – found himself hitting an actor with it. All of us were dealing in our own way with the horror of the dénouement, still ahead of us as we rehearsed the first two acts.

Our opening was set for March 1st, and with two weeks to go we had still not broached the final scene. In fact we were running out of time, and it was at this point that I proposed that we should hold a weekend 'act-in' at the theatre. It was planned with all the care of any large camping expedition, and on the Friday evening we assembled in the theatre foyer with tooth-brushes and sleeping bags. We worked that night till two in the morning, and then bedded down wherever we could find space. Saturday's meals were brought into the theatre by the University's catering department, and in between them we worked a fifteen-hour day, finishing once again at two, in the early hours of Sunday morning.

The sustained concentration and isolation of this period had a predictable effect on us. The community we created pulled together the separate parts of the play and for the first time bound all the company – 'old' and 'new' members – into a single group. It had the unreal, ecstatic atmosphere of our best moments from the fall Workshop, and the final gruesome scenes finally took shape, portrayed in mime and using all the effects that could be thrown at it: slow motion under strobe lights, with powerful sound effects and stirring music whipping the company on to do their dreadful deed. All in all, it was so powerful an experience that when it was over we felt as though our job was done – the production date lay ten days ahead like a tiresome afterthought, and a lot of effort was needed to pick ourselves up for the final stages. But the weekend had also done its work. When March 1st came, we were ready. I wrote in the program:

The Workshop wants it to be clear that no accusations are being made, or even implied, against individuals involved in any phase of the Centralia Incident. The names spring at us out of history and we attach to them our own honest ideas of how the persons thought and felt. To help us do this, we have used all the factual evidence we have found: where the evidence stopped, we carried on. Where named individuals appear in violent action, it is the violence not in them but in ourselves that we portray. We confess ourselves part of all men do and have done.

It was my belief at the time that we had created a piece of considerable power and significance. Ancient Wobbly members came up the mountain to see the production, and were heard tapping their feet and singing along with the Union songs. Students attended the performances in full force, and many audience members left the theatre in an emotional daze. Jerry Zaslove wrote an affirming if barely intelligible review for the campus newspaper. But reaction outside the University was minimal: one of the Vancouver newspapers gave us a couple of paragraphs in their scanty arts section, and that was all. It has always been a matter of regret for me that the whole project disappeared behind the Rockies, never to be heard from or about again. This was the first time, in fact, that I found myself wishing I were back on the eastern side of the continent, back in the swim of things. 'So nice to be out of the rat-race' was a sentiment you often heard in those early days on the West Coast. 'But I want to be in the rat-race,' I muttered to myself. It was to be another couple of years before I took action on that front.

CHAPTER TEN

MY NEW COUNTRY

That summer did in fact see me heading back for a few weeks to eastern Canada. The Canadian Conference of the Arts had arranged a national arts conference to be held at Queen's University in Kingston, Ontario, and this was to be followed by an international theatre conference in Montreal, set up by the Canadian Centre of the International Theatre Institute. I remember little of the proceedings in Kingston, except that Lester Pearson's Minister of Culture, Judy LaMarsh, gave the opening address, and that many of Canada's leading artists, critics and commentators attended. Murray Schafer and I represented Simon Fraser's Centre for Communications and the Arts, which many had heard of but few understood. We had a chance to speak of our western enterprise, and I found myself almost manically articulate in describing our work and our plans: "You're a poet," said Patrick Watson after one such discussion. Yes, I felt myself to be a poet, riding the English language like a motorbike, speeding and careering, absurdly self-confident. Perhaps I was even a little unhinged: the apocalyptic atmosphere of Simon Fraser was having its effect.

For many of us the Kingston get-together was an obvious stepping-stone to the major Canadian event of that centennial year: Montreal's Expo '67. The moment the conference ended, we made our way to the city.

Once there, I found myself in the midst of a gathering of theatre artists from all over the world: Jerzy Grotowsky from Poland, premier critic Kenneth Tynan from the UK, French playwright Armand Gatti, and so *ad infinitum*. Architects were also much in evidence, because theatre architecture was one of the conference themes. The visionary Irish theatre designer and architect Sean Kenny was a delegate, along with John Bury and Denys Lasdun, who were at that time designing Britain's new National Theatre and its stages. It was also at this time that Ottawa was building a National Arts Centre, and its architect Fred Lebensold gave an illustrated presentation on his plans and designs.

During these heady and exciting days, a chance meeting changed the direction of my life. In the bar of the rooftop Hotel Bonaventure (which had just opened that summer and was the principal venue of our conference), I met a playwright and director from Colombia, South America. His name was Enrique Buenaventura. I spoke no Spanish, but luckily he spoke quite respectable French.

Short, grey-haired and barrel-chested, with a craggily handsome face and a contagious laugh, Enrique held a group of us in his spell one evening as he told us about his work in Colombia's theatre. It was a country of which most of us knew nothing. Enrique described how Colombia had only recently emerged from a long period of bloody civil unrest, known as *La Violencia*, which had killed over 200,000 of its citizens. The conflict had pitted Liberals and Conservatives against one another, and almost everyone was ancestrally or regionally one or the other: if you wore a red tie in a blue-tie village you were likely to be gunned down in the street. But there was also a vigorous leftist movement in the country, supported by strong trade unions, and recently re-inspired by Castro's Cuba. In fact it was the 1948 government's assassination of a charismatic union leader, Jorge Eliécer Gaitán, who had been strongly tipped to be the next President, which had set the country on fire and inaugurated *La Violencia*, with ten thousand killed in the first week. The leaderships of the two traditional parties, though bitter enemies, were united in opposing the left: they were both led by a wealthy and firmly entrenched conservative elite, fuelled by money from the United States. It was this common cause of the old parties which in fact finally ended *La Violencia* after twelve years: one of the terms of the peace agreement between Liberals and Conservatives was that the Presidency would alternate between the two parties every three years, thus ensuring that the 'communists' would not get a look-in.

This was my introduction to Latin American politics, and for the first time I began to see 'the Americas' as a single continent, with Canada in the north and Latin America in the south, both seeking to resist the power and influence of the overwhelmingly rich, powerful and dominant USA.

Enrique had spent some years running what he called a 'bourgeois' theatre in his hometown of Cali, producing a string of European classics. But he had shifted gears, and his company, Teatro Experimental de Cali, was now devoting its energies to plays that confronted the political situation in Colombia. Most of these plays he had written himself, and he described how his actors were always on the watch for the arrival of the police to close down performances. The company's generous grants had of course been cut off, and it was only Enrique's personal reputation which had so far protected his company from the active hostility of the government: he came of a distinguished and prosperous Cali family, and had already served as a representative of Colombia in international conferences. Some of his plays had been performed abroad – in Mexico, Paraguay and Cuba. He was even known, he told us with a scornful laugh, as 'the Pope of Colombian theatre.'

The idea of a 'dangerous' theatre was irresistible to us Canadians, as we reflected on the placidly safe environment in which we lived and worked. But there was one story he told which fixed itself in my mind, and which did more to bring Colombian culture to life than anything else.

While he was till running his more conventional theatre, he told us, he had directed a production of *Oedipus the King*, which he presented in Cali and later took on tour throughout the country, offering it free with the aid of a government grant. One of their performances was scheduled for a poor and fairly primitive port town on the Pacific coast, called oddly enough by Enrique's own name: Buenaventura. The day came; the company arrived and set up their simple touring set in the town square, and as show time approached the square filled with eager townspeople, for whom theatre was almost completely unknown. Most members of the audience were black and very little educated, descended from the slaves brought to Colombia by the Spanish in the 17th and 18th centuries. Enrique and his actors were not sure how the play would be received, but the audience was rapt, following the unfolding tragedy with perfect understanding, and occasionally letting out cries of horror and sympathy.

After the final applause the crowd dispersed, and as the company was striking the set, a grey-haired, dark-skinned man came up to Enrique and congratulated him on a fine performance. 'But of course' he told Enrique, 'it wasn't quite accurate.'

'What do you mean?' asked Enrique.

'Well, they didn't get the story quite right.'

Enrique was intrigued and suggested they all go to a bar and talk some more. And it was there, over a beer, that the stranger informed Enrique and his troupe about the mistakes they had made. 'In the first place,' he said, 'Oedipus was not raised by shepherds the way you say: he was found and brought up by a fisherman and his family. I know this, because it was just a few miles up the coast from here.' Enrique and his actors looked at one another in amusement and disbelief. But the man went on: 'and I don't know how you got that idea about Oedipus and his father fighting 'where three roads meet'. That's not right at all: they met on a rope bridge above a gorge, where there was only room for one person to cross. Oedipus refused to give way, as did his father, and so Oedipus knocked him over into the gorge. The rope bridge is still there today – and it's still called '*El Puente de Edipo*'. If you had checked with us before, anyone could have put you right about this.'

The man went on to describe Oedipus' later wanderings, and the story seemed to get tangled up with the ancient legend of the Wandering Jew. But his conviction that this was a local story was what astonished his listeners, and we were equally amazed as Enrique recounted the incident to us. He wondered whether perhaps black slaves, often brought up in their master's household, might have heard the original story being told, which over time had become embroidered and localized.

This was my first exposure to something like the 'magic realism' of Colombia, now familiar through the work of Enrique's friend Gabriel Garcia Márques. Enrique told us that life in his country was so extraordinary, its daily events so unbelievable, so melodramatic, so full of murder and mayhem, that a playwright had a hard time inventing a story line that would not be upstaged by the day's realities. As an example, he told us how when the government in 1948 had killed off Gaitán they were anxious to appear to be doing everything they could to find the murderer. The President – who had clearly read his Agatha Christie – flew in two detectives from Scotland Yard to unravel the 'mystery'; but even before the two of them had left Bogota's airport their luggage had been stolen. Enrique broke into his high-pitched, cackling laughter, which we were beginning to realize carried more than a hint of the stress under which he and his fellow countrymen lived.

Before this conversation I doubt if I could have even found Colombia on a map. I was abashed by my own ignorance, and moved and fascinated by Enrique and his stories, which opened up an entirely new world for me. I spent much of the next two or three days in his company, and before he left he handed me a manuscript of his latest play, a series of unconnected episodes, which he called *Los Papeles del Infierno*, or *Documents From Hell*.

No one who had been in Montreal that summer could ever forget it. Not only was there the great Expo site to visit, with its pavilions and restaurants, but we were also celebrating the 100th birthday of Canada's confederation. The world was flocking to the city, and Canada was receiving surprised but fulsome praise for the quality, scope and organisation of its celebrations, and for their creative energy. It would be the last time for many years that the idea of Canada as a successfully unified bilingual country still seemed to be dominant, and that the century really did belong to us. The work of its artists was on full display, not only in our pavilions but on Expo's many stages, which they shared with orchestras, theatre companies, singers and dancers from all over the world.

I believe in fact that my decision to embrace Canada fully as my own country stemmed from those hot and vibrant days in Montreal. I was genuinely proud to be part of the national adventure. No doubt I was also changed by having crossed the

Rubicon of my sexuality. Though I had left my beloved far away in Vancouver, I still knew I was loved, and in love. There is nothing like love to give you power.

I returned west by road, having acquired a new MG 'hatchback' in Toronto, and feeling uplifted by my heady experiences in Kingston and Montreal. Immediately I set about looking for – and soon found – a good translator for Enrique Buenaventura's *Documents From Hell*. My plan was to mount the English-language premiere of the play in the spring term.

Meanwhile I remember little of that fall semester of 1967, apart from three interesting events. In October I was invited by Ralph Maud to join him at a celebration dinner to be held in downtown Vancouver. What were we celebrating? Nothing less than the fiftieth anniversary of the Russian revolution, the October Days that brought Lenin and the Bolsheviks to power. The walls of the union hall were gaily decorated with red flags sporting the hammer and sickle, and the speeches honoured Lenin and his leadership in grabbing power for the people. I'm astonished now to think of that naïve occasion, and the fact that even in Cold War days it could happen in capitalist Canada without police surveillance or even interest.

Then I recall a visit by Peter Dwyer, the first executive director of the Canada Council, accompanied by Guy Huot. They toured Simon Fraser, sat with us to hear about the aims and activities of our Centre, and later went downtown to a newly established 'Arts Factory' which was establishing a reputation as a hotbed of wild creativity. No doubt there were other places on their agenda. What was the purpose of their visit? They had come to Vancouver, said Peter, to 'look for some horses to back'.

When I think of the many-faceted bureaucracy that is now

the Council, I look back to that splendid moment of pioneering by the man who was its first leader, as he crossed the country searching for artistic enterprises to place bets on – knowing as with all bets that there is a sure risk of losing.

I'm also happy to remember the visit to Vancouver of the National Theatre of Great Britain, on their tour of Canada to celebrate the country's centenary. The company was led by Laurence Olivier, and the two productions they brought with them were *All for Love* by John Dryden and *A Flea In Her Ear* by Georges Feydeau, in the matchless translation by John Mortimer. Olivier was the shining star of Colin's firmament, and I made sure we picked up tickets for both productions: it was rare to see this quality and scale of production in western Canada, and wonderful to watch Colin's spellbound expression as he took in every moment of each performance. I also had the idea of inviting the cast up to Burnaby to see Simon Fraser and to talk to the students, and then to have lunch served up to them on our stage, with some of the students sitting down with them. To my delight a dozen or more accepted our invitation, and though Olivier was not of the party it was a distinguished gathering – which I remember included Geraldine McEwan.

The drama of Simon Fraser University's escalating conflicts continued as soon as term began, and I have to work hard at resisting the temptation to dive off into a detailed history of those tumultuous times. Sufficient to say that opposing forces were hardening: the Students' Union, led by Martin Loney, was becoming increasingly vocal, and had joined forces with the revolutionary elements of the faculty, located primarily in the Political Science and Anthropology Department. One struggle took place over whether chairmen (they were all men) of departments should be appointed by the University or elected by their department. No fewer than six chairmen – some of them distinguished scholars who had been tempted from places like Cambridge (England) to head up a new department at an exciting new university – were peremptorily voted out of office by their junior colleagues. The Student Union also called for the University's name to be changed to Louis Riel University, on the grounds that Louis Riel was a true hero and that the explorer Simon Fraser was one of the group of 'pirates, thieves and carpet-baggers' who had come west to exploit the land and dispossess the aboriginal inhabitants. At this distance it is hard to recall what other rights and freedoms were being fought for: only that passions were roused to bursting point, and that they led slowly but remorselessly to the insistence that the entire Board of Governors and the President McTaggart-Cowan be ousted. The Board of Governors was not to be budged, but they finally let the President go in the summer of the next year ('on his birthday, too!' lamented his wife), after massive assemblies of protesting students and faculty had filled the great steps overlooking the covered quadrangle at the centre of campus. The steps seemed positively designed for such events: perhaps they even helped to create them.

Meanwhile, with these ongoing battles for a backdrop, our 'Centre for Communications and the Arts' was still working to define itself. We continued to discuss how our different arts could work together, and had been exploring models like the Bauhaus School. Murray Schafer, whose interest in and knowledge of inter-artistic history far surpassed that of the rest of us, introduced us to Wagner's *gesamtkunstwerk*, the artwork that combines music, drama and visual art. The original group of our artists (Schafer, Baxter and Bawtree) had grown considerably, as a direct result of the trimester system by which faculty were required to teach for two of the three terms: the third term required a replacement Resident in each area.

This was what had led to John Juliani's original appointment in the summer of 1966, and he was now a full-time member. Iain Baxter had been joined by miniaturist painter Joel Smith, and Murray Schafer by composer Jack Behrens. Other Associates had also been appointed, and the interests and expertise of these talented newcomers were all added to the mix. In fact we had gathered together infinite riches in the little room of the Centre, but we were grievously lacking a master spirit, a Walter Gropius (founder of the Bauhaus) who could harness and direct our energies. We were still a part of the University's Faculty of Education, led by its messianic but not entirely rational Dean Archie McKinnon; we still had a group psychologist with no artistic interest as our kindly but reluctant and temporary chair; and, in the absence of visionary leadership, individual ambitions and competitiveness began to assert themselves for all our attempts at accommodation and compromise. The first excitement of being part of an uncharted new adventure gave way to more mundane concerns like tenure and pay. No one had thought to limit terms of employment, and now even those young men (no women) on short-term contracts were beginning to assume that the University owed them a permanent living, and that in the absence of strong leadership and rigid rules they could refuse to accept the decisions made up the line. This would soon be leading to trouble.

Meanwhile though, like good utopians, we at the Centre continued to try and plan a model society of our own design. We even came to an agreement that fall to test out one way of exercising our interdisciplinary inclinations: this was to decide on a theme for each term, with one of our number selected to mastermind and program the term's thematic activities. I offered to coordinate the second term, and chose my theme: 'BRIDGES.'

Looking back on it fifty years later, I still feel this was a happy choice. The bridge was after all an ancient and very physical communication device, but also heavy with metaphorical symbolism. We were all searching (with varying degrees of enthusiasm) for ways to link up our disparate activities, and for this we needed bridges to ease the passage between our very different artistic territories. The 'bridge' theme also brought together the two somewhat intractable parts of our title, 'communications' and 'the arts'.

I was concerned to begin by concentrating on the bridge as a physical object, an early example of fine architectural imagination and technique. I bought several books on the subject to fill in my ignorance; it was fascinating to be reminded that one of the Pope's titles (inherited from the Roman emperors) was Pontifex Maximus, the great bridge-builder, or pontiff. And I couldn't forget *El Puente de Edipo*.

I invited a bridge engineer to give us a talk, and he obliged; Vancouver was itself a fine example of the value of bridge-building, with Burrard Street, Lion's Gate, Second Narrows and Cambie Street Bridges linking the sprawling city together. He also entertained us with film footage of the oscillation and final collapse in 1940 of 'Galloping Gertie', the famous Tacoma Bridge in Washington State, not far to the south of us.

As part of the program, Murray Schafer made a presentation about Wagner's theories combining Music and Drama. I gave a pair of illustrated talks about the Bauhaus, from its inspirational rise out of the ashes of the First World War to its final closing by the Nazis in 1933.

But the bridge that I personally was most anxious to build was the one that I had begun to conceive, linking Colombia with British Columbia (the coincidence of the two names was not lost on me). Since arriving in the country five years earlier I had always shuttled physically and mentally between Canada and Europe, with one or two forays across the United States border: my cultural parameters were strictly limited to the northern hemisphere. Suddenly, through my meeting with Enrique in Montreal, my eyes had been opened up to the vast area of our continent to the south of us. I had been astonished by how little I knew of those millions of Latin Americans living out their lives. It was as though I had been given an Archimedean fulcrum outside my world with which, for the first time, I could imagine moving it.

The performances of *Documents From Hell* scheduled for May 1968 were of course part of the 'Bridges' program, and provided a springboard to introduce the campus to Colombia and its sufferings. I invited young director Tim Bond from Toronto to co-direct the piece with me, with each of us directing four of the eight episodes. Susan Benson designed the clothes. The central and longest episode, directed by Tim, was called *The Orgy*, and took place in a brothel, with beggars, a mute and a dwarf; strongly influenced it seemed, by the films of Buñuel.

Another scene, titled *The Hearing*, showed a set of corrupt hooded judges and police in red robes, accepting bribes to condemn an innocent man to death. For myself I chose among others a most telling episode, called *The Autopsy*, of a doctor who many times had been summoned to the local police station to sign a certificate of 'death by natural causes' for someone the police had killed in captivity. He had now just received another call from the station to do the same thing, but this time it was his own son, a revolutionary, who had been murdered. Should he go? We see him with his wife talking over the whole agonising dilemma, knowing that if he refuses he will probably be murdered himself.

In the program we reprinted Enrique's preface to the play, and it is worth recalling it:

> *This is a record of almost twenty years of violence and unofficial civil war. Many characters parade across it in different episodes. There is no order. There is no style. There is no unity. The only thing that brings these scattered papers together is the wind of violence, the hurricane that has blown almost ceaselessly upon our generation… You will see grand-scale violence and petty violence: the violence of history and of daily life: official violence and violence of the oppressed.*
>
> *Here you will find something of the monstrous struggle to preserve the status quo: and you will find peoples' reactions to it — sometimes a silence, sometimes a reply…*
>
> *What we are aiming to do is to show the foolishness of that struggle and what it costs us. And what it teaches us.*

During the play's production week we arranged a 'Colombia Workshop', with talks and discussions on the situation in Latin America, and of course including the role played by the United States through the CIA. Somehow I even managed to find the funds to fly Enrique up from Colombia to see his play, and to talk about his Teatro Experimental de Cali. This was a great coup, and it was fascinating to hear his responses to our production. He felt that it was generally over-designed and over-produced. He particularly disliked the judges' magnificent red robes, and emphasized for us the true shabbiness and banality of evil. Running a theatre of genuine poverty, in which technology was minimal and actors were often paid in cigarettes, he naturally found that the money we had spent on set design, costume and dramatic lighting was unnecessary. But he was generous in his criticisms, and spent time with the company sharing his thoughts about the play and its characters, and telling them about his work in Colombia. For the students it was an eye-opener.

One evening I recall from that visit, when Colin and I took

Enrique out for dinner at a restaurant in Vancouver. We chose a table and were beginning to sit down when Enrique asked that we move. He told us he couldn't sit in a restaurant or a café without facing the door. In sleepy Vancouver his insistence seemed comic, but he told us he had known too many friends gunned down in such situations, and it was something he couldn't change.

It was during that same spring of 1968 that sleepy Canada had in fact begun a major change of direction. In April Pierre Eliot Trudeau had become leader of the Liberal Party in a close vote, and so was now our Prime Minister. He called an election almost immediately, and in June, amidst the exciting furore of 'Trudeaumania', he won a comfortable majority. As Minister of Justice the previous year Trudeau had brought forward the Criminal Law Amendment Act, which among many other things decriminalized homosexuality, contraception and abortion. It was finally passed in a narrowly-won vote in May of 1969. So the domestic arrangements that Colin and I had initiated in 1967 were now legal. We were no longer criminals and no longer needed to obfuscate about our relationship – though the habit died hard.

Some time in that same term Bruce Attridge's wretched medical problems were finally accepted as permanent, and we received permission to look for and appoint a new director for the Centre. A number of names were tossed around, but it was a hard position to fill, and as the advertisements went out we were sceptical of finding a good candidate – who had to face not only the University's own mounting conflicts but the stresses within the Centre itself. It was then that I thought of my Toronto friend Patrick Lyndon. He was in the magazine publishing business, but he was someone of artistic sensitivity, and had even been a youthful concert pianist. He was highly intelligent, administratively experienced and with a sardonic humour which might suit our situation well. I contacted Patrick, and to my surprise and delight he expressed interest, and submitted an application, on the condition that neither he nor I let it be known that we knew each other, in case it affected his candidacy. Patrick's Curriculum Vitae was impressive and original, and he was invited to come west to be interviewed, when his articulateness and sharp mind soon won over the appointment committee. He was hired. I was immensely happy at the prospect, not only because he was a friend but because I believed he was the right person for the job. None of us, and he least of all, could have predicted the scale of the crises he would soon be dealing with.

I was also developing a project on my own account. I had been encouraged to apply to the Canada Council for an eight-month travel bursary, and it was only natural following the events of the last year that I would apply to travel to Colombia to observe and work with Enrique Buenaventura and his company. I also intended to write a report on *The Centralia Incident*, using the recorded tapes of many of our meetings. I filled out these plans with the intention to learn Spanish, and to organize my theatre lecture notes into a book. It was a rather over-ambitious proposal, but to my surprise (such things always surprise me) I was granted the award. In order to take it up, I had to take advantage of the University rule that if a faculty member worked for three trimesters running, he or she could then take off the next two. By working through the summer of 1968, I would be free to leave in September, and not to return to Simon Fraser till June of 1969. Even more happily, Colin had completed his two years at Vancouver City College, and was now eligible to become a mature student at SFU for the summer term. He would then be free to travel with me. Our plan was to fly first to Mexico for a few days, and then on to Colombia via Panama.

In the gathering storm of unrest in universities all over the world that summer of 1968, fuelled in part by news of the hunting down of Che Guevara the previous autumn and the assassination of Martin Luther King in April, Simon Fraser played its part. But in our own Centre for Communications and the Arts it was a fairly uneventful time, with our troubles simmering just below the surface. Patrick took up his duties in June, and before I left I put together a small cast of students who were not part of Juliani's troupe, and directed a production of Beckett's *End Game*. Then, after a quick August trip to Italy and back for a visit to my family (coinciding with the Soviet invasion of Czechoslovakia), I packed for the long trip south with Colin, giving up our apartment and selling my beloved MG. And just a few days before we left, we had a visit from Michael Langham. He was not alone...

It was over this year that changes had been happening in the Langham household. I had first become aware of them that spring when Michael had asked me to come to Boston, where he was directing Zoe Caldwell in the premiere production of *The Prime of Miss Jean Brodie*, slated to open a month or two later in New York. Helen was there with him, and I detected some tension between the two. Then one evening, at dinner in a restaurant, Michael started to talk about Ellen Gorky, a young woman he had met at Stratford. He went on about her specialness, and at one point said "Maybe we should adopt her: we always wanted a girl." Helen, whose intuition always served her well, replied immediately, "You just want to sleep with her". I think he had already done so, and his usual *sangfroid* buckled under her hostile gaze. The conversation moved on.

Sadly, the loving relationship between my dearest friends Michael and Helen had already started unravelling. Michael was terrified of leaving Helen, but clearly passionately engaged with the wonderfully nubile and street-wise Ellen, who was not much more than eighteen at the time: Michael was almost fifty. For a time he was imagining the possibility of having it both ways, and continued to hide the facts of the matter from Helen, which had not been difficult because with their home in London and Michael's work abroad they spent so much time apart. Michael told me later of a Feydeau-like incident that took place in Italy, earlier in the summer. Michael had been approached to direct a film of *The Merchant of Venice,* with Peter O'Toole in the title role, and had flown out to Venice to scout locations. Since Helen was busy in London looking after their son Christopher, he thought this would be a chance to invite Ellen to be with him. They stayed at a fine hotel close to the Piazza San Marco, and for three or four days their romance blossomed in that most romantic of cities. But the two of them were lying contentedly in bed one morning when the phone rang, and the front desk told him that his wife had arrived and was on her way up. Horror! In less than two minutes Ellen, wrapped in a towel, was bundled out on to the balcony, hiding just out of sight with her suitcase and clothes. As Michael closed the balcony and was putting on a bathrobe, he heard a knock at the door. Shakily he opened it, and there was Helen, with an enormous bouquet of flowers in her arms. "Darling! What a surprise! Come in."

After a few minutes' chat Michael had dressed, and persuaded Helen to come downstairs and join him at a neighbouring restaurant for a coffee and croissant (and for Michael probably a stiff whisky), leaving the coast clear for Ellen to dress herself, pack up and make an undignified exit. I can't now remember how Michael extricated himself – and Ellen – from the situation, but presumably she was put on a plane and removed from the scene.

The *Merchant of Venice* scheme fell through not long afterwards, and at some point later that summer Michael stopped leading a double life and summed up the courage to walk out. Their marriage was in fact just one more of the casualties of the sexual revolution of those years. In spite of his happiness at the time, Michael still loved Helen, and he told me he was shocked by the back-slapping support which greeted his decision. "Good on yer, Mike!" said his friends and colleagues. "She's a dish! Go for it!" A few years later the wife of one of my old teachers took off, afraid, she said, that her husband would leave first. No doubt my own sexual shift was part of the same Zeitgeist. Sexual experiment and promiscuity was in the air.

As a loving friend of both Michael and Helen I was deeply distressed by their break-up. Helen was often on the phone to me, full of tears and resentment, and while comforting her, I did my best not to take sides. Michael of course was only too happy for me to keep up my friendship and support for Helen, as it made him feel less guilty about leaving her; Helen on the other hand would have preferred me to cut Michael out of my life. This I could not do. In fact when Michael came out to Vancouver he had Ellen with him, and I met her for the first time. It was also the first time I introduced Michael to Colin, and so let Michael know (nearly two years after the event) of our relationship. He took it in his stride. After all, we were both making some sort of intimate confession. The four of us even went off on a trip to Vancouver Island, visiting the Butchart Gardens and staying overnight in a very rundown motel in Sooke. Ellen and Colin began a friendship that lasted for years. I continued to feel something of a traitor to Helen.

Michael and Ellen then flew on to San Diego – I think he was still involved with the La Jolla theatre project at the time – and the next day Colin and I set off for our own flight south. But there was a hitch: we discovered at the airport that whereas Colin had no problems entering Mexico as a Canadian citizen, I was still a British subject and needed a visa. It seemed absurd to return home – we no longer had a home. Eventually we managed to change our flight to end that day in San Diego, where we expected we could get consular help to arrange my visa. Arriving that evening, we took a taxi to a hotel on the water, which I remembered from my previous visit to nearby La Jolla, and where I guessed Michael and Ellen would be staying. Having confirmed that 'Mr and Mrs Langham' were also there, we booked into a room on the same floor. I then phoned Michael and told him that we had been delayed in British Columbia because of my visa problem. After a pleasant 'long-distance' chat I put down the phone, walked across the hall and knocked at his door.

It's satisfying when a practical joke pays off. Michael was of course stupefied, but also happy to see us again. We dined out together, and the next morning, through Michael's contacts, we were able to obtain my visa. Michael's advice to Colin and me, as we took off again to begin a new chapter in both our lives: 'Walk slow.'

Toronto in the 1960s, looking south. Note CIBC Tower (top centre left), then the tallest building in Toronto - and the Commonwealth

Martha Henry with MB as Ghost in *The Enchanted*. Crest Theatre 1962

The Crest Theatre, Mount Pleasant Avenue, in the 1960s

Bill Glassco 1960s: MB's first friend in Canada

J. Grant Glassco: MB's first employer in Canada 1962

Victoria College, University of Toronto, where MB taught 1963-4

MB in Queen's Park, Toronto 1964

On a visit to family, 1964: l. to r. Ray (father), Jenny (sister), MB, Tessa (mother)

Helen and Michael Langham Stratford 1963

Helen and Michael with son Chris at Grand Bend, Ontario 1963

Stratford Festival stage 1962

MB in his MGB, Ontario. 1964

MB above Lake Superior, travelling west, 1965

Simon Fraser University campus 1960s

Aerial impression of SFU campus 1965

Vancouver Harbour from Point Grey Road apartment 1965

The other 'Young Turks' at SFU: (l to r) John Mills, Jerry Zaslove, Ralph Maud

THE LAST OF THE TSARS
Stratford, Ontario.
July 1966

Fighting for control of Russia. (left) Grand Duke Michael (William Hutt); (right) Samoilov (Tony van Bridge)

The Tsar and his inner court. (left) Count Benkendorff (Max Helpmann). (seated) Tsar Nicholas (Joel Kenyon) and Tsarina (Amelia Hall;) (standing, l to r) ; Gen Voykov (Bill Needles); Ania Vyrobova (Frances Hyland); Count Frederieksz (Mervyn Blake).

Stratford, Ontario. July 1966

Controlling the Tsar. Rasputin
(Powys Thomas), Tsar Nicholas
(Joel Kenyon)

The dining room at 19 Trow,
Stratford, where MB wrote *The Last of
the Tsars* in 6 weeks

Tsar Nicholas declares war on Germany and Austro-Hungary (end of Act One)

Centralia poster SFU 1967

Centralia rehearsal SFU 1966-7

MB 1966

Colin Bernhardt 1966

Rosita Sanchez

Enrique Buenaventura

View from home in Cali, Colombia

Rosita and Colin with R.'s grandchildren

By train to Machu Picchu

Machu Picchu

Protest meeting at SFU 1968

Turkish kiosk, West Vancouver 1969

MB with student at SFU theatre 1968　　　*Two Soldiers* SFU 1969

Two Soldiers SFU 1969

Colin at the Gordon farm 1969

Colin in USSR 1973

Colin as 'William' in *As You Like It* 1972. l. Ted Atienza
r. Elizabeth Shepherd

House on
Douglas Drive,
Stratford 1970-1

House on Birmingham
St, Stratford 1971-6

Pushkin in living room,
Birmingham St.

Design sketches by
DESMOND HEELEY

Final sketch:
Mr. Hardcastle
(Tony van Bridge)

Preliminary sketch:
Tony Lumpkin
(Alan Scarfe)

Preliminary sketch:
Mrs. Hardcastle
(Mary Savidge)

Goldsmith's
SHE STOOPS TO CONQUER
Stratford Festival, Ontario 1972-3:

My dear Michael —
hope that these jottings bring back pleasant memories for you — !!
I loved doing it
Thank you for letting me!
love.
Des.

The Hardcastles (Amelia Hall and Tony van Bridge). 1973

Preliminary sketch: ideas for Act Two

Phyllis Mailing in Patria II: *Requiems for a Party Girl*. 1972. In background: Don Lewis

PATRIA II by R, Murray Schafer

STRATFORD THIRD STAGE 1972-4

THE MEDIUM by Gian-Carlo Menotti

Madam Flora (Maureen Forrester) in *The Medium*. 1974

143 Gerrard Street E., Toronto (third from right)
Lithograph by Irene Powell

Living Room 143 Gerrard St E.

Cast of *The Rivals*

Sheridan's
THE RIVALS
Roundabout Theatre
NYC 1974-5

Gene Feist 1974

Christopher Hewett as
Sir Antony Absolute

Dress Rehearsal. Left: MB. Cast l. to.r.: Philip Anglim, Jeanette Landis, Linda Alder, Eric House, 'Hob' Hobson

MB in rehearsal

Joe Orton's
WHAT THE BUTLER SAW

**Playhouse-in-the-Park
Cincinnati 1976**

Beggar's Opera final scene: Ensemble with Emile Belcourt as Macheath

THE BEGGAR'S OPERA
Gay, arr. Britten Guelph Spring Festival 1976

Don McManus (Peachum) and Alec Gray (Lockit) with MB:
Beggar's Opera rehearsal

MB and Niki Goldschmidt
with Judith Forst (Polly):
Beggar's Opera rehearsal

COMUS Music Theatre of Canada 1976

COMUS Music Theatre of Canada 1976

Harry's Back In Town: Judy Marshak and Martin Short

Judy Marshak, Nora McLellan and Ruth Nichol

COMUS Music Theatre of Canada 1976

Len Gibson　　　　Ruth Nichol　　　　Nora McLellan

Maureen Forrester and MB: 1976

Ray and Tessa arriving in Tuscany 1965

The home of their dreams: Casa del Bosco, 1975

The view from Casa del Bosco

A family lunch at Casa del Bosco 1973
l. to r. Jo (sister), Tessa (mother), Ray (father), MB

MB with Helen and Michael Langham 1978

CHAPTER ELEVEN

LATIN AMERICA

September 1968. Mexico City. Clutching our *Mexico on $5 a Day*, we arrived in a city bursting with people and teeming traffic, its smoking exhausts making our eyes sting in the intense heat. We made our way to a hostelry recommended by our guide: the Hotel Monasterio. A converted monastery, it was a good choice: cool, dark and airy, and right in the centre of things.

We had also arrived in a city that was simmering with social unrest. Since the early summer, university students had been demonstrating with ever-increasing numbers and confidence, like their counterparts in Paris, California, New York, Belgrade, Madrid and scores of other cities around the world. Mexico was to host the 1968 Olympic Games the following month, so that the government had a particular concern to keep the lid tightly closed on protests, which in August had mobilized over half a million students. Classes at the Autonomous University of Mexico (UNAM) had been closed down by the government a few days earlier (so much for autonomy), so that when we visited the spectacular campus a few days later it was deserted.

In spite of the tense political situation, we were able to do many of the things that visitors do. We visited the recently fire-damaged

Metropolitan Cathedral, built on the site of an Aztec temple and slowly sinking into the ground as the water table dries up. We took a bus out to the pyramid of Teotihuacan, and climbed to the top. We visited the newly-opened Museum of Anthropology in its striking building. But our most memorable time was not Mexican at all: it was an evening spent at a performance of *The Constant Prince* by Grotowski's Theatre Laboratory company from Poland, who were visiting as part of the Cultural Olympics. I had seen Grotowski in Montreal the previous year, and even attended one of his workshops. An English translation of his book *Towards A Poor Theatre* had since been published, and was already becoming a bible for alternative theatre everywhere. It was an extraordinary piece of luck that we were able to see his work, and even to meet briefly with him afterwards. For both Colin and myself it was the most 'experimental' theatre we had ever seen, and we talked of it for days afterwards. So different, so very different from Laurence Olivier and the National Theatre of Great Britain.

While still in British Columbia we had been told by friends that if we were to be in Mexico we must not miss the little town of San Miguel de Allende, which had its own School of Fine Arts, and had begun to be a haven for international artists. After a week in the bustle and heat of the capital this seemed a good idea, and we enjoyed our brief stay there enough to imagine returning for a few months some time in the future. We then bussed back to the city, and within a day or two were off to the airport to continue our journey to Colombia. It was only two weeks later that the terrible massacre of October 2nd took place in Mexico City, with the army opening fire on a mass of protesting students and killing untold hundreds and maybe thousands of them. The government, determined not to harm the country's image a few days before the Olympics opened, suppressed all details of the incident, passing it off as a little skirmish with communist students. Its true story has still never been told.

We took off in a small plane bound for Panama City, with a stopover in Guatemala. As our plane was descending into Guatemala City airport in a violent storm, it hit an air pocket and suddenly dropped what felt like hundreds of feet. Passengers' belongings flew, and those who had their safety belts unbuckled hit their heads sharply on the ceiling. There was huge commotion, with babies howling, men and women screaming, and a general sense of imminent doom. But we survived, crashing on to the runway and lurching this way and that before recovering direction. I often think of that violent moment as our introduction to the wild unexpectedness of South America. I also have a special reason for remembering the stopover, because while we were waiting at the airport to continue the flight we were approached by an old native woman selling small appliqué designs, of exquisite workmanship. I chose one of these, a so-called *mola*, for which I think we paid $3. Nearly fifty years later I have it still, framed and glowing in my kitchen.

After one hot tropical night in an airport hotel in Panama, enjoying the pool and the palms, we took off again for the direct flight to the even hotter and more humid town of Barranquilla, on Columbia's Caribbean coast. From there we boarded a shabby little bus to take us along the coast to the town of Cartagena. On the way, we had a first view of the country we would be calling home for the next few months. Beggars everywhere. Whenever we stopped hawkers would run to the bus screaming 'ai yai yai yai!' and offer trays of food through the open windows. Images kept flashing by: a golden bird singing in a cage on the cab of a truck in the street.... the cigarette passed through the bars of a bus office for a quick drag... the decay of the houses, roads, kerbs, everything... cactus fences... half-hearted crops... cows grazing unhobbled at the roadside... donkeys... palm-trees... huts we could look into and see earth floors, a bed, a rocking-chair... and the people: blank faces pitted and hollowed, eyes cast down, sagging spines. I looked over at Colin. He was utterly absorbed taking in this desolation; like a precious stone set in mud, I thought. What had I got him into?

We stayed a couple of nights at a many-storeyed but desolate hotel on a strip of land jutting out into the sea outside the town, in which we were more or less the only guests. It was our first experience of Colombia's then ubiquitous scattering of buildings – hotels, stadiums, bullrings, apartment blocks – that had been started with grand ideas but without the funds to finish them, let alone sustain them in operation. Our glossy bathroom was mouldy. There was no hot water. The air-conditioning didn't work. The food was poor, the staff hostile and slack. Not a good start.

Why had we come to Cartagena at all? Because we had read that it was a historic old town, with its Spanish fortifications – which we visited. But also, I must confess, because I had originally dreamed up the idea that we might travel up from the Caribbean coast to the capital of Bogota on the River Magdalena, the waterway which had first brought Europeans inland in their search for El Dorado. Sadly the last steamboats to make the journey had ceased operations a few years before we arrived. There was little if any traffic now on the river: people and goods travelled by road.

Or they flew, as we did a day or two later. Bogota, rainy and cool at over 8000 feet, was a lot more welcoming than Cartagena, but a gloomy place, full, it seemed, of people dressed in black, and hemmed in by the mournful mountains of the Andes, which we now saw for the first time. After a three or four day stay, we were happy to take off for the short flight to our final destination: Santiago de Cali, known to the world as Cali. We were warmly greeted at the airport by Enrique, the first familiar face we had seen in Colombia. He drove us in his knocked-about Volkswagen to a pleasant old-fashioned hotel by the river, where we stayed until we moved into a modern and attractive furnished house that he soon found for us in a fairly smart residential area. After a wandering few weeks, thanks to Enrique's kindness and hospitality, we were finally settled again.

Within a week or two we were even offered a housekeeper, and were happy to bring Rosita Sanchez into our household. She was a handsome black grandmother of fifty or so, and came every day to clean for us, do our laundry, cook lunch, and even wait on us at table. For all this I remember we paid her the equivalent of $3 a week. (A bourgeois neighbour was outraged that we were so generous: she paid her 'help' no more than $2.50.)

We became devoted to Rosita, and she to us, and through her we began to know at first hand something of the harsh divide between the rich and poor of Colombia. Rosita had never married, but had had eight children by different men; only two of them were still alive. She lived in a single-room shack in a slum area of Cali. This she shared with one of her daughters, who had not been married either but had given birth to four children, now aged between two and ten. How Rosita was able to leave that impossibly crowded home every day in spotlessly clean white blouse and skirt, walk the several miles to work and arrive with always the same enchanting smile on her face, was a matter of amazement to us.

Enrique invited us to his apartment for dinner, where we met his attractive French wife Jacqueline and their six-year-old boy Nicolas (who grew up to become a noted actor and story-teller in both Paris and Colombia). There for the first time I realized that Enrique was not only a playwright, poet and director but also a fine draughtsman and artist: his pictures crowded the walls. A day or two later he brought us to meet his company and watch them in rehearsals, which took place in the concrete skeleton of a never-finished auditorium in the town. They were preparing a performance of *The Orgy* from *Los Papeles del Infierno* – the play we knew well as *Documents from Hell*. But we soon found that the barrier of language made closer involvement difficult, and we decided to concentrate for the first month or two on our Spanish. Colin found a sad but intelligent teacher called Gerardo, who taught him conscientiously: Colin was not a natural learner. I taught myself from a Spanish reader, and stumbled my slow way through the whole of Gabriel Garcia Marques' *Cien Años de Soledad (One Hundred Years of Solitude)* with the aid of a dictionary. I built a vocabulary, and was even able to give a short talk in Spanish before we left. Colin could understand and make himself understood, but as much through sensitivity as knowledge. Years later I had forgotten much of what I had learned. But Colin, though he had learned less, never forgot a word, and Spanish became a shared private language between us from then onward: '*Te quiero*.'

We revelled in the city's mild air. Cali lies in the fertile Cauca River valley, and at sea level it would be steamy and tropical. But it sits at 3000 feet, and has hardly discernible changes of season. Its milky temperature never went much above 30 or below 15 degrees centigrade. Occasional heavy rainstorms, especially in late fall, kept the city's greenery lush. We could not have hit upon a pleasanter climate.

While I got to work on *The Centralia Incident*, Colin would go off and wander through the town. He signed up with a swimming pool. He found a pleasant bookshop with a café attached, where we would often meet. And he made friends, especially among the devotees of the café, who made up a kind of Cali intelligentsia.

THE BEST FOOLING

They included bourgeois young writers who did not write much, and painters who did not paint much, but who all talked at great length about art and the coming revolution before strolling home through the sad streets to their parents' comfortable houses, where they could add a line or a brush-stroke to their latest work.

> *The young man, a touch stout*
> *rises at dawn*
> *to work on his bad play,*
> *tires at ten*
> *and paces to the square*
>
> *At coffee he will discuss*
> *importances with Jorge:*
> *whether the new literary magazine*
> *can replace the one that failed.*
>
> *Returning he halts*
> *to finger curious fluting*
> *on the statue of his country's Liberator.*
> *Its form will help him in his work, he fingers.*
>
> *To a ghostly black with no hands*
> *he insists he has nothing. Nada.*
> *It is the morning's first truth.*

Both Colin and I were made wretched by the depth of poverty that confronted us daily: men in rags lying on benches with newspaper covering them; women with ghastly facial injuries pleading for a peso or two; a young fellow with no legs at all using his hands – covered in leather – to propel himself around town on a little trolley. Beggars were a part of everyone's everyday life: Enrique told us not to give them anything. 'Why?' asked pitying Colin. 'Because as long as they manage to scrape a living from charity the system will never change.'

These destitute folk often found their way to Cali because the temperate climate made their outdoor life less harsh. Enrique told us that a few years before the city council staff had gone through the streets one night packing beggars on to trucks and shipping them a hundred miles down the valley to Popayan, where many of them had come from. It was a hopeless exercise: they soon made their way back.

The weeks passed productively for me, with not only my work on Centralia but writing up my theatre lecture notes, which I found were taking the form of a series of poems. I also wrote a few poems about life in Colombia, like the one above. Enrique's own poetry and paintings and his ceaseless work in the theatre, gave us a powerful example of a life dedicated to art, and both Colin and I were learning a lesson from him that we carried with us always.

As always, memory lets the daily routines pass by without leaving much of an impression. But then there are incidents that stand out in astonishing detail. We were approaching one of these.

It was in early November that we decided to travel south, to see more of the continent. Our money was tight. We took just one small suitcase between us, and travelled by *bus popular* – the buses that the poor people used, brightly painted, stubby and noisy, gaily decorated with tassels and the inevitable crucifix: open windows, hard seats, no leg room, but wonderfully cheap. We had no problem leaving our house: it had been built like a fortress, and anyway our bourgeois *barrio* boasted its very own watchman, who would wander around and every so often blow his whistle:

THE BEST FOOLING

Around the grand houses
of the Colombian rich
nightwatchmen walk

And at each turn
whistle that all is well
for the Colombian rich

The watchman here –
because we are rich
have things to steal
to buy beer and bread,
guard these things pitilessly
like the Colombian rich –

Is so old, so hungry
he must totter first
to the bench by the guardia tree

Before he can muster the breath
to whistle that all is well
for the Colombian rich

Our first stage took us down the valley to Popayan: I remember the bus once having to swerve to avoid a recently-dead horse, its entrails being torn apart by dogs, with vultures flapping overhead. We spent a night in an elegantly-converted monastery hotel somewhat above our price range, and the next day, after an hour or two looking round the attractive old town, we continued on our way to the very primitive little *pueblo* of Tulcan, on the Ecuador border. There we learned that we had three or four hours to wait before the bus took off for Quito at 6 pm. We ate a fairly unpleasant meal in a local tavern; unable to leave our case anywhere, we could not do our usual exploring, and simply sat in the square over a beer as the hours passed. I remember we saw there a woman with a violent case of the shakes, her head jumping up and down, her whole body jolting and quivering. At one point a man came out from the café with a plate of food for her, and after putting it into her shaking hands he whipped out a cloth and threw it over her head and face. This was clearly a routine: her eating was evidently something no one could stand to watch.

We were already in the high country and surrounded by mountains, and as evening fell it rapidly became cold. We had not expected this and were ill dressed for it, but managed to find a store where we could buy a blanket for the journey; I still have it. What we were not prepared for, though, was the high adventure we were about to stumble into.

The old and diminutive bus stood in the square, slowly filling up as six o'clock approached, and the two of us got on board with our luggage, managing to find a couple of its diminutive seats together. Our departure time came and went, and it became clear that something strange was going on. There was no driver in sight. We asked, and a passenger pointed him out to us, sitting in the café, together with our ticket collector and the armed policeman who was going to ride in the bus with us. What we learned through a mixture of signs and our vestigial Spanish was that for the last hour they had been in the process of buying the policeman drinks. Why? Because the bus passengers, most of them Ecuadorian, were nearly all of them carrying goods to smuggle from Colombia to Ecuador. These were not criminals on the grand scale, simply poor people who wanted to avoid paying customs duty on things like canned peas, face cream, coffee, toy dogs and detergent. But even this petty smuggling was against the law, hence the policeman, and hence the driver's efforts to get him well and truly smashed.

They seemed to have been successful. An hour or so later, amid general laughter, he was helped on to the bus with a half full bottle of brandy still in his hand. They made room for him along the back seat and laid him tenderly down, where he sang, drunk as an owl, before drifting into sleep. Our journey finally began, with our fellow passengers looking forward to a trouble-free ride to Quito. It was already dark.

Our dirt road ran immediately into the mountains, negotiating one hairpin bend after another as we toiled up a mountainside and then giddily descending into the next valley before climbing again. At the start of each of many terrifying descents over the next hours, the bus stopped and the ticket-man came through with a small bag, collecting a few pesos from any of the passengers who could afford it. He then got off the bus, walked over to a convenient shrine a few yards away, knelt down, left the money as an offering to the Virgin Mary, and returned to the bus. We started down, well insured against misfortune, with Colin and me made a little more panic-stricken by the whole exercise.

We reached the Ecuador border within a few minutes. Our passports were looked at cursorily, and for some reason the bus was waved on without a search of any kind. But sadly our petty smugglers' worries were not over. Even departments in Ecuador and Colombia at that time had customs restrictions between one another. So every fifteen or twenty miles there was a checkpoint, manned by armed guards. As we approached the first one the lights in the bus were extinguished, and all the passengers feigned deep sleep. As soon as we were stopped, two or three guards climbed aboard. The driver spoke to their *Jefe* in a low voice, and they left together for the office by the roadside. Meanwhile the *Jefe*'s underlings called for the lights to be turned on and began to search the bus. They soon found some packets of Fab detergent, and went on poking under men's legs and into women's bundles for more. But they searched without conviction, as though almost afraid to find things, and kept looking over their shoulders until their *Jefe* returned and called them off. Matters had been arranged. The guards left, the barrier was raised, and the bus bumped through. There were laughs aboard, and a collection made to compensate the driver.

More checkpoints were ahead and again we got off lightly. But just after midnight, as soon as we left the mid-journey *pueblo* of Ibarra, it was a different story. The bus was stopped and the men were ordered off the bus so that a proper search could be made. Pandemonium broke out. People begged us to put their face powder, their oil, their cans of food into our cases, telling us that as *gringos* we would not be searched. We could not risk this, but we did stuff a few items into our pockets for them. One large old lady wearing a voluminous skirt which went down to the floor lifted up the edge of it with a wink to show us a whole pile of goods stacked round her feet. She moaned to the guard that she was too old and ill to stand up and be searched, and after some hesitation he let her stay where she was: as she knew, there was no way he would lift her skirt. A young girl had been carrying a giant new, articulated plastic doll which was evidently contraband, because her mother had torn it out of her hands, dismembered it, and handed out arms, legs and head to different passengers, stuffing the doll's clothes into her underwear, and leaving the girl clutching a wretched torso and sucking her thumb.

The guards finally sent in their secret weapon, a huge, severe woman in uniform, who had no compunction in searching the females on board. A lot more goods were discovered and confiscated before the search was over, but even so most of our new friends felt they had got off with a few treasures as we started away again, roaring with laughter at their successful ruses. We gave back the things we had pocketed for them. The doll was reassembled and returned to its young owner.

And then at some point the policeman finally woke up. They tried to calm him, but he got belligerent, stood up drunkenly and pulled out his revolver, waving it in all directions. He staggered to the front of the bus, and then in a change of mood began to get everyone to sing a popular song, '*Vivan los solteros!*' ('*Long Live Bachelors!*'), conducting it with his weapon. He then shuffled back through the bus, shouting '*Canta! Canta! Sing!*' and making sure everyone did. Of course neither Colin nor I knew the words or the music, so when he came to us and found us not singing, he started to threaten us with the revolver, holding it a few inches from our faces. The passengers came to our rescue, telling him we were ignorant *gringos*, and he eventually moved on. But it was a scary moment.

I remembered Enrique telling us how real life in Colombia was so unbelievable, so melodramatic, that playwrights had a hard time matching it. We now knew exactly what he meant.

Nothing in the rest of our trip south could match the excitement of this night's goings-on, which ended at dawn as we crossed the equator and arrived in Quito. We spent two days recovering here, journeyed happily through sugar-cane country to wretchedly steamy Guayaquil, and from there took a 35-hour coach-ride to Lima, crossing through Peru's 'driest desert in the world'. We stayed in the capital a few days, trying to make contact with the University's theatre people, but there had been student demonstrations there too, and the University was closed. We then flew to Cuzco (where I haggled for and bought two alpaca rugs), and took the tourist train to the astonishing ruins of Machu Picchu, something both of us had set our hearts on seeing. We thought of taking another train on to Bolivia. But our money was running out, and back in Lima we were already bracing for the long haul back to Cali, when I had the idea of seeing if we could find a ship to take us back along the coast.

We struck lucky. An Italian boat was just then making its way from Santiago in Chile to Genoa in Italy. We took a taxi down to Lima's port of Callao, and in another hour were in the luxurious surroundings of an ocean liner, with our own cabin, superb Italian food, an amply-stocked bar, and even a swimming-pool. Our fellow passengers included a large party of excited nuns, off to Italy to see the Pope. (I even managed to persuade the purser to take charge of one of my alpaca rugs, and post it to my parents in Italy when he got to Genoa. Months later I heard it had arrived safely. An honest man, that purser.)

After our cut-price three weeks in '*popular*' buses and flea-ridden hotels, our two-day boat-ride was paradisal, and we arrived in the port of Buenaventura wonderfully refreshed. We landed by lighter, met by the now familiar wall of steamy heat at sea level. There was a bus to take us a hundred miles up through the jungle to Cali. And we were home.

Rosita, who in her fifty years had probably never left the city, had been doubtful we would ever survive such a journey, and was overjoyed to see us. While we were away, she said, one of her grandchildren (here she cradled her arms) took very sick and nearly died (here she crossed her arms over her chest). Rosita had this wonderful gift of matching words with gestures. Once, when warning us to beware of '*ladrones*' (thieves) in the marketplace, she accompanied the word '*ladrones*' with a gesture, running her nails down the side of her face. I asked her why she did this. She seemed to be quite unaware that she had done it. She thought a bit, and said 'maybe because they have beards.'

Our Spanish slowly improved. We met and got to know the noted Colombian constructivist sculptor Edgar Negret, who divided his time between Cali and New York; very urbane and very gay… We accompanied Enrique's company on a visit to a factory, where they entertained the workers in their cafeteria with a short play, and a series of powerful, militant poems by Enrique… We went with Enrique for a five-hour taxi-ride to the annual arts festival in Manizales, where a university troupe was performing one of Enrique's plays *En la Diestra de Dios Padre* (*On God's Right Hand*). We had hoped to hear and even meet Pablo Neruda, who had been reading his poetry at the Festival, but he had left the previous day.

And so the weeks passed, and Christmas was upon us. Colombia at that time didn't really do Christmas – Santa Claus and Christmas trees were almost unknown. But Colin and I decided that for our Christmas lunch we would do things the North American way, with a turkey and trimmings and a plum pudding if we could find or make one. We also decided to invite a delighted Rosita to bring her daughters and grandchildren.

About five days before the big day, we asked Rosita to go down to the market and buy us a turkey. She had never bought one before but was happy to take on the commission. She was away some time, and when she returned she had the turkey, but it was walking behind her on a string; she thought it would be a good idea to fatten it up for a few days. Our shock and surprise were impossible to conceal, and I asked her who was going to kill it. 'Oh, that's easy,' she said, making the gesture of wringing the bird's neck. There was nothing we could do, so for the next few days we fed the turkey, and would hear it gobbling away in the courtyard.

It was around that time that a parcel arrived for me; a Christmas gift from my mother in Italy, wrapped in the normal brown paper and string of those days. It turned out to be a small round tray from Florence, all gold and red, and somewhat 'antiqued'. Rosita admired it, and I was throwing the wrappings away when she asked if she could take them home. 'Of course,' I said, 'What do you want them for?' I imagined her recycling them for presents of her own. But no: she told us that the brown paper was just the thing for her windows, which were missing panes of glass. And the string was ideal for her grandchildren's shoelaces. It was a sharp lesson in the meaning of poverty.

The day came that the bird had to be dispatched. Rosita went down to the courtyard to do the deed, but after a few minutes she came back and said that after looking at the turkey's neck she realized it was too big to be wrung.

'So what are you going to do?' I asked in dismay.

'It's easy,' she replied brightly. 'The people next door have a *machete*. We can borrow it and just cut the head off.'

'I see,' I said dismally, guessing this would be more than a one-person job.

So, twenty minutes later, there we were all three of us in the courtyard. We had caught the bird, and Colin and Rosita were holding it, each of them with a hand holding down its long red neck, and – yes – I was wielding the machete. Terrified of cutting their hands, I suppose I was less decisive than I should have been: it took several strokes to sever the head, and when I did so the headless turkey took a last turn round the courtyard before collapsing. Any doubts about the pagan origins of Christmas were put to rest that year in Colombia. We had held our very own sacrifice.

For all our attempts to fatten the turkey, it was a scrawny creature, and with an inefficient oven we had not used before and which barely accommodated the bird, it took hours to cook. Colin had bought presents for Rosita and all the children, and when they arrived looking enchanting in their very best clothes, we gave them a good time. But the lunch was not really a success. The children had never eaten turkey before and poked at it suspiciously, concentrating on their roast potatoes. The older ones left most of theirs uneaten, wanting to take their portions home to give to their brother and sister who had not been able to come. I can't remember whether we ever got a plum pudding together; we no doubt filled them up with ice cream. But, for all the awkwardnesses, we had given them a day to remember; they had sat up at the table and behaved like angels. Rosita was ecstatic, and treasured the photographs we took to record the event.

A few days later the New Year came in, with bells ringing and firecrackers popping all round us and throughout the town. 1968 was finally put to bed.

I had a special reason for being happy to be living far away in Colombia that fall. I had received two or three letters from Patrick Lyndon, telling me that the whole simmering trouble at the Centre had exploded in his face a few weeks after I had left. It had been decided to cancel the position of Centre Associate, and the Associates already on staff had been told they were being let go. They said they would refuse to leave. John Juliani came to their defence and delivered a long letter of resignation, which included declarations as to his loss of confidence in the Centre and in the University, and even in himself. Patrick wrote to him accepting his resignation, which made John furious. Patrick said he would withdraw the letter if John withdrew his resignation. John said he certainly would not do so. John also said he would continue to put on plays at the Centre whether he was on staff or not. Patrick told him that this might be possible, though the Centre might have its own programs and not be able to accommodate his plans. John continued to haunt the University and stir up his flock of devoted students, and eventually the security people arranged for a court injunction against him appearing on campus. And so on. And so on.

Living in the midst of Colombia's extreme political and social situation, I received this news with maybe less seriousness than it deserved. Simon Fraser's turmoils were far away, and seemed insignificant compared to the genuine distresses of the people around us and in the rest of Latin America. The rapturous espousal of Che Guevara by our students (and middle-class students all over the world) as the icon of their revolutionary inclinations seemed also an insult, given the very real horrors against which Che and Castro had fought, and fought successfully, ten years earlier. I was obviously concerned at the stresses that Patrick was dealing with, and felt mildly guilty at my part in inviting him to the Centre. But I also felt confident in his handling whatever might be thrown at him.

It was perhaps now that I began to question seriously whether my future lay in British Columbia. For all the idealism with which we had begun, it had become by now a place of enormous stress; a bone being fought over by animals of all colours. I remembered the excitement of my years in Ontario, and the many opportunities I had been given there. Surely Colin and I could start a new life together back in the east, free from the travails of Simon Fraser? We discussed the idea at length over the next months, and though Colin loved BC we were agreed that a move probably made sense.

We were to leave Colombia at the beginning of March, deciding to re-enter North America up the east coast and spend some weeks in New York before returning west. In preparation for our departure we began to buy as many authentic Colombian artefacts as we could find: a *ruana* for each of us, two fine blankets, primitive musical instruments (one made out of a gourd), and a splendid little Indian stool, carved out of a single block of wood and crudely hand-painted in a pattern of black and dark red. We soon realized that we could not take these things with us when we left, so arranged for them to be transported by ship to Vancouver in a chest, which arrived on the docks there many months later, battered but intact.

Meanwhile we had two months of our Colombian adventure still to run. I had completed my report on *The Centralia Incident*, and was moving ahead with my lecture-poems. I still have the originals of these, with wormholes bored through the yellow paper: bookworms were a regular pest in our house, along with the occasional scorpion. And of course we always had to be careful of the 'amoebas' in our food. Lettuce had to be washed leaf by leaf. Enrique told us that his own amoebas were permanent residents in his body, and that most Colombians were the same way, giving them chronic stomach-ache. All this teeming microbial and insect life seemed to mesh with the country's politics, and with the permanent atmosphere of danger in which Colombians lived from day to day.

Some time into the New Year, Enrique's domestic arrangements changed. Perhaps he had been having an affair; for whatever reason, Jacqueline threw him out. He took a room in a house quite close to us, and as a result we began to see more of him, occasionally inviting him to share lunch with us. He told us stories of his life, one of which became a poem:

A man I love
who writes plays
for his Colombian people
when a boy
mixed toy explosives in his room

which on a hot evening
as his mother entered
blew up in her eyes

They say that after that
she turned slowly mad
I guess that after that
he turned slowly sane

Mixing explosives in his room
which on hot evenings
as the public enters
burst in their bloody eyes

To make them mad
to make their children sane

We also saw more of Colin's teacher Gerardo, who was keen for us to know the local country and organised trips for us into the area outside Cali. Once we visited the home of the 19th century writer Jorge Isaacs, whose only novel, *Maria*, is a landmark of Latin American literature. The house, now a museum, was built in classic Colombian *hacienda* style, and its covered verandahs and closed courtyards always stayed in Colin's mind as an ideal structure for a home. It was called '*El Paraiso*'.

On another day we took the bus to nearby Palmira, and from there to a distant mountain village, where Gerardo had grown up, and where his sister was the only teacher in the little primary school, with its statue of the Virgin Mary outside the door. We visited the one class, who were full of excitement at meeting two folks from Canada – wherever that was. We also visited the *pueblo*'s very simple and shabbily beautiful white church, quite unadorned by the usual Catholic statuary, and met the grave and simple village priest, obviously a dear friend for Gerardo and an important figure in his life. The village was amazingly rustic, with one-room adobe houses built around one or two unpaved roads, and goats nibbling along the verges. The water supply came from a single well, and women lined up to fill their jugs and buckets. Gerardo was staying that night with his sister, so Colin and I took the bus back alone, along with a peasant family and a few other passengers.

Not long after we started down we came to a halt, and were met by farmers with sacks of onions strapped on to the backs of their mules. They proceeded to load these sacks on to the top of the bus. We then continued for another few hundred yards before stopping again for the next consignment, and then again, and then again. Soon the roof of the bus was piled high, and as we drove on we could see farmers running down the side of the valley ahead of us, urging on their laden mules to reach the road in time. When the roof could take no more, they started stashing the sacks inside the back of the bus, on the empty seats. By the time we reached Palmira the sacks of onions filled half the bus. And our eyes were streaming.

We talked with Enrique about our charming but sad friend Gerardo, who was in his forties, had never married, and lived with his mother on a pittance. He seemed incapable of finding a job, and Enrique told us that he was a common type in Colombia: he was not homosexual, but the society with its wretched inequities deprived men of so much of their self-belief that they became listless and asexual.

One evening Enrique, whom no one could describe as asexual, took us to a brothel in the poor part of town. It was very decorous. We were ushered into a kind of shabbily genteel drawing room with red velvet armchairs and sofas, and the madam asked us if we would like a drink. We took a beer and sat there rather uncomfortably while young and not-so-young women came and went by an inner door covered with a bead curtain, looking at us invitingly as they sashayed through. I seem to remember that at one point Enrique retired through the curtain for ten minutes or so, but maybe I am wrong. Certainly Colin and I politely declined, hoping to give the impression that regretfully we had not seen the girl we wanted. We were glad to get out of there.

We had made another friend, a Canadian called Tony Sampson, who had married a Cali woman and had settled there, teaching at the Universidad Santiago de Cali. On our last day in Colombia he invited us to a theatre seminar at his university. Enrique's theatre as a co-sponsor and he was present with his usual force and articulacy, as was Danilo, one of his lead actors. Our familiarity with Spanish had made strides by this time, but it was still difficult to follow the cut and thrust of a lively meeting:

They are talking in a language
that I hear only through water
talking of theatre in their town
of whether to bring workers
into their theatre committee

Danilo who looks like a 19th century Russian
insists on their participation
The delicate Merino
who has worked with Ionesco in Paris
flutters his hands and mutters
'absurd' to his neighbor

We sit in the university theatre
open-ended
shabby and inefficient
the lights missing bulbs
the large fan still
on a Sunday afternoon
In Colombian heat

And while the voices fade and return
I wander in the corridors
between Colombia and my Canada
clashing obrero with Canadian worker
and the shrieks of their poverty
with the hum of mechanized welfare
searching the bonds of amity

And the far-future poem of us
laughing together.

We hurried home from the seminar to prepare the house for a farewell party, to which we had invited all our friends, now numbering perhaps fifteen or twenty. Rosita had done some cooking, but she was in such a state over our imminent departure that she spent a lot of time sitting in the kitchen crying into her newspaper.

There was a lot of wine and beer to drink, and the get-together was convivial. But it was raised to a whole new level by Gerardo, who had used some of his scarce resources to engage the services of a well-known local musical group to serenade us on our last night. The *Trio Maguar* began singing and playing outside the door, to our astonishment and joy, and then came inside and gave us their whole repertoire of energetically sad songs. We bought their LP, *Miel de Caña*, which they had brought with them and signed for us, and they joined the party. They had heard that our next stop was New York, and they begged us to try and use their disc to get them known there. We promised to try, knowing the hopelessness of it all.

It was this same desperate dream that so many poor Colombians nursed and which we were exposed to again and again, of escaping out of their country into a place where there was money and hope. Rosita begged Colin and me to adopt as many of her grandchildren as we could, knowing the life that was ahead of them in Cali. We felt we had to refuse, but often wondered in the years that followed what became of them, and whether we could have handled such a project. The youngest of them would now be fifty…

Rosita insisted on accompanying us to the airport, and told us that she loved us forever. We told her the same thing, and never forgot her beauty, her dignity, her warmth. Though we sent her occasional messages of love through our Canadian friend Tony, we never saw her again.

CHAPTER TWELVE

TRANSITIONS

We flew to Miami on March 3rd, and once there searched the ads in the newspaper and picked up a drive-away car to take to New York City. Edgar Negret had given us the name of a playwright friend, Paul Foster. As soon as we had delivered our car to somewhere in Brooklyn Heights and returned to Manhattan we got in touch. Paul recommended we stay at the Hotel Albert in Greenwich Village, and we were able to settle into that historic hostelry, following in a long line of artists like Mark Twain and Hart Crane.

A day later Paul welcomed us into his apartment, and we began to realize that we were in the presence of a distinguished and prolific young writer. Through Paul we were introduced to Café La Mama, met its founder the mythical Ellen Stewart, and attended a production there – I think it was Foster's *Tom Paine*. I also contacted Richard Schechner, whom I had met at Stratford, and we were able to get tickets to his production of *Dionysus '69,* which was beginning to make waves all over the city. Andy Warhol tore our tickets at the door. We were also able to take in Peter Brook's now legendary production of *A Midsummer Night's Dream*.

As I recount these distant memories, I realize now that we had stumbled into the midst of a seminal time in New York: Andy Warhol in the ascendant, the beginnings of the off-off Broadway movement, the sudden proliferation of productions at Café La Mama by young playwrights like Foster and Lanford Wilson, the pioneering of the environmental theatre movement by Schechner, with its breaking up of the traditional actor/audience space; even the breaking of taboos by the entirely naked cast of *Dionysus*. Unfortunately I don't think we were in a state to take advantage of this amazing *apertura* into new ways, and of the luck we had in meeting some of its guiding spirits. We were not sure who or where we were, returning from six months in a now already sadly distant Latin American country and culture, living out of suitcases, and on our way back to western Canada, with our future there very uncertain.

We did not know it at the time, but we were in fact at the start of a time of considerable upset and dislocation – mental as well as geographical.

After a couple of weeks we managed to secure another drive-away commission, and set off across the USA to Seattle in a handsome Chrysler, which we delivered to its owner before taking the train up the coast to Vancouver, checking into a motel by English Bay.

The events of that summer of 1969 are soon told. Colin and I went to live in a house right on the sea in West Vancouver, rented from a history professor who was away for the summer. He was a specialist in Middle East affairs, and on the rocks by the water he had built a Turkish-style *kioski* as a writing studio. We coveted it, and for years afterwards would talk of building a kiosk wherever we happened to be living. The house went on the market at the end of the summer, for $90,000, and we – well, Colin – thought of buying it; but our plans were to take us elsewhere. (The house's site alone would no doubt now be worth several millions. Colin always had a good instinct for a deal.)

I returned for the summer term to Simon Fraser, teaching my theatre course and directing two one-act Colombian plays, one of which, *Dos Soldados ('Two Soldiers')*, I had translated from the Spanish. Colin signed up for a couple of courses.

The University was in its usual turmoil, under an interim president, with demonstrations and protests and plots and counter-plots taking up the precious time and attention of scores of highly intelligent people. The absence of John Juliani's presence was clearly felt, and, I have to say, appreciated. But after spending six months in a genuine revolutionary atmosphere, under genuinely authoritarian rule, and with genuine oppression and deprivation being suffered by a disenfranchised population, I found the struggles at Simon Fraser absurdly childish. By the middle of June I went to Patrick Lyndon and handed in my resignation. Having had time by then to be fully familiar with the workings of Simon Fraser, he assured me I was doing the right thing. For me, it was the end of what had been an extraordinary but unrealisable artistic dream. Murray Schafer stayed on, but applied to have his Resident status switched to the academic rank of Associate Professor. So, I think, did one or two of our other residents. The idealism of our beginnings as a beacon of the independent arts in academia had died.

Colin and I planned to head east at the end of the summer, and we made our preparations. Our minimal furniture we sold to my successor as theatre resident – the Newfoundland actor and theatre visionary Chris Brookes (later to return home and make major contributions to Newfoundland's theatre and life as a documentary maker and story-teller.) I cashed out my accumulated pension, giving us enough money to start out on our new life.

To make the trip we needed a car, and found one at a garage in West Vancouver. It was a 1959 Mercedes four-door sedan, and we bought it, I remember, for just $450: the first of many tired Mercedes cars that Colin acquired over the next many years, and of all of them the most reliable.

Only one thing stood in our way. My friend David Gardner, who back in 1963 had directed me in the TV play of *A Resounding Tinkle* (in the course of which I had met Helen Burns), had just become artistic director of the Vancouver Playhouse, and offered me a season of parts in three plays. It was a tempting idea. But there were two good reasons for turning it down. In the first place our sights were now set on a return to eastern Canada. Secondly I had made something of a commitment to myself that from then on I would work as a writer and director, and Colin would be the actor in our partnership. David had not proposed a season to Colin, whose work as an actor he had no way of knowing.

We remained close to David and his wife Dorothy, and the day we left they were the last people we dropped by to say goodbye to, our car filled to the gunwales with all the possessions we could carry.

Once back in Toronto we took a cheap, furnished attic apartment just off Parliament Street. And somehow, within a few weeks, we had hooked up with the young director Clarke Rogers and a handful of out-of-work Equity actors and put together our own little group, which we called 'Poorhouse Theatre Company'. Still fresh from our Colombian experience, Colin and I imbued the group with some of our enthusiasm for a socially and politically motivated theatre, and we created a forty-minute Colombian program, which included the one-act play *Dos Soldados*, along with my translation of Enrique's sequence of militant poems which we had first heard in a factory in Colombia. We used a German

Expressionist sketch of capitalists in top hats as our poster, and with Bill Glassco's help managed to borrow the old gym at Victoria College as our theatre space.

As soon as we began advertising our two or three performances, we were contacted by Larry McCance of Actors Equity (still at that time part of American Equity), who wanted to ban the production because of our status as Equity members. Clarke and I went to see him to plead our case: we were showcasing our talents in order to attract work, we said – and American Equity was already approving what they called 'showcase' productions, for which Equity actors were not paid. Larry was receptive, and we were allowed to proceed. In fact I believe ours was one of the earliest 'Equity Showcases' (if not the earliest) to be approved in Canada.

With no money for publicity, our audiences were sparse. But I did manage to persuade Jean Gascon, now artistic director of the Stratford Festival, to attend, along with my friend John Hayes, now the Festival's Executive Producer. I think our militant leftist stance struck a chord with Jean's own youthful rebelliousness, a time he had now left far behind as the leader of Canada's most staid and even bourgeois theatre. And he had a chance for the first time to see Colin perform, as one of the Two Soldiers.

Our Colombian program was to be the first of a series, and we were beginning to plan for our next. But as with so many ventures of this kind, when its members get offered paying jobs they have no alternative but to accept. Within a few weeks three of our six members had left for work elsewhere, and our brief life as one of Toronto's first alternative theatres came to a dwindling end.

A few weeks later I seemed to be heading out myself. Michael Langham was returning to Stratford as a guest director (he had given up the Festival's artistic directorship two years previously), and was preparing a production of Sheridan's *The School for Scandal*. He asked Stratford to offer me a position as his assistant director. The production would start rehearsing in Stratford just after Christmas, and was slated to make a short American tour to Chicago and Urbana, Illinois, then on to the National Arts Centre in Ottawa, before returning to the Festival as part of the 1970 season.

I can still remember the turmoil in my mind when this offer came through. My time at Simon Fraser had aroused my interest in all things new and experimental, and I still thought of our collective work on *The Centralia Incident* as unfinished business. Grotowski's *The Constant Prince* still resonated with me, and our brief time in New York had brought me face to face with all the exciting things now happening in America's theatre capital. Even in Toronto things were on the move: Theatre Passe Muraille had been founded the previous year to provide a home for new Canadian plays (within two or three years it would be joined by Factory Lab, Bill Glassco's Tarragon Theatre, and other initiatives). It was impossible not to be influenced by the excitement of the sixties, with their promise of making all things new.

Meanwhile our months in Colombia had radicalized Colin and me in a revolutionary direction. We still felt strong fraternal links with Enrique and his brave troupe, and had been proselytizing for the idea of a 'dangerous' political theatre such as we had witnessed in Latin America. And now came an invitation from Canada's centre of classical dramatic tradition. Was I going to return to the world of the classics – to the old English culture that had been nurtured in me from my school days? It was a world in which I had even become something of an expert, and valued as such by one of the world's great Shakespearean directors. But it would surely mean saying goodbye to my links with 'all things new', and to the dream of a 'dangerous' Canadian theatre.

In the end, the need for funds forced the issue, and I accepted Stratford's offer. I was excited to be working once again with Michael, and pleased in many ways to be returning to a place I knew so well and where I had many friends. We moved out of Toronto a couple of days before Christmas, having found an upstairs studio apartment in Stratford – on King Street, next to a funeral parlour. Colin with his usual flair ensured that we had a Christmas tree, and presents. And a few days after rehearsals began production manager Jack Hutt offered Colin a position in his backstage crew. We were both once again working and making some money.

It had been over three years since I had spent time at Stratford, and there had been several changes. When Michael Langham left (under something of a cloud) in 1968, the Board was under strong pressure to appoint the Festival's first Canadian artistic director. There were two leading candidates for the position. Jean Gascon, founder of Montreal's Théâtre du Nouveau Monde, had first come to Stratford in 1956 when his company played the French king and court in Langham's *Henry V*. That first year Jean spoke almost no English. But he had persevered, and Michael hired him several times as a guest director, first with opera and operetta, more recently with Molière, and then with his first Shakespeare productions. In his young days Jean had trained as a medical doctor, but had broken away from the profession to follow his love for theatre. He was a bull-chested extrovert, charming and very French: a man who liked a party, who flirted with women, who laughed a lot, who fiercely needed the love of those around him, and yet who hid a deeply melancholy soul beneath all this bonhomie.

And then there was John Hirsch, who had first made a name for himself as artistic director of the Manitoba Theatre Centre in Winnipeg. A survivor of the Holocaust (which had done away with all his immediate family), John had found his way from Hungary to Canada in his late teens, learnt English, completed his education, and then begun directing. He was a highly intelligent, extremely sensitive, tortured soul, and discreetly homosexual.

It was a difficult choice for the Board to make. But they hit on the very worst solution: they appointed these two candidates as joint artistic directors. It would be hard to imagine two personalities so different, and the arrangement only lasted one season. I'm not sure of the details, but John withdrew, eventually finding a senior position in the drama department of the CBC. Jean was now the Festival's sole artistic director.

At the same time as making the short-lived double appointment, the Board had come to the conclusion that Michael's role as artistic and executive director had to be split into two, in order to provide the Festival with stronger financial and administrative leadership – and perhaps also feeling that these artistic types needed to be balanced by someone who could keep a close eye on the money. Bruce Swerdfager, who had been Front of House Manager in my first years at Stratford, was now Comptroller. But the Board's major move was to bring in William Wylie as Administrative Director, reporting directly to the Board. Bill's primary business experience had been in a mail-order company, but more recently he had been managing the Manitoba Theatre Centre. He was astute and well-organised, and had immediately begun to effect some much-needed changes in the areas of the Festival's budgeting, box office and publicity. He was also a great believer in the value of touring for the Festival company, as a way of expanding the Festival's reputation. It was he who had arranged the winter tour for which I had been hired, in which Langham's *The School for Scandal* was to be paired with Jean's production of *The Merchant of Venice*, with Donald Davis as Shylock and Maureen O'Brien as Portia. Leo Ciceri played Antonio.

There was one other addition to the artistic team. Tom Hendry had been hired as Literary Manager. Tom had co-founded the Manitoba Theatre Centre with John Hirsch, and his appointment had probably been John's initiative. But when John had left, Tom had stayed.

In spite of all these changes, the Festival's staff members, as well as many of the actors, still remained largely the same as those I had known and worked with during my previous stints at Stratford, in 1964 and 1966. It was good to be back. My new acquisition of a partner was also noted – maybe to the surprise of some; but Colin's sweetness and good looks and earnest high-energy soon began to make him friends.

Our apartment was only a short-term rental, and it was not long before we started looking around for more permanent accommodation. It was then that Bruce Swerdfager's wife Mary, who worked as a real estate agent, suggested that instead of renting another apartment we buy a house. In those days this was not too extravagant an idea, and I still had some dollars in savings from my pension payout at Simon Fraser. We eventually settled on a modest little brick-built, three-bedroom home on Douglas Drive, which we bought for $18,000, with a down payment of something like $2,000 and the rest supplied by a mortgage. It was the first home we had owned, and we were excited and proud. We immediately set about furnishing it, initiating the collection of cheaply bought but attractive antiques that we continued to accumulate over the years. Southwestern Ontario at that time was a treasure trove of such things, and I can still remember the prices we paid for pieces I still have: a mahogany chest-of-drawers for $90, a cherrywood writing desk for $6, a 19th century pine hutch for $75 – and so on. We also planted a weeping willow in the back yard – something that became a tradition at all our future homes. Within a few weeks

Colin also realized another of his dreams, purchasing a golden puppy from a breeder of Afghan hounds in London, Ontario. We named him Pushkin, and for the next twelve years our Pushkin, who grew into one of the most beautiful dogs I have ever seen and known, was a loving member of our family and part of our lives.

A few weeks after we began work on *The School for Scandal*, Jean Gascon sent for me and told me that his literary manager Tom Hendry had announced his intention of leaving, and that Jean would like to offer me the position of assistant to the Artistic Director, which would include the role of literary manager. I was honoured: though it was a job I had already undertaken for a season six years back, this was a full-time post, and I could imagine that I could be of real help to Jean, whose self-confidence as leader of this 'Anglo' organization was always a little fragile. At the same time I realized that the experimental course I had been pursuing at Simon Fraser was now fading somewhat. Perhaps I was fated to remain a 'classical' theatre person: there was not much room at Stratford for collective workshops and anarchic experiments.

Meanwhile, the work on *The School for Scandal* progressed. I soon took on the same role as before, working as Michael's assistant director, literary advisor and general sounding board. The cast he had assembled was superb. Robin Gammell played Joseph Surface like David Garrick come again, with the elegant, lightly-posed gestures familiar from eighteenth century theatre prints. For Sir Peter Teazle he had brought in Scottish actor James Donald, best known to North American audiences for his performance in *Bridge on The River Kwai*. Donald caught just the right mixture of fury, bafflement and helpless attraction as his not-so-innocent young wife from the country (played by American actor Helen Carey) was tempted further and further into town ways. Michael lavished all his wit, and his comfort with the extremes of acidity, on the 'school for scandal' scenes, with Eric Donkin's campery as Sir Benjamin Backbite, Bunny Behrens' deliciously crabby Crabtree, and the amazing Jane Casson as Mrs Candour. Colin, who had been invited to join the company as an apprentice, always relished Jane's delivery of Candour's most biting lines, and for years afterwards would bring them out on occasion: "How have you been this centu-ry?"… "By the way, is it true that your brother is <u>absolutely ru-ined</u>?" With Leslie Hurry's costumes and the racy, rock-and-roll influenced music of New York composer Stanley Silverman, it was an extraordinary production, and I was happy to be part of it.

I also continued to learn some basic theatrical lore from Michael: "The end of the first half must send the audience out buzzing with excitement, while the opening of the second half must knock 'em over". And I have always remembered the moment when Oliver Surface and Peter Teazle meet after Oliver's return from long years in India. Michael set them apart the whole diagonal width of the stage. Oliver enters, and when they catch sight of one another they stand still, arms outstretched, their affection electrifying the distance between them as they hold and relish the unrepeatable moment: "My old friend!" "Sir Oliver!" – before finally rushing together in a handshake and an embrace.

I went with Michael and the company to Chicago, Urbana and Montreal as he continued to tinker with the production. When it toured later to Ottawa, Helen Carey had to leave the part of Lady Teazle because she was pregnant, and I was responsible for coaching her understudy Blair Brown into the part.

It was while I was in Ottawa, staying with the company at the Beacon Arms (always referred to by our actors as 'the Broken Arms'), that Jean came to see me in my room after a performance. He was highly distressed: Tom Hendry had told him that he intended to stay on as Literary Manager, so that Jean's offer to me had to be withdrawn. I wondered why Jean did not simply terminate Tom's contract if he felt he could not work with him. But for Jean, with his reluctance to upset anybody, this was a step too far. (For some reason poor Jean went on that evening to bemoan to me his declining sexual prowess. "It used to be three or four times a night, but now…")

Since we had just bought a house in Stratford, the news was disappointing. But Jean went on to say that he had been talking to Hamilton Southam, Director-General of the National Arts Centre, who might have something for me. The newly-completed National Arts Centre had been built to house three theatres. The largest, seating 2,300, had a proscenium stage and full fly-house and was designed for opera, ballet and symphony concerts; it was also to be the home of the newly formed NAC Orchestra, under Mario Bernardi. The smallest was a hexagonal studio theatre for experimental work; and the second, middle-sized stage, with 900 seats, was for drama. Southam had been pressing the Stratford company to take over this second stage as a winter home, and to become Canada's English-speaking national theatre – the stage had even been designed to accommodate Stratford's thrust stage configuration. Stratford was reluctant, but the pressure, both economic and political, was intense, and the company was even being billed in Ottawa as the 'Stratford National Theatre of Canada'. After two or three years of trial the plan was dropped and the Centre created its own companies (English- and French-speaking) to occupy this stage.

Meanwhile there was the Studio. For this space Southam had dreamed of two separate small theatre companies, francophone and anglophone, to create experimental work.

A few days after my meeting with Jean, I was invited to Hamilton Southam's office at the Centre. He told me he had heard good things from Gascon and Langham of my work at Stratford, and he asked whether I would be interested in taking on the leadership of the experimental English-language company at the Studio. I would have the funds to hire up to twelve professional actors for a six-month season, and would have absolute freedom to choose the company's repertoire. There would be sufficient funds to hire composers and designers, and enough production money for two productions.

It was a fine offer, and a unique opportunity. What young director would not jump at the chance to be given his or her own theatre company, with complete artistic freedom and a mandate to experiment, an open and flexible theatre space in which to work and perform, and a generous budget? After discussions with Jean and with Michael, and with Colin back in Stratford, I accepted. This seemed to be the chance I had been waiting for, to return to the ideas I had been mulling over since *The Centralia Incident*. At Simon Fraser our initial collective creation methods had gradually been replaced by traditional theatrical forms, with a playwright, a manuscript and a director. I had always thought of this shift as an act of cowardice on my part. This time, though, I would pursue the dream of 'un-led' theatre to the very end, without compromise. And I would accomplish it not with a random group of young students but with a group of talented professional actors. The anarchist philosophies I had gathered up during my time on the West Coast came flooding back. I would resist any temptation to take control. Out of our collective creativity and intelligence we would finally shape for our first production a new kind of play, a new kind of theatre.

There was another immediate advantage in the plan. Since there was no set cast of characters – no play script – I was able to hire actors without regard to the specific needs of a play. I would simply choose a likely group of good and intelligent actors. I could also break the usual dominance of male roles, and hire six men and six women to make up our troupe of twelve.

For our second production I planned an 'experimental' version of Shakespeare's *Pericles*. Since the play was so little known, I felt we could be free to develop something interesting and original. But this was still months in the future, and nearly all my energies were concentrated on our first creation.

I cannot remember, but no doubt I shared these thoughts early on with Hamilton Southam, and apparently was able to present them with enough fluency and conviction for him to support the plan. It is always hard for an administrator to stand in the way of artistic convictions on any grounds other than finance. Hamilton, who had spent time in the Department of External Affairs and had served as Canada's ambassador to Poland, was a tall, fine, patrician gentleman with considerable inherited wealth, and a war-injured face that twisted his smile. He had been the force behind the creation of the Centre, and was passionately keen for its success. Devoted to music and theatre, he knew little of the workings of either profession, and so was heavily dependent on the advice of others. He welcomed me warmly to the Centre, recommended as I was by two of Canada's leaders in theatre. He had studied at Oxford and loved literature (he was learning a new sonnet every day at that time, he told me), so my own university and literary background found in him a responsive chord. We became friends even to the point of my being invited during the summer to his lavishly simple cottage (complete with tennis court, gardener and cook) on an island in Rideau Lake. There were times when I felt almost a filial relationship with this powerful but oddly sensitive and romantic man.

I was back in Stratford that spring for the new rehearsals of *The*

School for Scandal, which involved the adaptation of the production for the Festival Theatre stage. Jean was also beginning to rehearse Shakespeare's *Cymbeline* for the summer season, and he invited me to serve as assistant director to him on the production. I was thrilled with this assignment – not least because it was being designed by the legendary Stratford designer Tanya Moiseiwitch, with music to be composed by Gabriel Charpentier. It was a great excitement to be part of the creative discussions on the play right from the beginning, and with my familiarity with the play and the period I believe I was able to make some quite valuable contributions to the look and sound of the production. I was happy too that Colin was to be a member of the cast.

Jean's choice of this play was in line with his increasing preference to direct lesser-known works by Shakespeare and his contemporaries: works in which he felt his limited knowledge of the language was less of a liability. "When I direct Molière," he used to say, "he is right <u>here</u>, beside me," and he would slap his left shoulder. "But with Shakespeare, well…" The following year he was to direct a brilliant production of Webster's *The Duchess of Malfi*.

In fact, while Jean had a flair for powerful stage effects and strong contrasts of colour and mood, his approach to character in all his productions tended to be broad-stroke and one-coloured. "You are a whore," he would say to the Patricia Galloway playing the Queen in *Cymbeline*, or "You are a butcher," to Robin Gammell as the violently stupid Cloten in the same play. In this he showed his comfort with human archetypes, like those familiar to him from the *Commedia dell'Arte*, with its stock characters like the braggart soldier, the cunning servant, the old lecher, the quack doctor (these in turn deriving from the Roman comedies of Terence and Plautus). This meant that he was most comfortable with the plays of Shakespeare most influenced by *Commedia*, like *The Comedy of*

Errors; even his *Taming of the Shrew* production of 1973 was interpreted in heavily *Commedia* style. He felt comfortable too with a Commedia-influenced comedy of Ben Jonson, like *The Alchemist*, in which characters' names suggest their personality traits. And he responded well to the melodramatic in Jacobean tragedy.

But Stratford actors were used to Michael Langham's explorations of Shakespeare text, revealing the rich nuances of character and motivation, and accustomed to the idea of character slowly developing and changing in response to events during the course of a play. For them, Jean's one-line summaries were strangely unsatisfying and difficult to work with, inviting caricature. Surely 'whores' and 'butchers' come in all shapes and sizes and colours like the rest of us. Their life experiences shape every one of them differently. How do you play 'whore'?

It was in this area of textual interpretation, with its clues to character and motivation, that I was most able to contribute to *Cymbeline*, and as rehearsals progressed I was more and more assigned to private sessions with one or two actors at a time, providing something of the sounding-board they needed. Some of their speeches were tough-knotted, as in Shakespeare's other late plays, and we enjoyed untangling them together. Those actors were grateful, and Jean was very much aware of the help I was giving them: in the talk he had with the company the day we opened, he was good enough to give me a special thanks, and to say that really I should be credited as co-director of the play. Generosity again; it was Jean's great gift.

The play opened that night to fine notices: Stratford had introduced the audience to a play they barely knew, and revealed its power. Maureen O'Brien shone as Imogen, Robin Gammell's Cloten was an extraordinary creation, and Powys Thomas as the weak and indecisive King Cymbeline ("I am amazed with matter") made an appropriately odd match with Pat Galloway as his witch-like and thoroughly decisive Queen. The final scene, in which one discovery after another is made and wondered at, has often been cited as a ridiculously unbelievable ending to one of Shakespeare's failed plays. But it was fascinating to see the smiles on the faces of the audience, not scoffing but rooting for each new wondrous discovery, like all our childish wishes come true as in a fairy story.

It was during that summer that Stratford suffered an exceptional and tragic blow. Leo Ciceri, a long-standing and brilliant member of the company, had taken a priest friend of his to the airport on a foggy evening, and missing the road on his way back had driven over an embankment on Highway 401. He died more or less instantly. Stunned as we all were by the news, our shows had to go on, and we had to replace poor Leo immediately in all his parts. His role as the treacherous friend Jachimo in *Cymbeline* was taken over by his understudy, Malcolm Armstrong, whose part as 'a French Gentleman' was in turn being understudied by Colin, who now for the first time had a few lines to speak on stage. It was poor comfort for the loss of a fine actor and good friend, and the whole company was in mourning for many weeks as we went about our business. I accompanied Jean to Montreal for the funeral, which was taken – shakily – by the very priest he had taken to the airport right before his death.

We drove homeward
after the funeral and the flight
passing on either hand the fields he passed
the signs
the blades of grass

and at the cut of the fence

where his life stopped we stopped
to gaze down the bank of his last moving

then climbing back into the car
moved softly to our own ends

passing on either hand
the fields he did not pass
the signs
the blades of grass

Increasingly, as the summer progressed, my major preoccupation was with my preparations in the capital city. The summer involved a lot of shuttling between Stratford, Toronto and Ottawa, as I developed plans and budgets. I auditioned actors, and hired a composer, designer and stage manager – to all of whom I expanded on the excitement of creating a production together, with script, designs and music being created as we went. Once again I presented my ideas with a great deal of passion and articulacy, and managed to stimulate some of the same excitement in the company I chose.

I was also concerned to make a real connection with our work on *The Centralia Incident* at Simon Fraser University three years earlier. One of our very bright writing group in the workshop had been Brian Freeman. I invited him to join us in Ottawa as dramaturge, and was glad when he accepted. Here, I reckoned, would be one ally who understood the concept and had even seen it playing out. I also invited Paul Bettis, who had directed *Centralia*, to be a member of the acting company.

As the weeks went by I began more and more to feel that, as with *Centralia*, we were going to have to start with some kind of a theme to focus our ideas. After casting around I chose the Spanish-

American War of 1898, in Cuba. It was a topic I had begun to research following my stint in Colombia, and I had become more and more fascinated with it. The subject seemed also to satisfy my desire for a political element in our work. It was after all the first 'imperial' war engaged in by the United States of America – the first time an American army had left North American soil. With the Vietnam War still raging, there was a very real point to be made – if we could make it.

I contracted Brian to begin work in August, and tasked him with preparing a dossier on the War, including a brief history, a summary of some of the major characters involved, and extracts from memoirs and journalists' reports. Copies of this dossier would be handed out to each of our actors on the first day of rehearsal. We also had to provide a title for our non-existent play, so that the Centre's marketing department could start advertising it. It was a time when long play titles had something of a vogue, and we hit on '*How the Company Went to an Island, What Happened and Who Came Back*'. The name was more prescient that we might have imagined.

Colin and I sub-let our Stratford house to friends Leon and Sharon Pownall, and at the beginning of September we packed ourselves into the old Mercedes, together with Pushkin and a stack of suitcases. After two or three days in an Ottawa motel room (leaving the poor dog there for hours at a time) we found an attractive sub-let at the top of an old house on MacKay Street. We were settled again.

Naturally I had hired Colin to be one of the company, and had put together a fine group of actors, including Jackie Burroughs, Blair Brown, Beth Ann Cole and Maureen Fitzgerald among the women, and Dominic Hogan, Neil Munro, Richard Donat and Bob

Silverman among the men. We were all invited to a generous welcome gathering at Hamilton's spacious house in Rockcliffe, along with Mario Bernardi and his new orchestra, and our parallel French language studio theatre company under the leadership of Jean Herbiet. We seemed to be truly at the beginning of a starry trail.

There were also less auspicious signs. The National Arts Centre, with its brutalist concrete exterior, its endless hexagons and its Kafkaesque labyrinth of corridors, its bureaucracy and its elaborate security arrangements, seemed strangely stony ground in which to seed and nurture any kind of delicate new plant; and looking back from forty years' distance, I guess I was pretty crazy to think I could relaunch my west-coast, anarchist ideas in such a setting. I was also naïve to think I could carry a bunch of professional actors with me on the adventure. But I was evidently determined to lead the idea of leaderless theatre to its conclusion, blithely unaware of the paradox involved.

It was shortly after our arrival that I received a visit from Paxton Whitehead, artistic director of the Shaw Festival at Niagara-on-the-Lake. Paxton invited me to his Festival for the following year, to direct a French play called *Summer Days (L'Eté)* by Romain Weingarten, newly translated and adapted by Suzanne Grossmann. The play's four characters consisted of two young children and two cats – the cats to be played by adult men. I read the script swiftly, was suitably charmed by its very French campery, and accepted the offer. The play could not have been more different from the adventure we were about to embark on, but it was many months away. Sufficient unto the day…

The first days of our rehearsals in Ottawa were full of excitement. We spent the first hour of each morning on movement and voice exercises, using as a final spoken choral piece a passage from Claude Levy Strauss's *Tristes Tropiques*:

THE BEST FOOLING

"It is a system adrift, after cutting the cables by which it is attached. It is like a sail-less ship, driven out to sea by its captain, who is personally convinced that, by subjecting life aboard to the rules of an elaborate protocol, he will discourage the crew from thinking nostalgically either of their home or of their ultimate destination. It is not a question of sailing to other lands. The proposed revolution is much more radical: the journey alone is real, not the landfall, and sea routes are replaced by the rules of navigation."

We then sat in a circle, took up the dossier of Spanish American War materials and discussed how we might approach the putting together of a play. The actors each chose a historical character to concentrate on, and we improvised, and discussed, discussed and improvised. Meanwhile our costume designer went out to the second-hand stores and came back with a pile of old clothes and accessories: uniforms, dresses, a sword or two, canes, a sunshade, toy guns, and lots of hats. To develop the theme of free play, our set designer proposed a pit full of sand, and in due course this was installed. It inspired some interesting improvisations as generals sat in the sand, acting like children.

Our composer wrote some incidental music to be played if I remember on a keyboard, with some actors joining in with percussive instruments.

As the days went by, the actors kept looking to me to take the lead, to make a plan, to decide what we should do next. And each time I refused. "What do you suggest?" I would ask. It was natural that they should look to their director, the person who had hired them and got them involved in this company: what did he want? I wouldn't say. I had made quite clear from the beginning that this was to be a truly collective enterprise, and it was up to them to take responsibility. They knew the truth of this, and that they had committed to it. Day after day, they tried to pick up the baton. But nothing came of it. Each day they improvised scenes, dressed up, played in the sand, enacted disorganized battles. There was no order, no plot, no plan. And of course they became frustrated. I guessed that this was a necessary first stage, and I continued to say nothing.

And all the time the clock was ticking, and the Centre was calling urgently for a news release describing our play. They were even beginning to sell the odd ticket. There were requests for interviews with myself or with one or two of the better-known actors. The Centre's whole machinery for publicizing our work was getting into gear. And we still had no idea what the end result of our work was going to be.

Towards the end of the third week, when I had for the tenth time refused to take a lead, the actors made a plea: 'At least develop some rules for us, so that we know what we can and can't do. If we are free to do whatever we want, then you might get a situation in which we all just walk off the stage, and refuse to go back. What will you do then?'

We discussed the idea at length. I realized, perhaps for the first time, that although I was determined to shed my personal artistic responsibility for the shape and character of what we were trying to create, I was still responsible by the terms of my contract for producing a play, and for holding the company together. So in the end I agreed – reluctantly – that I would write a set of rules – Levy-Strauss's "rules of an elaborate protocol". I have no record of these, but they went something like this:

1. The playing time would be divided into two periods of 45 minutes each. A whistle would sound at the beginning and end of each period. There would be a 15-minute intermission.

2. A two-faced digital clock would be set up above the middle of the stage, so that the actors could check the time.
3. No one was allowed to leave the stage during the two periods.
4. Each actor must choose and sustain a character.
5. No one was allowed to speak as themselves, but always as their character.
6. Three of the company of twelve would supervise the action, to ensure that no one broke the rules. They were referred to as 'caretakers'.
7. The caretakers had whistles, which they would blow when there was any infringement of a rule.
8. If an actor was whistled out, he or she would be taken to the sand-pit and placed in it, and would there be subjected to interrogation.
9. Certain punishments would be meted out by the caretakers if the accused was found guilty.

The rules did have some connection to the subject we were dealing with. The stage stood for the island of Cuba, which the characters could not leave. As in armies, there were penalties for disobedience and desertion. Interrogations were a routine part of the campaign, as Spanish soldiers were seized and compelled to reveal their army's whereabouts and battle plans.

I returned the next morning with my set of rules, and shared them with the company. The actors responded positively, feeling that they at least had some kind of framework within which to work. From then on, as the advertised time approached for our opening night, the actors spent each day bravely improvising action, dialogue, battles, speeches. And each day two or three of them were whistled out and led into the sandpit for interrogation. Our designer rigged up a platform ten or twelve feet above the stage, reachable by a ladder, and here the caretakers sat watching the action for signs of rule-breaking. And I watched, and said nothing, except occasionally to tinker with some rule that we felt was being counter-productive. There was still no plot, no story, no shape. This was a true collective.

For the actors, I have to say it was a time of enormous strain. Accustomed to learning a role and playing it within a predictable setting among other actors who could be counted on at each performance to reproduce their rehearsed actions and words, this valiant group found themselves in a no-man's-land, in which nothing and no one could be counted on.

At the end of the day, while Colin and I returned home to walk the dog and talk and eat, it was natural that most of the company adjourned to a pub, where I can imagine that as the beer flowed their talk grew increasingly turbulent. I found out only later that a few of the group were also fairly heavily into drugs: something quite outside my experience. Naïve? Yes, no doubt.

I still retained my connection with the administration of the Centre. I was once invited to the home of Mario Bernardi and his wife Mona Kelly, and remember sharing my ideas of leaderless art with Canada's most distinguished conductor. Why did he not try it with his orchestra – step off the podium and let them create a work by improvisation? He was genial, but not to be persuaded. Perhaps he thought I was a little mad.

I also reported regularly to Hamilton Southam, assuring him that the experiment was going well; that like all experimentation it was open to failure, but that we were working hard, and creating something unique. He was nervous, but was staying the course. He trusted me.

Opening night came. Hamilton arrived with a small entourage of his office staff. Thirty or forty audience members showed up, as well as some friends and partners of the company, and of course a handful of critics. The Company was extraordinarily nervous, since neither they nor anyone else had any idea what would happen. One of them told me afterwards it was the most agonizing ninety minutes of his life.

The audience was made fully aware in the program of the improvisatory and haphazard nature of what they were about to experience. We could not guarantee them an entertaining evening. We had done nothing to build excitement, or mystery, or surprise. What they saw was twelve actors having the courage to appear in front of them and make things up as they went along. The actors were as much in the dark as the audience.

There was ragged applause as the show came to an end. I went backstage and congratulated the cast on their pluck and staying power. What we had created was indeed a new kind of theatre, in which for lack of a directing hand the action sprawled along with no rhetorical flourish, no lesson, no climax, even no meaning beyond what it revealed about theatre with no playwright and no director. Was this what I had been imagining for our end result? I no longer knew.

The Ottawa Citizen's review excoriated our show: boring and stupid, an utter waste of the critic's time, "laughingly referred to as a play". *The Ottawa Journal's* review was similarly dismissive. One other critic though, when his piece finally appeared in *Octopus* (an 'alternative' newspaper of the time), reacted very differently. He had at once understood what we were trying to do, and he applauded the experiment. Soon afterwards that critic made himself known to me. His name was Jeremy Gibson, an Englishman then living in Ottawa and writing and directing plays. Neither of us could have known it at the time, but we were to become friends and colleagues for life.

I believe that if our experiment had culminated in three or four performances in front of an audience, all might have been well. We could have licked our wounds and discussed the whole adventure with some detachment. Unfortunately we were locked into a production schedule laid down long in advance by the Centre, which committed us to play a full three and a half weeks: a total of something like twenty-five performances. And these performances would be entirely in the hands of the actors, with the director having to withdraw in the normal way after the opening night.

Somewhere around the beginning of the first full week, things began to go wrong. Whatever belief they initially had in the experiment and its methods, the actors' confidence in it – and in me – began to shatter. The caretakers' enforcement of the rules became increasingly aggressive, and there was mutiny in the ranks, which led one evening to the company of nine storming the three caretakers' tower and replacing them with a new trio, while the original three were brought down for interrogation in the sandpit. The interrogations became increasingly personal: actors began to be questioned about their private lives, about their sexual relationships. The play between actors became more cruel and anarchic from one night to the next. There were further assaults on the tower, and further takeovers of power. The order of things, such as there was, was unravelling.

The plan was to start rehearsing our second production during the days, and performing *How The Company* at night. But the license given to the actors by night was impossible to shed in daytime rehearsals for *Pericles*, and having given up my director's authority in the first production, there was no way I could re-assert it in the second. Poor Colin as a company member was exposed to a lot of angry and hostile talk about me, which he felt he had to let me know about. I began to lose all self-confidence, and hovered on the edge of a nervous breakdown, barely able to proceed with rehearsals of the new show.

A crisis came one night in the second week of performances. Colin had broken some rule, and when he was being interrogated the company asked him searching questions about his private life, and about his relationship with me. He was traumatised, but used his quick wits and ready anger to survive. However, at some point during the performance the following night a group of actors started chasing Colin, and he escaped from them by running into the audience. This was of course an infringement of the rules, and one muscular member of the company ran after him, tackled him, and brought him back on the stage. But Colin had hit his head during the tackle, and appeared to be unconscious. Eventually he was taken off stage and an ambulance called, and he was taken to hospital to be checked for concussion. He returned home late at night, shaken but unhurt.

It was by now clear to all that things had got seriously out of hand, and Colin was obviously being attacked as a scapegoat for me. I asked to see Hamilton the next day, and had to report the imminent disaster. It was agreed between us that the play would be taken off at the end of that week. But I also had to report that I was in a serious mental state. I felt I could no longer continue with the second production, and proposed that it be taken over by another director. I asked for a two-week leave to recover.

Hamilton was wonderfully sympathetic, but clearly I had disappointed him. Joel Miller, who had worked at the National

Theatre School and was known to some of the company, was available and was asked to take over. He agreed to do so, though he preferred to scrap Pericles and direct a work of his own creation.

Colin resigned from the company on the last night of *How The Company*, and somehow I mustered the strength to say goodbye to the actors, and even to apologise for any distress I had caused them. I don't think I received any apologies for the distress they had caused me, though I couldn't resist the thought, which I have shared often since, that 'if you try to play Christ you get crucified'.

It is worth mentioning that the critic of the *Ottawa Journal* came back to see our work a second time, and that he wrote a column in which he took back his earlier condemnation. He praised the courage of the actors, and the boldness of the production. It is the only time in my experience that a critic has returned to a show and publicly revised his first judgments.

One other writer a few months later also took a positive tack. Dr. James Flannery, Coordinator of English Theatre at the University of Ottawa, wrote a paper about the production, saying among other things:

"Make no mistake about it, How the Company *was important and it was original. Nowhere else, to my knowledge, has a contemporary theatrical work so boldly and powerfully mirrored the vulnerability of modern man, caught in absurd power structures, forced to improvise his way out of one oppressive situation only to find himself caught in another. The actors nightly improvised their roles, at times brilliantly, at times less so, but at all times with integrity. Those few of us in the audience were aware of their continual danger — the danger at the root of stage fright which is, in reality, symptomatic of much greater human fears. Like the actors in* How the Company, *we all perform our lives without texts, improvising as best we can our daily roles, trying to hide as much as we reveal, calling upon what*

experience we have gathered as a defense against a pushing world, struggling to define our worth to ourselves and others, fearful of being found wanting, and, in turn, aggressive out of the reaction to our very fears."

We decided to spend my leave in Jamaica: a couple of days after the play closed we flew south for two blessed weeks in the heat and luxuriance of the tropics. My mental balance began to be restored. When I returned, I met with Hamilton. He was cordial but firm. In his opinion I was 'a commander who had lost control of his troops', and there was no alternative for me but to resign – with the obvious implication that if I refused I would be fired. But Hamilton had gone further than that. He had discussed the situation with Jean Gascon, who told him that his Literary Manager, Tom Hendry, had resigned a few weeks earlier, and that Jean would be happy to invite me back to Stratford to replace Tom and to serve as assistant to the artistic director. So, in asking me to leave, Hamilton was able to assure me that I had a new job to go to. I was more than happy with the proposal, and delivered my letter to Hamilton that same day. I did not meet with my company again, and within a few days we shook the dust of Ottawa off our feet and drove back to Stratford. The nightmare was over.

I have had many years since then to reflect on the *débâcle* of those days in Ottawa. Whatever the production's supporters said about it, it was a wretchedly public personal failure, with articles in the papers and a great deal of scuttlebutt bandied about in the acting fraternity. Even after I had moved back to Stratford and taken up my duties at the Festival, it was some months before I could sit in my office with the door open; a sure sign that paranoia was still lurking.

But the experiment had its instructive side. What began as a group of well-intentioned artists working together to create a play had become, in the absence, of directorial leadership, a 'behavioural sink', in which struggles for power, vindictiveness, and cruelty both mental and physical, took over. Was this what happens when leaders refuse to lead? Was this a prime example of 'original sin'? Were people inherently bestial, and only prevented from playing out their beastliness when kept firmly in control by a leader?

The experience certainly brought my love affair with anarchy to an abrupt end: all power may corrupt those who wield it, but a refusal to exercise power seems to invite a more general corruption. Perhaps a group of people is inherently unable to share power and responsibility equally or even equitably for any length of time. But then it has to be remembered that this particular exercise in anarchy had been stitched into the highly hierarchical context of the National Arts Centre, in which my refusal to direct could be considered simply perverse, rather than idealistic and courageous. In the end, whatever I said and however I acted, I was responsible, and paid the penalty.

CHAPTER THIRTEEN

BACK TO STRATFORD

I shall be forever grateful to Jean Gascon for taking me into his administration at the Stratford Festival after I had fallen on my face in Ottawa. I seem to remember at some point sitting down with him at his home and recounting my version of events. It had been an aberration, an act of rash courage. But in recognizing my foolhardiness I didn't want to lose my preparedness to put myself on the line again in the future.

I must also recognize here the unhesitating love and loyalty of my dear friend and partner Colin, who stood by me through the crisis, and supplied me with the strength over the next months to restore the self-confidence I had lost. After all, I had thrown away a fine opportunity for him as well as for me. But never once did he throw blame at me, reserving his anger instead for those members of our Ottawa company who he felt had betrayed and deserted me.

Having leased our house for a full year, we had the added complication of having nowhere to live in Stratford. Once again Mary Swerdfager came to our rescue, finding us the top floor apartment of a handsome old home on Birmingham Street. We soon learned that the owners who lived below us were in the process of separating, and that the house was for sale. Again through the skillful advocacy of Mary – involving not only a hefty mortgage but also a bridging loan – we were almost immediately able to buy the place, for $21,000 or so. A few months later we sold our original house, and were now in possession of a duplex, with the added advantage of having rental income. This became our home for the remainder of our time in Stratford. With its large bay-windowed living-room, two bedrooms (one of which doubled as a study) dining-room and attractive kitchen, it served our purposes well. Back steps led down into the garden, which we soon surrounded with a high enough fence to keep the long-legged Pushkin safe.

It was soon clear that Jean's rescue of me was not simply an act of kindness. He had felt increasingly alone at Stratford, seeing his colleagues Tom Hendry and Bill Wylie as John Hirsch's men, and never feeling sure that he had their loyalty. He really needed someone to talk to, someone to share his artistic ideas with. His wife Marilyn, vivacious and party-loving, avid for her daily crossword puzzle, was a fine and loyal partner – and a skilled cook – but not an artistic thinker. John Hayes, his executive producer, was again wonderfully loyal, but saw his job as a facilitator of Jean's program rather than a co-creator: he was much too self-effacing to debate or contest whatever plans Jean might share with him. Bill Hutt, who had been named associate artistic director, was able to contribute from his extensive experience as an actor. But the only friend with whom Jean could exchange original creative ideas was the composer and poet Gabriel Charpentier, who had been a central creative force at the Théâtre du Nouveau Monde during Jean's years there. Gabriel was still Jean's composer of choice for his productions in Stratford, and was working there more and more. But he still lived in Montreal.

Within a few days of my arrival, Jean called me in to discuss an idea. There had been increasing pressure on the Festival for some years to produce new Canadian work. But the Festival's two theatres, one with 2,250 seats and the other with 1,100, were considered far too big to house untried new plays (my *Last of the Tsars* in 1966, with its epic scale and theme, was one of the rare exceptions). The previous summer Tom Hendry had been responsible for putting together a season of 20th century plays at the Avon, including Arnold Wesker's *The Friends* and Mrojek's *Vatzlav*. The season had been something of a financial disaster, and it seemed that Jean did not want to go further down that route. But down by the Avon River stood a large hall called the Casino, built some time in the thirties, belonging to the Stratford Badminton Club and used for badminton, but also for dances and other social get-togethers. The Festival had rented it for occasional events over the years, and Jean was now considering that we should hire the hall for the summer to present a season of three or four modest-scale productions, perhaps including one piece specifically for children. Influenced by Charpentier maybe, he was particularly anxious that some of the work be musical, in the form of intimate opera – or, as we were beginning to call it, 'music theatre' – providing opportunities for Canadian composers and singers as well as actors. And he invited me to be the artistic director of this third stage – soon in fact to be advertised as 'Third Stage'.

Of course, I embraced the offer. It was a chance to continue building my experience as a producer, but also to direct a show or two of my own – now that I had discarded my rash forays into leaderless theatre. It meant I could still be involved with creating and fostering new work. And it gave me a chance to redeem my shaky reputation. I am still amazed at the way in which Jean so rapidly showed his continued faith in me.

That first season at the Third Stage was more a pilot project than anything else, and it was such a last-minute plan that I had only ten days to pick a play to direct. I proposed a new play by Enrique Buenaventura, which he had recently sent me. It was called *Il Convertible Rojo* (*The Red Convertible*), and was a play-with-songs in the low-life Brechtian style. To translate it I engaged our old friend in Colombia, Antony Sampson, though because of difficult communications and deadlines being missed as the summer approached, I ended up having to translate most of it myself. I was also forward enough to take on the job of writing the music for its songs. To play the lead – a raunchy, tragic prostitute – we engaged a remarkable American actor named Mari Gorman, with the other three actors – David Schurmann, Patricia Grant and Ed Henry – playing multiple roles. We rounded out the Third Stage season by bringing in a production for children, presented by the Marionettes of Montreal, followed by a week of performances by the recently-formed Canadian Mime Theatre.

In response to the failure of the previous season at the Avon, Jean had also changed the direction of Avon productions, concentrating on comedy and large-scale music theatre. Thus my literary duties also involved me in making a new translation (book and lyrics) of *An Italian Straw Hat*, by Labiche and Marc-Michel, for production at the Avon under the direction of Stephen Porter. This light-hearted nineteenth-century musical frolic was to be played in tandem with a Feydeau farce, *There's One in Every Marriage*, in a new translation (by Suzanne Grossmann and Paxton Whitehead) of Feydeau's *Le Dindon* (very sensibly it was thought inadvisable to title and promote it as *The Turkey*).

Somehow in the midst of all this activity I also had to prepare my production of *Summer Days* for the Shaw Festival, taking off for three weeks in the early summer for rehearsals in Toronto, and for a short run in Ottawa before opening in Niagara-on-the-Lake.

The action of *Summer Days* takes place in the garden of a house where two children, a brother and sister, live with their cats. The cats inhabit the garden. By day they are more or less amiable if catty, but by night their characters change into thoroughly tigerish felines, and their dialogue turns into poetry. The two cats, played by middle-aged men, wear black suits with white gloves, and are given floppy bow ties, much resented, to wear on Sundays.

I had had a chance to audition the two 'children' for my play, but the cats had been cast by the artistic director. I was delighted that one of them was to be played by my friend Eric House. The other cat was to be Jack Creley, a good actor whose name I knew well, but whom I had never met or worked with.

I well remember the first day of rehearsal. I was thoroughly prepared, but understandably nervous, since this was the first directorial job I had undertaken since the Ottawa episode. My stage manager and I had met early to plan the rehearsal schedule, and it was just before ten o'clock when the first actor arrived. It was Jack Creley. We introduced ourselves, and then Jack asked, "By the way, who's playing the other cat? – I never heard." "Oh, it's Eric House," I replied happily. Jack's face fell. "Oh God," he muttered: "I was afraid so." "What's wrong?" I asked. "Can't stand working with him," said Jack: "Oh well…"

It was an inauspicious start. But Jack was nothing if not professional, and rehearsals went forward with few problems. In fact the very catlike spitefulness and hostility between the two cat characters was probably well served by the lack of fellow feeling between the two actors who played them. Rehearsals proceeded enjoyably, and the play opened to mostly warm and friendly notices both in Ottawa and Niagara, appropriate for the slight and charmingly camp little piece it was: '*Summer Days* – gloriously funny, truly imaginative, optimistic, and a beautiful way to spend an evening' (*Ottawa Journal*); 'Bawtree has built a haunting mood, sometimes amusing, sometimes rather touching' (*Buffalo Courier Express*); 'Michael Bawtree has done wonders...' (*Globe and Mail*). I had passed my first professional test as a director who actually directed!

Back in Stratford I was soon busy finalizing the text for *The Red Convertible*, working out the very basic but effective stage design with Art Penson (two bare trestles in front of black curtains was all we could afford, and really all we needed), and composing the music for the songs, which were pulled together by the wonderfully talented Alan Laing. I remember little of the rehearsals, except the pleasure of working with my small and clever cast: the play opened in late July for just ten performances. The work had revealed itself to be somewhat thin and derivative, but we 'improved' it considerably in rehearsal, and it was sustained by a really remarkable performance by Mari Gorman. Notices were definitely mixed, from 'rather compelling' (Chusid, *Vancouver Sun*) to 'utter calamity' (Kareda, *Toronto Star*). But the dismissive reviewers were mostly dismissive of the play itself, and nearly all were impressed by Mari Gorman. (It was no surprise to us that she won an Obie in New York the following year for her performance in *The Hot L Baltimore*.)

Meanwhile, I enjoyed the fact that I was the first person to have directed plays in the same season at both Shaw and Stratford Festivals.

In September of that year, Colin and I celebrated the fifth anniversary of our first meeting. It had been a tumultuous time, with our move from the west, our brief stay in Toronto, and our two settlings in Stratford with the Ottawa safari in between. There was no diminution in our love and care for one another. But there was no doubt that the relationship was sometimes under strain. For one thing, Colin was subject to violent mood swings, by which a pleasant conversation could turn in an instant to vituperation and sometimes even physical assault, often followed by a rapid exit from the house. He would eventually return, and would slowly change his tune from self-justification to apologies. I assumed that these attacks were the result of emotional stress and guilt at the loss of his son, and perhaps this had something to do with them. It was many years, though, before we discovered a more elemental reason.

Meanwhile, both of us were still young and sexually ardent, and Colin's erratic behaviour – known only to myself and never displayed in front of others – sometimes made intimacy difficult. After all, neither of us had had any experience of other male partners. To add more strain, we were living at a time when new and highly-trumpeted sexual freedoms were beginning to overpower many social relationships, heterosexual and otherwise. Since homosexuality was no longer illegal in Canada (even though still considered a treatable disease by the psychologists' lexicon), promiscuity had become much more open and even acceptable. Gay bars proliferated in the big cities. Every urban centre had its areas where gay men would cruise, often teaming up with someone and walking off to make love.

To make matters more difficult, Colin and I were now living in the theatre world, where for centuries the actor's freedom from moral rigidity and a necessity for emotional availability have made casual sexual encounters all the more usual and accepted. Fidelity to one's partner is heavily tested in such a world, and many relationships and marriages founder there. Alcohol often fuels these encounters: liquor provides a heavily-used way of relaxing after a performance, and many actors hover on the edge of alcoholic addiction – or tumble over it. Colin was no drinker, and had inherited from his mother a lifelong antipathy to bars. I on the other hand had been brought up in a pub culture, and it was natural for me to gravitate to some drinking-hole or other in my off hours.

While never failing to keep the care for one another firmly at the centre of our thoughts and feelings, we both of us found ourselves looking out in other directions, and since I was both more self-assured and had more opportunities, it was I who initiated at Stratford two or three amours, meeting guiltily, and occasionally driving out of town on hot summer nights. Though I kept these assignations secret from Colin, he was far too astute not to know that something was afoot. But slowly, during the rest of the torrid seventies, it became a mutually accepted behaviour between us. We once in Toronto even went out cruising together, with the aim of each making a separate conquest.

My job at Stratford entailed more and more travelling, and over the following years of the seventies I learned to know the whereabouts of gay activities in every city, from New York to Chicago to Los Angeles, from London to Paris to Rome. I am not particularly proud of this activity, and many of my friends might be surprised that I am admitting to it here. I can only say that sex can become as much an addiction as alcohol or drugs, and that for several years I was quite simply a secret addict. The truth is that when we are trying to be good the sexual urge often gets irresistibly in the way, and very few of us are successful in damping it down. Nor, incidentally, are women exempt from the same primal urges. Prominent folk all try to exclude their sexual adventures from the public story of their lives, and are shamed and hounded in varying degrees if the truth comes out. Not all their misdemeanours are illegal, but all are against the moral code that society has set up for us, and that we – and the tabloid newspapers – claim to live by

So what kept the two of us together during this time? I have to say that our relationship in the early years was a little like parent and child. Colin had had a rocky childhood, with an aggressive father and a mother who was too protective, a twin he did not feel close to, and a much older brother whose career in the NHL kept him far away from the family. He had been poorly educated, having achieved very little in the classroom, especially after the death of his parents. His handwriting was immature and irregular, his capacity to write a good sentence almost non-existent. He was impulsive and found it hard to concentrate – he probably had what we would now call Attention Deficit Disorder. He had a hard time listening to or analyzing what he heard. He read little.

His triumphs, I gradually learnt, were in other fields. When tickets were to be sold for a school performance he would be indefatigable, going from door to door and charming everyone into surrender. He could sell anything, and had a line of patter that along with his charm and good looks was irresistible. He was a brilliant mimic, and would keep his family on a roar with his imitations of neighbours and TV personalities – especially women. He was also passionate about learning to play the piano, and tried to persuade his parents to buy an instrument, but they refused – even when one was offered by a neighbour as a gift. Above all, he wanted to be an actor, and became involved in every theatrical opportunity going. When he was recovering from the accident in which his parents lost their lives, a nurse once asked him how he had found the strength to recover from his terrible injuries. "I want to be an actor," he replied, "and nothing is going to stop me."

What kept us together? There was something about the rawness and vulnerability of Colin's personality that attracted and held me fast. I had never encountered anyone so uneducated who was also so quick and sharp. There seemed to be no filtering process when he spoke – he could talk inventively and off the cuff for minutes at a time with barely a pause for breath, let alone for thought. His gift of mimicry was endlessly enthralling: he had a whole range of voices he could slip into, his favourite being a strong middle-European accent belonging to some older woman of huge social pretension and utter stupidity. He could also reproduce exactly the tones of a small child, who was often hiding nastiness under a veneer of sweetness. ("Mummy! Baby's crying!" he would call out in his lisping child's voice. "Don't cry, little baby," he would say quietly to me, and then give me a sharp pinch. "Baby's still crying!" he would call out.) I was dumbfounded and reduced to helpless laughter by his power of observation and his sheer fluency. Unfortunately he was also shy, and in the early days it was only I who knew of these exceptional gifts.

What kept us together? Colin was in desperate need of direction. I was able to be the parent he never had as an adult: someone to talk to, someone to advise, someone to make things happen for him. He became deeply dependent on me, and was always bracing for the possibility that I would desert him; always ready to harden his heart, to thrust me out before I could leave of my own accord. I could never let him down; never confirm his fears of abandonment.

Colin was exceptionally handsome, and would tell me that he found me the same. We took pleasure in each other's looks as well as company. He was also passionately keen to create a home to replace the one he lost when his parents died, and it was this that would send him out to the antique and junk shops and to country sales. He had an unerring instinct for a bargain, and innate, unconventional good taste. He bought second-hand clothes of name brands, for myself as well as for him. Our apartment filled up with attractive old chairs, tables, fine china, carpets, silverware, even old pictures. Christmas and birthdays were high points in his calendar – excuses to decorate, to send countless cards and to buy presents. He always had far more gifts for me than I had for him. And there were always presents for Pushkin the dog.

The fall of 1971 saw the Festival's administration sitting down to plan the season for the following year, which would once again be housed in three theatres. At the Festival Theatre Jean Gascon had chosen to direct Alfred de Musset's *Lorenzaccio,* and decided to cast Pat Galloway in the title role. It was an audacious move, but followed the tradition established by Sarah Bernhardt, who had played the same 'trousers' role for the premiere of the play in 1896. (The play would require some careful cutting and re-arranging, and Jean asked me to recommend someone who could handle this. I suggested Jeremy Gibson, formerly of Ottawa, now living in Toronto, and he happily accepted, serving the production with skill and dedication).

Bill Hutt would direct *As You Like It*, and guest director David William, who had been directing for Stratford since 1966, would return to mount *King Lear*, with Bill Hutt as Lear. The fourth production on the Festival stage was to be *She Stoops To Conquer* by Oliver Goldsmith. Jean had not yet chosen a director for this play, and I suspect he was hoping Michael Langham would be available, but he had recently taken over as artistic director of the Guthrie Theatre in Minneapolis and could not come.

It was at this point that I asked for a meeting with Jean, and proposed that I direct the Goldsmith play myself. I am still astounded by my pushiness, given my still recent disaster in Ottawa. At Stratford I had developed a reputation for being able to work with classical masterworks in the role of assistant to the director, and as dramaturge, having served Jean well on *Cymbeline* the previous year, and having developed a close working relationship with Langham over nearly ten years. But taking responsibility for a full-scale production on the main stage, with a company of experienced and talented actors, was another thing again. Jean hemmed and hawed, and did not give me an immediate answer. He no doubt discussed the idea with others. But a few days later he called me in and offered me the job. I was ecstatic. I was even more thrilled when Bill Hutt, with whom I shared an office at the Festival, told me he had decided to cast Colin in the small but significant role of William in *As You Like It*.

It remained to establish a program for my Third Stage. Jean and I worked on this together, with the help and advice of Gabriel Charpentier. We were already in consultation with my old Simon Fraser colleague Murray Schafer about my directing his extraordinary – and as yet never staged – *Patria II: Requiems for a Party Girl*, with Montreal's brilliant composer/conductor Serge Garant as music director, and Murray's wife Phyllis Mailing singing the lead. We also decided to present Charpentier's own opera *Orphée*, to be translated by myself and directed by up-and-coming Quebec director André Brassard, under the music direction of Ursula Clutterbuck. For our children's production we chose a production of The *Adventures of Pinocchio*, first performed at the Manitoba Theatre Centre, directed by John Wood, with music by Stratford's Alan Laing, and with the still more or less unknown Michael Burgess in the title role.

We rounded off the program with a production of a play called *Mark* by Betty Jane Wylie, to be directed by Bill Hutt. Jean reckoned it was prudent to do this, in deference to Betty Jane's husband Bill, who continued to be someone Jean was afraid and distrustful of – – and with some reason. John Hayes, Bruce Swerdfager and I were aware of Jean's wavering self-confidence, and his tendency to drink himself to sleep at night. He would arrive at the theatre in the morning hung over and morose, and it was our job to bolster his spirits. We loved him and were staunchly loyal, doing a lot to cover his lapses. More than once I had to stand in for him at a board meeting - once even to announce his plans for the season: he was in a real funk. Wylie also knew of these lapses but was much less forgiving. We believed, in fact that he was badmouthing Jean behind his back to the Board. And he was.

So many biographies of theatre people contain interminable lists and descriptions of productions and actors that I have thought twice about sketching out Stratford's 1972 program in such detail. But that year was an extraordinary turning point in my life. It brought to a head my many years of work on the Festival stage, by giving me a chance to direct for it for the first time. It also exposed me to music theatre, both as a director and a producer. I had been fascinated by the possibilities and needs of home-grown opera ever since the Simon Fraser days with Schafer and his interest in Wagner's music-drama. Now for the first time I could help to provide a home for Canadian music theatre, and I was starting with Schafer's own highly original piece. I will not test my readers by giving blow-by-blow accounts of all my theatre productions over my years of directing plays, but my fortunes in the productions of that year are maybe worth recording in some detail, because they were part of my apprenticeship as an ex-anarchist director.

I had always loved Oliver Goldsmith's *She Stoops To Conquer.* Whereas Sheridan's *The School for Scandal* is an urban piece, full of spite and gossip and even cruelty, in which country ways are scorned and mocked, Goldsmith's play by contrast is set in the countryside, with London and its fashions and manners looked at as a distant and rather laughable foreign world. Sub-titled *The Mistakes of a Night*, the play's central 'mistake' is made by Charles

Marlow and his friend George Hastings, who have ridden into the country from London to visit Mr Hardcastle so that the painfully shy Marlow (whose father is old Hardcastle's friend) can pay court to his daughter Kate. They get lost, and ask directions at an alehouse, where Hardcastle's stepson Tony Lumpkin happens to be enjoying a pint or two with his villager friends. When Tony finds out who these posh visitors are he decides to play a joke on them, telling them that Hardcastle's place is miles away and that they will have to stay the night at an inn which is hard by: the 'inn' in fact being Hardcastle's house. They arrive and are warmly welcomed by Hardcastle, but they assume he is a pretentious old buffer of a landlord, and treat him accordingly. So the night's mistakes begin.

To design the play Jean kindly gave me Stratford's Desmond Heeley, who had worked at Stratford for years under the tutelage of Tanya Moiseiwitch, and had now come into his own as a designer of some genius. This collaboration was to be a privilege for me. As a director, there is no part of the process of preparing a play that I find more exciting and enjoyable than the first brainstorming meetings with its designer and composer. During *Cymbeline* the previous year I had been able to sit in on Tanya Moiseiwitch's initial meetings with Jean Gascon and Gabriel Charpentier, and had watched how Tanya in her humble but authoritative way had done so much to help Jean shape the look and feel of the production, a contribution that went far beyond the mere visual aspects of design, affecting its mood and its dramatic effects. Now, with Desmond, I found myself learning so much about the play from his careful reading of it, and so much too about our Festival stage, with the limitations it placed on pictorial stage design. With Desmond's long experience he had learnt how a whole world could be suggested with just one or two stage elements. These pieces also had to be designed for rapid removal by actors, in full view of the audience:

there could be no long and complicated scene changes.

With *She Stoops* we had a challenge. Our play, first produced in 1773, had been written for a proscenium theatre: how could we place it on the Festival stage, with those uncompromising Doric pillars and its whole classic severity? I had also added a further complication by wanting to place the very first scene out in the garden, to which we would return later in the action.

We wanted to suggest a run-down country mansion, the comfortable and unpretentious home of our Mr Hardcastle, who liked 'old things: old books, old wine'. Desmond began by sketching a gnarled old mulberry tree to wrap around the stage's permanent central pillar, to be made of fibreglass for lightness and quick removal. Then, to suggest an eighteenth-century terrace, he proposed just a single and somewhat broken-down balustrade, which ran up the steps on stage left. We now needed something to sit on for Hardcastle near the centre of the stage. I imagined a conventional garden seat. But Desmond suggested that we follow Hardcastle's unpretentiousness, and make a seat from an old and broken wheelbarrow. He then added a random assortment of flowerpots and a watering can to sit beside the barrow, and a rake and bucket to sit alongside the balustrade, giving the whole scene the feeling that this was a working garden, and that there was a gardener or two just round the corner. All these humble accessories were built into each piece, so that the whole thing could be removed in a flash as we moved into the mansion's front parlour.

It was this masterly humanizing of space that was Desmond's gift to the production; his instinctive feel for the 'rambling old mansion that looks for all the world like an inn,' where we imagined hens and dogs wandering in and out (his first rough costume sketch for Mrs Hardcastle showed her with hens around her feet); his sense of the difference between the front parlour with its formal old furniture, and the back parlour with its round rag rug, its simple table carrying pottery ware, and its high-backed Windsor chair.

The same feel for character went into the clothes he designed: I particularly remember that he imagined Hardcastle wearing an infinite number of layers, 'like upholstery.' He also designed Hardcastle's special armchair, outsize, slightly shabby, and massively comfortable like its owner.

It was in the later stages of preparation that I saw a problem with the play: I found it ended rather perfunctorily with Hardcastle looking forward to the marriages of his daughter and Constance, and saying 'the mistakes of the night will be crowned with a merry morning'. The original production no doubt ended with a stately dance. I tried to imagine a more festive finale, foreshadowing the joyous three marriages that were shortly to be celebrated. Reading the play for the umpteenth time, I came to realize that there was a lot of talk about the meal that was to be served up for Marlow and Hastings – they were handed a menu and given a glass of wine when they first arrived, but no dinner ever appeared. It occurred to me that we could extend this theme somewhat. So I added a few lines to emphasise their growing hunger, and wrote a brief extra scene in which Marlow asks tetchily about the meal, and is told that it will be a while because 'Bridget the cook took a turn in the passage, and they be still at pains to revive her'. All these delays added up to an impression of the rather chaotic household over which Hardcastle presides, but also led into a joyous finale, when dinner is finally served, and the whole company comes together around a long table groaning with food and silver, with Tony Lumpkin bringing in his mates from the alehouse, along with his girlfriend Bess Bouncer the barmaid.

Jean had also ensured that I had a splendidly talented cast, led by the inimitable Tony van Bridge as Hardcastle, and with Mary

Savidge playing his tiresome wife, who hungers after the high life of London, and spends the play trying to marry off her own son Tony Lumpkin to Kate's friend Constance, much to Tony's and her discomfort. Lumpkin was to be played by the enormously fine actor Alan Scarfe. To play Marlow, Jean had brought in Nicholas Pennell, a British actor of some standing, whose youthful good looks and attractive voice made him a perfect male ingénue, and who was to stay in Stratford and become a fixture there, before his sadly early death. Kate was played by Pat Galloway, and to play her friend Constance (with whom George Hastings intends to elope) we imported another British actor, Carole Shelley, who had recently appeared in the stage and film versions of *The Odd Couple*. Barry MacGregor was our George Hastings.

My composer, Raymond Pannell, was a native of London, Ontario. A child prodigy as a pianist, he had become an accomplished composer with a passionate interest in opera/music theatre. A master of many different styles of musical writing, he was happy to compose a score for our eighteenth-century play which reflected the music of the time, but with a buoyant contemporary feel. Unlike some composers (Schafer for instance!), he was quite content to write the kind of 'incidental' music that theatre needs – and especially a theatre with no curtain like Stratford's Festival stage, where scene changes have to made in full view of the audience, and where the music must pick up on the mood of the scene just finished, carry the audience through the scene-changing, and then deposit them in the right mood for what follows. My knowledge of music helped in what became a fruitful collaboration.

She Stoops To Conquer started rehearsing in June, after the first three plays had opened on the main stage (my Colin charming audiences with his simple and innocent 'William' in *As You Like It*, and terrifying even his own colleagues as a murderous retainer helping to put out old Gloucester's eyes in *King Lear*). Confident though I was of my grasp of Goldsmith's text and the strength of our designs and music, I was wretchedly nervous as we set out, having never had to marshal such a big and starry cast, and never before having had to face alone the challenges of the Festival stage, where the mechanics of entrances and exits, and the continual need for movement in order to give the wrap-around audience an equal share of the action, had to be managed with special skill. As a result there were times when I became indecisive, and unable to give the firm directions that actors require. I was also having to deal with certain actors' temperaments, and found that my small bag of directors' tricks was lacking in this department. Once, when I was trying to prepare for an entrance on stage right, I asked Carole Shelley whether she could move a few paces down left as she said a particular line. "No," she said. "What's the problem?" I asked, taken aback. "I don't feel it," she replied. "If I can't feel it, I can't do it." I was stumped. With the help of the other actors on stage we worked out a solution. But it was a long time before I learned how to combine the practical needs of staging with the vital necessity of giving actors motivations for every move. She was right, of course, but she would probably not have responded in that way to Michael Langham, or any more experienced director. Like animals, actors can easily sense their director's lack of self-confidence and in their own insecurity somewhat enjoy taking advantage.

    I learned another similar lesson at the beginning of a scene when Alan Scarfe, our superb Tony Lumpkin, had to burst out of the upper right entrance. When the moment came I said "All right, go!" Alan came fiercely out of character, and said "Don't just tell me to go, like it's an order! That's not the way I work. It's not the way any actor works!" I had bungled again, and soon learned the vital formula, "Thank you, Alan: when you're ready." But meanwhile I had once again showed my inexperience. Nor was I good at standing up to such hostility, still plagued with the expectation of politeness I had been trained up to. Acting is a wretchedly difficult and exposing business after all, and actors naturally want to feel they are in competent hands. It was a long time before I learned to act aggressiveness in response to challenge.

My stalwart ally throughout was Tony van Bridge as Hardcastle, who was of course the star of the show, and who continually and very publicly acknowledged my authority when others were near to flouting it. Tony was an actor from the old school, trained up in the old British repertory system, a master of comic timing, and with a vast compendium of traditional 'stage business'. There is one point in the play when Hardcastle enters in a total baffled rage at young Marlow's condescending behaviour towards him. He plumps himself down angrily on a chair. It was Tony's suggestion that after a few seconds he should grab off his wig in his fury, revealing a shining bald pate: "Michael, I had an idea for this bit. Let me try it, and tell me what you think. If you think it's too much, let me know and we won't do it." I thought it was a wonderfully funny and yet truthful idea, and as expected it brought the house down. Few audience members took in the fact that at every performance from then on Tony had given himself the intricate job of preparing two wigs, one on top of the other.

It was above all Tony's discipline, creativity and kindness that helped me to survive some very difficult moments, and his example to younger, less patient and respectful cast members was invaluable.

In spite of all our stresses, the production came slowly together, with the actors often chiming in to make suggestions and to sort out staging difficulties. By the time we had put together the lighting plot, rehearsed and re-rehearsed the lightning and often comic scene changes with Hardcastle's servants (including Colin as

'Thomas'), incorporated Desmond's brilliant costumes and accessories, and reached the great day when Raymond's driving musical score suddenly lifted the whole tone of the play, it was clear that we had a show.

But no one was quite prepared for what happened at our opening in late July. The first-night audience roared with laughter throughout the piece and gave it a long, standing ovation, and the joy of that final dinner scene capped the evening beyond my highest expectations. The notices, when they came out, were quite the most remarkable and unanimous I have ever seen, with all Toronto's newspapers in agreement as to the splendor of the production, and eventually every other newspaper and magazine from Canada and the United States echoing their praise. I had an amazing success on my hands. ('Canadians excel in *She Stoops to Conquer*... Michael Bawtree's staging of the play has a speed and grace all its own... With this kind of playing, this kind of teamwork, the Stratford company can be matched by very few theaters in North America' (Clive Barnes, *New York Times*); 'Stratford's 'Conquer' a glory'... Bawtree has staged Goldsmith in perfect style and with unflagging energy' (*Boston Globe*); 'She Stoops to Conquer filled with dizzying theatrical joys... The man most responsible for this engaging, thoughtful mayhem... is director Michael Bawtree... Bawtree's achievement is to demonstrate a sensible authoritative understanding of the play while resisting the temptation to translate that comprehension into a tight, flashy stylistic affectation' (*Toronto Star*).

There was talk backstage of course about how the actors had saved the show. The fact is that Stratford had been run for years by directors (including Michael Langham) who had a faintly colonial attitude towards their Canadian company, and did not particularly expect or encourage creative participation on the part of their actors. As someone who believed in collective creation, I was glad of suggestions, but did not at that time have enough experience to welcome them while still fully maintaining my own authority. I would learn.

My program note (quoted approvingly by several critics) still sums up my feelings about the play. It says in part:

"Though *She Stoops to Conquer* was not designed as a lesson in anything other than fun, it offers to our speedy, anxious age a picture of eighteenth century pre-industrial society life which for all its divisions of birth and class cannot be too far from our own fading dreams of happiness on this earth. There is a splendid assurance, a superb solidity of spirit, in almost every character, from the fellows in the alehouse who consider themselves 'gentlemen', to Mr Hardcastle with his unashamed love of 'everything that's old.' And those who have not this assurance find it in the course of the play. Marlow learns confidence in the presence of 'women of modesty and reputation'; Hastings and Constance Neville discover that instead of eloping they can appeal successfully to the humanity of Mr Hardcastle. Mrs Hardcastle's yearning for the manners and fashions of London gets a distinct jolt when she discovers the true intentions of her idol Mr Hastings. And when Tony Lumpkin, the anarchic, animal spirit of the play, is freed from his mother's apron-strings and becomes 'his own man again', we can feel the release of a great burst of bucolic energy, generosity, truth and good spirits, which will sustain the people of England well into the industrial darkness and psychological deprivations of the nineteenth century. Surely this is the true paradise – a paradise not of mystical experience and chemical fantasies but of practical social harmonies, based on self-trust and trust in others. It looks like being some time before we find it again."

The moment that *She Stoops* opened I had to turn my attention to the very different world of Murray Schafer's *Patria II: Requiems for a Party Girl*. The opera, set in a mental hospital, requires a cast of a dozen actors and only one singer: the schizophrenic 'party girl', Ariadne, played by Phyllis Mailing. My designer for the production was Eoin Sprott, who lived in New York, and I had already travelled down more than once to work with him on the show. One of the great advantages of the Casino building in which the Third Stage was located was that it was vast enough to house more than one stage set. We had already presented Charpentier's *Orphée II* (now *Orpheus Two*) in its own setting, and done the same for *Mark* and *The Adventures of Pinocchio*, moving around our eight modular units of 32 seats each to fit each configuration. For *Patria II* we were able once again to conceive a complete miniature theatre. We decided that the piece should be set in the round, with the audience up high on bleachers, looking down into the stage action. The orchestra was placed beneath a section of the audience, more or less hidden behind a curtain of scrim. This arrangement gave the sense of Ariadne being imprisoned in a kind of pit, surrounded by walls, with her paranoia and helplessness growing after she first submits to a brain operation, and then searching for an exit as she hears voices discussing her condition in languages she does not understand. The piece ends with her suicide.

Eoin Sprott, who had designed all over Canada, had yet to establish the career that was to make him famous as a designer of special props and effects for many films (*The Wiz*, *The Producers* and Woody Allen's *Zelig* among them). But with his extraordinarily inventive and quirky talent and his strong architectural sense, he was the ideal person to create the world of *Patria II*, and it was a pleasure working with him. We were not only creating a theatre space, we were dealing with the perennial operatic question of what you do with the musicians when you move away from the usual proscenium configuration with its orchestra pit, and with the conductor commanding both the pit and the stage. Our solution was successful enough for us to re-use it – with slight adaptations – for music theatre pieces over the next two years.

Phyllis, with her beautiful contralto, her musicianship, her fine stage authority and her technique, was one of the few singers in the country who could master Schafer's exceptionally demanding score, much of which she had already sung in concert performance. And Serge Garant was one of the few Canadian music directors with a rich enough feeling for contemporary music to be able to conduct it. We were enormously lucky to be able to bring this team together, and with a fine acting company (though soon-to-be stars like Michael Burgess found their supernumerary involvement not always to their liking) the result was a major success, superbly reviewed, and sold out for all its three performances.

When Murray found out how cheap the tickets were (General Admission $3!), he wrote to Stratford asking to buy up the entire lot, with the intention of inviting friends and students – and, so he said afterwards, scalping the tickets for a higher price. Stratford understandably refused. I was of course nervous of his reaction to the production, since he was not easily impressed. But he seemed delighted, and wrote later in his autobiography that 'the production was excellent'.

I wrote in the house program for all four productions that this first season was "in no way a blueprint for forthcoming seasons. At the same time, the Festival intends to maintain in future years the variety and innovative quality of this its first full-scale Third Stage season, with its emphasis on new forms of musical theatre, its employment of a mixture of young and experienced Canadian talent, and its bringing together of artists from both English Canada and Quebec."

It was around that time that Lord Harewood was commissioned by the Ontario Arts Council to tour Canada and review the state of opera in the nation. He wrote a gloomy report, but noted that the one light in the gloom was the Third Stage program at Stratford, Ontario. 'Present thinking,' he wrote, 'has produced an exciting scene... Canada's present operatic situation urgently requires experiment of some sort. Stratford should provide exactly the right milieu' (*Opera in Canada*, 1972, p.32).

Somehow in that year of 1972, with all its bumps along the way, I had managed to satisfy my desire both to develop my skills as a director of one of the classics of dramatic literature, and at the same time to continue being associated with the new and experimental. It was thanks to Jean's belief in me that I had been able to turn my career around. And for all his personal frailties, I was happy to be loyal to him, and deeply sad when he announced his resignation to the Board, effective at the end of the 1973 season.

CHAPTER FOURTEEN

'AND AWAY HE SHALL AGAIN'

In January of 1973, as I sat in a bar in Montreal, I began for the first time in my life to keep a diary, writing in my first entry: *It is another determination to pull a few straws from the river's flotsam as it goes past. From the straws, bricks; from the bricks – etc.* Ever since that day, I have jotted down thoughts, recounted events, recorded jokes and odd sayings and copied quotations, making what the Victorians would have called a 'commonplace book', and providing an occasional glimpse into what I was thinking or doing or responding to at the time. So from now on in this memoir I will occasionally call up a diary entry, to bring a new angle on the story.

Early in 1973 the Stratford company was on the road once more, with our most ambitious tour to date. We would remount David William's *King Lear* from the 1972 season, couple it with a new production of *The Taming of the Shrew* directed by Jean Gascon, and take the two plays to Holland, Denmark, Poland and the Soviet Union. Since I was not part of either production I had little involvement in the trip, apart from preparing program material. But I was delighted that Colin got to be a member of the touring company, giving him a unique opportunity to visit Europe for the first time, and even to be exposed to the mysterious world behind the Iron Curtain. The company was travelling by Aeroflot via Paris, and I arranged to meet Colin in Paris on their return, so that we could spend a week or two together exploring the city.

The tour was to be led by Bill Hutt, as associate artistic director and of course the lead actor in *Lear*. Bill had recently been raised to the Order of Canada, which gave him enormous satisfaction. Like many an actor, Bill was always somewhat self-preoccupied, and Jean was amused during one administrative meeting with Bill Wylie and John Hayes, when they were discussing the very complicated details of the tour, especially the problems of transportation in Poland and Russia. Bill Hutt was barely participating – just looking absent-mindedly into the distance. At one point Jean said, "What is it, Bill? You look worried about something."

Bill replied, "I am just wondering whether I should take my white tie and tails."

"Whatever for?" asked Jean, amused and incredulous. "They're communist countries!"

"Well, but if we have a formal occasion, I'll need them in order to wear my Order of Canada sash."

The tour went well, though indeed transportation turned out to be a headache: the company flew from Krakow to Moscow, but the set was to be transported by road. When the Polish truck arrived to load up the travelling set, it turned out to be much too small for the job, and the set's longer sections stuck out two or three meters. Solution? Get a bigger truck. But not in communist Poland, where they simply sawed off the overhanging pieces, chucked them on top, and were on their way.

Colin's gregariousness became almost legendary on the tour.

THE BEST FOOLING

Whenever he had an hour or two to himself he would apparently dive off into the city, and somehow would pick up friends everywhere, all fascinated by his warmth and friendliness and good looks, and not much impeded by language problems. Fellow actors would describe how in Moscow and Leningrad he would return with a retinue of ten or twenty young people crowding into the hotel lobby alongside him, and how he would have to extricate himself from them all.

I remember little of our brief French holiday, except our excursion to Versailles, where Colin finally saw a home that matched up to his dreams for us. One brief image from those days:

Through the white-tiled arch that separates the two Metro lines, a group of three, framed and lit against a green background. Boy in black velvet, boy in brown, girl in blue. A roar, and the arch fills up with old red train. Stop. Pause. Start. A blur, and then the red curtain is pulled. The stage is empty. Someone plays a flute. And the Metro smells sweet. Magic.

Before long we were back in Stratford for the summer. But within a few days a deeply disturbing event shook the comfortable world of the Festival:

Last week Bill Wylie's food went down the wrong way, and within two minutes, aged 44 and in the pink of jogging, dieting, golfing health, he died.

It is a strange sensation for us who are left running the theatre. His power was so daily a thing to grapple with, his poor taste so continually a frustration, his insensitivity so galling, that we had built him of adamantine rock in our minds. It is when a man dies that you see the frailty of his drive, the child behind the hard man, the velvet fist behind the mailed glove.

If we are to learn anything from him, it is his calm authority. He confided once to John Hayes that he came through a Board Meeting knotted with nervous tension. But to watch him at a Board Meeting was to watch a master. He had something Machiavellian – in the most neutral and even complimentary sense – about him, practising Realpolitik packed in ice. The fact that he inwardly juddered adds to my admiration. "Never show anyone that you are hurt," said Noel Coward – no great philosopher, but what he said is at least true in our profession. Bill never showed he was hurt and so it was reckoned that he was invulnerable to hurt. And so we longed to hurt him. "He bent me. I can bend. I ain't the City Hall. He bent me." So Raymond Chandler. We longed to bend Bill, to be sure he was not the City Hall.

And yet it's clear that he felt hurt. He was almost certainly vulnerable about his origins in the mail-order vitamin business – something I knew nothing about until I read the obituaries. He was vulnerable also to rudeness, to the cold shoulder. But he would never show it and his hurt would find its expression in some apparently inexplicable crudity of behaviour some days later.

He longed to be in on our discussions of artistic program and policy. But his (quite proper) impatience with Jean G. led him to make his own use of the information. Time and again it was he – not Jean – who was the first to inform the Board members of some change of plan or new idea or stroke of success. And who knows with what cast of cynicism he gave the information.

I said to the Ad Hoc Committee of the Board (looking for a successor to Jean as Artistic Director) that Bill could not endure illness: that in the presence of a sick member or an old and no longer well-operating member his first impulse was to lop it off. When Jean was going through one of his phases of chronic malaise – inefficiency, getting drunk, indecisiveness, such as we saw at Christmas – Bill was calling the Board to be rid of him, telling me that the Board was awaiting a medical report on Jean and so forth, and that in the Board's eyes Jean had to go "as soon as a successor could be found."... He finally learnt tact in many areas. But it was his *impatience with indecisiveness and gutlessness and inefficiency that above all made him crude. I once asked him whether he lived according to any moral principles. He said "Yes." I asked him if he could define them. "I try," he said, "to live my life according to the principles laid down by Jesus Christ." It was a brave and beautiful answer, said partly perhaps for the benefit of his wife Betty Jane who sat close by, crying at the virulence of my attack and of the debate between us. Since then I had always, I felt, had a special relationship with Bill, because he knew I could hit, and because I had a mind. And in a strange way it was only with Bill in this whole organisation that I found I had met my match.*

Betty Jane said at the funeral parlour where we milled about in disbelief in front of that big fluted coffin that I had only begun to get to know him. I replied yes, but that he was a friend, and that I had learnt much from him, and that what I had learnt I would keep. Though I would probably have said this lyingly without a quirk of conscience, it was in fact truthful. I had above all learnt the extraordinary power of calm.

His mentally challenged boy of 11 said hello to everyone as though they were coming to a wedding, and told Marilyn that Bill would laugh if he found himself lying "in that box with flowers all around – wouldn't he?" Yes, he probably would.

Owing to the success of *She Stoops to Conquer*, it had been decided to remount it as part of the 1973 season. There were a few changes: Carole Shelley had not returned, and was replaced by my old colleague Patricia Collins from *A Resounding Tinkle* ten years earlier. Mary Savidge was replaced by Amelia ('Milly') Hall (my Tsarina!), and Powys Thomas (my Rasputin!) by Bill Needles as Old Marlow. All three newcomers were a delight to work with, and Milly, small and plump with an enormously high wig, made Mrs Hardcastle very much her own, bringing a less spiky, more cosily stupid warmth to the role. There were none of the problems of the previous year: everyone knew we had a hit on our hands. And indeed, so it proved. The critics repeated their enthusiastic approval. And I seem to remember that the average attendance for our twelve performances was 96% – in a house with a capacity of well over 2,000 seats.

For the Third Stage I had commissioned from Michael Ondaatje a stage version of his extraordinary and highly dramatic long poem *The Collected Works of Billy the Kid*, with my old Ottawa company member Neil Munro in the title role. Incorporating the marionettes of Montreal's Félix Mirbt, we also mounted the premiere of a play for children by Montreal writer Henry Beissel called *Inook and the Sun*, about an Inuit boy whose father is killed during a mid-winter hunt: Inook goes in search of the sun, finds it imprisoned in an iceberg and finally succeeds in setting it free. And we commissioned a music theatre piece from my *She Stoops* composer Raymond Pannell. This was to be my own production.

The libretto for Raymond's piece was, at Raymond's request, commissioned from his wife Beverly, a photographer as well as a writer. Titled *Exiles*, it was scored for four opera singers and five actors, a chamber ensemble, and a pre-recorded tape, thus using instrumental and electro-acoustic music, which combined with improvisation, poetry, and Beverly's photography to 'depict the ordinary world with a new vision'. Raymond was determined to break new ground with his piece, for which we re-assembled the previous year's *Patria II* theatrical configuration, adjusting it for the new work. Perhaps his most radical decision was to project the full orchestral score (white on black, with colours) on to a screen, from which the orchestra, seated at one end of the acting area, could read their parts. This did away with the necessity for the distraction of individual lights over each music stand, but put a heavy responsibility onto the technician handling the projections. There were several terrifying moments for the players when their new page arrived late on the screen.

Exiles has been described by Raymond as having no plot, but suggesting 'a place between two worlds... mysterious, disturbing and limitless'. When the libretto arrived it was indeed mysterious, and in June, after the revival of *She Stoops To Conquer* opened I decided to go away for a few days to live with it and try to decipher it before preparing the production.

I soon made a startling discovery: that the libretto, ostensibly written by his second wife Beverly but in fact clearly a collaboration, seemed to be inviting us to forgive Raymond for leaving his first wife, whom in a sense he has 'murdered'. This put me in a fascinating position. I could direct the show as an accomplice after the fact – or as a police detective. My detective work in fact placed me in a unique moral dilemma: for the first and only time in my life I found myself obliged to direct a theatre piece which I seemed to have found to be morally reprehensible. At the same time, it was far too sensitive a discovery to share with its authors. I did my best, battling as much with the complicated stage technics as with the plot. But I also believe that the personal workings-out of Raymond's life in *Exiles* got badly in the way of its dramatic structure and characterisations: the actors and singers all had a hard time with it, and their belief in it, like mine, became more and more tenuous. At the last performance, when actor Gary Reineke was free to improvise a speech, he shouted merely: "This is a turkey!" I could not find it in my heart to chastise him. I believed he was right.

Above all, I had an exceptionally hard time dealing with the husband-and-wife team of Raymond and Beverly. If I questioned Beverly about problems in the libretto, I had to deal with

Raymond's indignant defence of his wife. I vowed never again to put myself in this position.

Meanwhile, there had been problems over on the Festival stage. David William was to direct *Othello*, and had insisted on our hiring the distinguished Israeli actor Nahum Buchman to play the title role – a part he had already played with the Habima company in Israel.

Nahum was a straightforward, charming man and a fine actor. But it was soon apparent in early rehearsals that his ability to pronounce English, and especially Shakespeare's English, was very limited. Coaches were brought in to work with him, and he toiled hard to improve. But even on opening night it was soon evident that the audience was straining to understand him. "It is the cause, it is the cause, my soul" sounded wretchedly like "it is the cows, it is the cows, my soul". There were even titters at the most inappropriate moments. The production was met with a polite but half-hearted reception, reflected next day by its critics. As a result, *Othello* was a rare Stratford failure, and poor Nahum received much of the blame.

Of course the source of the problem was David William's insistence on using Buchman, an error of judgment which I know he regretted himself, and which Jean Gascon found it hard to forgive. The problem was that David was more or less assumed to be coming in as Jean's successor at the end of the season. But Jean, after discussing the situation with us, decided that to appoint David as artistic director after he had led Stratford into such a disastrous situation would be to add insult to injury, and he finally summoned up the courage to tell the Board that he could not agree to the appointment.

There was a further consideration. After the death of Bill Wylie, Bruce Swerdfager had been promoted from comptroller to administrative director. The administration now consisted of Jean, John Hayes, Bruce, Bill Hutt and myself. This was in fact a team of friends, and it was soon clear that, while we were all saddened by Bill Wylie's loss, Jean was in fact far more comfortable in his position that he had ever been, and even confided to me that he now regretted his resignation. Unfortunately, Bill's disparaging view of Jean had been firmly instilled in the Board. They agreed that the appointment of David William was not a good idea, but they then set about a search for a new artistic director. It was to be another seventeen years before David finally returned to lead the Festival in 1990.

One visitor from New York City to Stratford that summer was Gene Feist, artistic director of the off-Broadway Roundabout Theatre, which he had founded a few years earlier. He and his wife had set up a tent in a camp nearby, and proceeded to see all the plays. He was particularly thrilled with *She Stoops*, and got hold of me to tell me so, saying that he would like to talk. I invited him home, and soon after he arrived, he asked me if I would consider joining him as an associate director at the Roundabout Theatre. We had good talks about theatre, and I enjoyed his swashbuckling manner and his generosity. I of course told him that I was happy at Stratford and not contemplating a move. But he persisted, saying that things could change. I promised to keep in touch. (It was just at this time that Colin and I were giving a party for the entire cast and crew of *She Stoops to Conquer*, and I have an abiding memory of Gene helping us prepare lasagna for fifty people, slopping the pasta into plastic buckets as it was cooked, and then assembling the dish in eight or nine tinfoil baking tins. The party was a fine success.)

At the end of that season Jean recommended me for promotion as an associate artistic director, alongside Bill Hutt. It looked as though I was now well dug into the Festival's establishment. And I was ecstatic when Jean also invited me to direct *Love's Labor's Lost* in the 1974 season.

It was in the summer of that same year of 1973 that Michael Langham, now ensconced as the artistic director of the Guthrie Theatre in Minneapolis, invited me to come and direct *Tartuffe* for him. The play was to start as a winter touring production, before being incorporated into their following season. This meant that I could fit it into my Stratford schedule. The job entailed several trips to Minneapolis – my stage designer was Eoin Sprott, who had collaborated with me on *Patria II* and was now working in the Midwest – and also to New York, to work with my costume designer Sam Kirkpatrick and to audition actors for the production. Some time that fall I was also flown to Los Angeles to meet with Richard Thomas ('John-Boy' of *The Waltons*), who had shown interest in joining the Guthrie Theatre company. This was a pleasant occasion, but did not lead to anything. My Tartuffe was to be the Canadian actor Bernard (Bunny) Behrens, who had been my Kerensky in *The Last of the Tsars*. The well-known American actor Larry Gates was to play Orgon. Soon after I arrived to start rehearsals in mid-December, I noted in my diary:

Very happy with the chats with Sam, Eoin, Larry Gates, Bunny Behrens, and for the first time begin to feel on top of the play, as Tartuffe slowly emerges from a mist of pre-conceptions. He seems ineluctably Irish at present, a petty criminal, who began to show off to Orgon at church for a half-dollar, and found he had met the great sucker of all time. Think of him improvising his way through the play, until the point where he must either leave or go for broke. 'No, I am the master here,' and he sweats with the strain of his life's first important decision, a little man suddenly in the big time. Orgon, Christian Scientist, his clothes going to seed.

THE BEST FOOLING

I was also not above responding to my surroundings in Minnesota:

It is just before midnight, and I open my window. The winter's first snow began falling last evening and when I came home from the theatre it was falling still. But now, with Mendelssohn's Violin Concerto (slow movement) playing in the room behind me, the sky is washed clean and clear — Orion stands in the air behind the trees, upright for a change, his rather piddling sword almost heroic in the majesty of the moon's light. Cars move gently and 'piano' over the snow. A plane's light rises from the horizon and climbs west. The bright cold laps me round for two lovely minutes. Then tea, and bed.

My stay in Minneapolis turned out to be short. A week into rehearsals Michael told me that they had decided to cancel the winter tour and postpone the whole production of *Tartuffe* until the end of August. It was a disappointment, but mainly because I had geared up for the show, and was beginning to enjoy it. I stayed over a few more days to work with Sam Kirkpatrick, who was also to be my designer for *Love's Labor's Lost* in Stratford, before heading back home.

I was back in Stratford for another heart-warming development: the Festival had come to an agreement with the CBC to create a television version of my production of *She Stoops To Conquer*. They chose their premier theatrical director Norman Campbell to direct the television adaptation. Realizing the need of a live audience for so rollicking a comedy, Norman decided that it should be shot right on the Stratford stage, with a full auditorium of spectators. This entailed kidnapping the television crew of CBC's *Hockey Night in Canada* and bringing them down to Stratford for the two-day shoot. Somehow Norman pulled it off. They covered the entire stage with carpet to deaden the noise of footsteps, and covered the difficulty of sound pick-up on the open stage by having technicians sitting around the front row of the audience holding long sausage-shaped microphones. It worked.

Unfortunately, Colin was not to be available for the shoot. Tony van Bridge was directing *Love's Labor's Lost* at the Neptune Theatre in Halifax, and had invited Colin to play Longaville. The play opened early enough in January 2004 for Tony to return to repeat his triumphant performance as Hardcastle in February, but Colin was still away performing. In fact it was around this time that Colin made a life-changing career decision. He had already been invited to join the company on their tour to Australia that spring, with Gascon's production of Molière's *The Imaginary Invalid*. But he continued to feel the need to improve his education, and rather than returning to the Festival for another season, he decided to apply to a university and work towards a degree. This may have been partly because he had the feeling that his Stratford work was to some extent dependent upon me, and he wanted to be more self-reliant. After some thought of attending in Toronto, he decided to settle for the University of Guelph, only forty minutes' drive from Stratford. And, after much discussion between us, he applied not to the newly-formed and apparently rather academic Drama Department, but to study for a degree in Art History. He was accepted as a mature student. We found a room for him in a house near the campus, and he took off at the beginning of the summer term. Pushkin the dog was to stay with me, and Colin would return on weekends.

Meanwhile the search for Stratford's new artistic director proceeded. The Board invited Australian director Michael Blakemore out from the UK, but after some consideration he declined, because he had recently been appointed associate director of the National Theatre. I also put my own name forward, with no expectation of being considered seriously, but the Board's search committee at least gave me a courteous interview. I believe that John Hirsch also applied, but was not interviewed, and there was dark talk of anti-semitic sentiments in the Festival Board. In the end, their first choice fell on a young actor/director who was making something of a name for himself in Britain. He had played Nicholas in a BBC-TV production of *Nicholas Nickleby*. He had directed at the Chichester Festival and in the West End. His name was Robin Phillips.

Phillips was flown out to Stratford for an interview with the Board, and a chance to see the Festival. It was arranged that as an associate director I would have lunch with him, and we went to a restaurant on the edge of town. We talked of the Festival and its problems and potential. He was a little enigmatic, but charming, and I was suitably charmed. He told me that at the interview with the Board that morning they had asked him how he saw his possible role as artistic director at Stratford, and how he had said pointblank: "I don't". He enjoyed their surprise and consternation, which he then proceeded to allay. But he regarded them, it seemed, as a fairly ignorant bunch, and had enjoyed playing with them as though they were children.

After lunch I drove him back to his motel. He invited me up to his room, perhaps for a drink, I don't remember. But within five minutes he suddenly started to grope me, putting his arms around me and pulling me back on to him on his bed. I was astonished, and worked myself free. I told him that I had a partner I was happy with, and had no wish to stray. He cooled down, and shortly afterwards I left. It was a remarkable way to introduce himself, and it took me a long time to analyse this strangely crude behaviour. I told no one of it apart from Colin.

A week or two later it was announced: Robin Phillips was to be the next artistic director of the Stratford Festival. There were grumblings in the press and the theatre community about yet another Englishman talking over Canada's premier theatre. But the appointment was firm, and it was agreed that Phillips would spend much of the summer at Stratford to get to know the place and its work before taking over from Jean in September.

There was one more piece of planning to complete for the 1974 season, and that was the roster of works to be performed at Third Stage. I had already been in touch with Charles Wilson, the Canadian composer who had written an operatic version of *The Summoning of Everyman*, and we agreed to present it. We also chose Sharon Pollock's *Walsh*, set in Alberta, and Sandra Jones' play for children, *Ready Steady Go*. We were discussing other possible operas by Canadian composers when we were approached with an idea by Raffi Armenian, who had recently become Director of Music for the Festival. As conductor of the Kitchener Symphony he had been working with the great Canadian contralto Maureen Forrester, and in fact had just completed a recording with her. He now suggested that we invite Maureen to play the lead, Madame Flora, in Gian-Carlo Menotti's opera *The Medium*. He felt confident that she would accept. The American opera would be a divergence from our concentration on Canadian work, and we hesitated. But the chance to bring the celebrated Canadian singer to the Third Stage was too great to pass up. I drove up to Toronto to meet with Maureen, and before long it was settled. A great coup for our modest little stage.

I was able to get away in March for a three-week holiday in Europe, which included a stay with my parents in Tuscany. My father Raymond's emphysema had progressed inexorably, and he had become irascible and melancholic, with my mother Tessa gently coping. It was difficult to have a conversation without tensions: he had no enjoyment of disputation, and seemed to regard any disagreement with him as an affront. Nor could he endure the idea of doing things on the spur of the moment – everything had to be scrupulously planned and worried over until the enjoyment of it all had quite evaporated. Full of my own affairs, I was resentful that he showed no interest in them, and escaped back to Rome as soon as I could. It was only after his death several years later that I was powerfully reminded where his love of life had always burned. Among his diaries and correspondence we found the carbon copy of a letter he had written about this time to a bird-loving friend in England, and I quote it in full because its story brings me closer to this strange and difficult father of mine:

A final anecdote: one day last October a very old friend of ours telephoned me from his home, about 50 kilometres from here, to tell me that a woman who works for him had picked up a kestrel, apparently injured, in one of his fields and had brought it to him. He hadn't any idea how to feed it or treat it, and asked if he might drive over and bring it to me. I wasn't very keen, because I don't know that I'm particularly good with injured birds, but of course I agreed to do what I could.

My friend arrived within an hour or two with the bird in a cat basket. I found it was an adult female. Putting on gloves, I examined her carefully: the beautiful wings were certainly not broken, and I could find no trace of an injury on the body – not even blood on the feathers. This seemed to rule out the possibility of her having been shot at by a cacciatore, but left me with no clue as to the cause of her weakness; when released in the room she could only flutter along the ground.

With Tessa's help, I stuffed some pieces of raw liver down the bird's throat – a slightly painful operation thanks to her strong, curved bill. I got a little water down too, and then put her in a basket lined with hay for the night. I more than half expected to find the bird dead in the morning.

But she wasn't dead, and I released her in an empty room upstairs where we used to dry the olives. I put a dish of small pieces of liver, and some water, on the floor, and left her in peace until the early evening. I found the food untouched, so Tessa and I did some more forced feeding, adding a chicken feather or two for "roughage".

The next day she seemed a little stronger, and could flutter up as far as the low windowsill; but she still refused to eat, and had to be forcibly fed again.

She was certainly stronger the following day; in fact, when I tried to catch her to feed her, she flew quite violently against the low window. As I was afraid she might injure herself in this way, I left the dish containing twelve small pieces of liver and twelve mealworms, on the windowsill, and went out of the room. I went to look at her in the early evening. To my delight, only one small piece of liver and one mealworm remained in the dish.

The next day – the fifth since her arrival – she was flying quite strongly about the room. I put the food on the windowsill as before, left the room, but put my eye to a knot-hole in the old door. I was pleased to see her fly straight to the food dish and start eating.

On the sixth day, Tess and I decided, not without some misgivings, that the kestrel was ready for release. It was a "no-shooting" day (there are two each week) but nevertheless we took her high up in the Chianti hills where cacciatore are few and far between. We chose a clearing in the woods where the nearest tree, a very tall oak, was about a hundred yards from where we stood. We wanted clear ground so that we should have a chance of re-capturing her if she still proved too weak to fly properly. I felt that if she could reach the higher branches of the oak, we could safely leave her to look after herself.

With considerable trepidation, we lifted the lid of the basket, and the *bird flew straight out without a word of thanks for all the trouble we had taken with her. Ignoring the oak, she soared gracefully upwards until she was far, far above us, then flew strongly to our left and remained in sight for several happy moments as she described a great arc in the sky and disappeared into the distance. Tess and I could have wept with joy.*

I weep with them too, imagining my two old parents rejoicing up on that windy hill. For my father, birds always came first.

We began rehearsing *Love's Labor's Lost* in mid-April, but after three or four days had to interrupt our work for a day in order to accompany Robin Phillips to Toronto, where a press conference had been arranged to introduce him to the Toronto press, and where he could make an announcement about the 1975 season, with his future staff around him.

A few more days of rehearsal go by (the time being shared of course with the other two opening plays) and it soon becomes evident that I have a problem. At the heart of *Love's Labor's Lost* are four young men and four young women. The men are the King of Navarre and his friends, who have just sworn to abjure the company of women for three years, and to live a life of study in 'a little Academe'. At that very moment arrives the Princess of France with her retinue of young women, on a kind of state visit. This creates a serious problem for the King and his friends, but it is agreed that the Princess and her people will have to camp outside the castle, and that while they will have to be received and welcomed formally, there will be no further communication. Of course, the plan falls apart. Each of the four young men conceives a passion for one of the young women, and secretly breaks his oath. The whole deception is eventually revealed, and the young men hope they can forget about their oath and marry their loves. But the Princess reminds them that they are all forsworn, and tells them that they will have to wait 'a twelvemonth'. If they are still wanting to wed their sweethearts, then maybe...

This brief summary is enough to make clear that the men are very much under the control of the women, and that in turn the Princess is very much the women's leader. And this in turn means that the strong personality and intelligence of the Princess is vital to the effectiveness of the whole play, giving direction and leadership to the other seven lovers. This was my problem. Jean had given me Dawn Greenhalgh as the Princess. Dawn was and is a fine and competent contemporary actor. But it soon became evident that she was entirely at sea on the thrust stage of the Festival Theatre, and uncomfortable with the language of Shakespeare. She never took notes, never appeared to be learning her lines, and each day had to be reminded of the work done the day before. Nicholas Pennell (playing Berowne) and Pat Galloway (Rosalind) were the stars of the lovers' octet, and they found Dawn's apparent incompetence and laziness intolerable. I believe Pat was also discovering that the Princess's role was much more interesting to play than her own.

Almost a year later, I found and recorded into my diary a page or two I had handwritten at the time, outlining the whole sequence of events, and I can do no better than repeat it here:

April 30: Informed JH (John Hayes) and JG (Jean Gascon) that I didn't feel Dawn G. could play the Princess and that she should be replaced. JG attended no rehearsals to check on her, and told me that the only reason DG was hired was that she had a 12-year-old daughter (to play the child in 'Malade Imaginaire'), and that therefore, on the tour in Australia, Stratford would not have to pay extra for a chaperone. She was, in his words, 'Jello between the ears.'

May 4: Nick P[ennell] blows up against Dawn in rehearsal.
May 7: Asked WH (William Hutt) to attend rehearsal. He felt it was the others who were not giving her anything. I had a 15-minute row with Dawn on stage in front of the company. She began to work.
May 8: I tell JG we are 2 or 3 days behind schedule because of Dawn.
May 10: Run thru' of Act One for lighting designer. Phillips and JG both attended – nothing said. Michael MacOwen [former director of LAMDA, the London acting school, and in Stratford to give a workshop]: *'very promising indeed' and later, in a letter, "I think you have a very good production if the Dawn problem can be solved."*
May 11: Work-thru' most of Act 2. 1 catch JG after - he says (of Acts 1 and 2) "I think we have a disaster on our hands. No one knows who they are" (a Robin Phillipsism). I urge him to have confidence in me.
May 12: I have an hour with Pat Galloway at home, to talk about Rosalind. She is taciturn and unresponding. Says nothing of any problems.
May 13: I talk to JH and JG about replacing Dawn by her understudy. I talk to the understudy (in secret) and audition her. I then have an hour with Dawn. I try to see whether she wishes to continue. She does. She is slow, she says, she will get there in the end. She doesn't know the stage, the language is hard to cope with. I ask her why there is a communication problem. We make it up, agree to go on, using every available hour out of hours.
On Tuesday, May 14, I am phoned up by JG to come in and attend a meeting in his office. There are there Bill Hutt, Robin Phillips, Pennell, Galloway, Gascon and myself. Gascon says we have a time problem — then hands over to Pennell and Galloway — who talk about the time problem and then say "Can Robin help?"

It becomes clear that this meeting is the result of 4 or 5 days' talk, none of it with me. I remember seeing Jean G, Bill Hutt, Pat Galloway in Bill H's dressing-room after Act I run.

I listen. It is suggested that if Robin comes in we can double-rehearse. I agree to invite him as my assistant (I am told that Pennell talks of resigning unless some such arrangement ran be made). I decide to give Phillips responsibility for detailed work on the lovers' scenes.

I meet with him after and he suggests various "improvements" – chiefly a set of gates to go under the balcony. That evening I talk with the company, announcing the brief but happy news that Phillips is coming in to help with the lovers' scenes, double-rehearsing as my assistant. Phillips himself has said that we will be playing roles – him as assistant, I as director – in other words implying that the true state of affairs is the reverse.

End of the affair, but for another 3 weeks of abject misery.

As I copy this I find myself stirring angrily, but mostly at my own astonishing naivety. Even after that meeting with Galloway and Pennell I still had the feeling – like a dog after a beating – that Galloway and I were my friends. And after the company meeting I go up to her and say 'how was that?'" Ugh!

This was the sequence of events. And this is what I wrote when coming back to my diary just after the play opened:

A two-line gap, and into each compressed more anguish than in the last four years of myself. A coup to take away my play, Gascon feeble, Phillips concerned to please actors and show off his superior skills, Galloway her own self, I too stunned to offer her resistance, and then sliding through sleeping pills and cigarettes away from the picture I was painting, the brush dropping, picked up by Robin for a few carefree daubs and swirls, and then handed back to a paralytic, holding on with stiff upper lip but limp, sucked imagination, not eating, sips of Scotch for breakfast, endless coffee, off-time soon becoming caverns of peace – a two-hour break before an evening runthrough and I would watch the hands held back by the priceless load of an hour and a half; slowly the pressure lightening – more cigarettes, more coffee – until even the last five minutes were a blessed green field, even the last minute a flower, a scent too sweet to leave. And then the tumbril ride to the theatre. Better once there and going, but the joy of the evening's end, stars or rain, Scotch and tea and life beginning again – only to lay stones in my stomach at five in the morning.

At the height of the shock it was the signs – familiar from Ottawa – of wanting the body to disappear into the wall, the old rictus of face, the silent scream, the clutching of genitals that means death is stalking. Passive endurance is stronger in me than defence by attack.

The play opened and was given good reviews by the critics ('What a work of theatrical grace Michael Bawtree has fashioned out of all the artifice!': TIME Magazine), but for me it is the ugliest of bastards – I hate both my own work in it and Robin's – I had lost the gift of myself, and am still fighting for it back. But at least the play was on, and not an amateurish disaster – though in my eyes it is and will always be just that.

I won't go on – there is still too much to say – pull only from the fire the acute noticing of such a time – the treasuring of Colin and the dog, the comfort of the piano, the hatred of news and newspapers – for three weeks I could not endure the radio for ten seconds – the swerving driving that imagined trees coming happily to rescue me with oblivion, the prayers to Jesus Christ on the first day, Colin working to fix me up with a mantra...

So this was the start of my last summer in Stratford. Recalling it now over forty years later, I still suffer a rumble of angst. But I can also see that I was the victim of a particular circumstance. Phillips had arrived in Stratford that spring, in readiness for his take-over in September. The very moment he arrived, the loyalty of the acting company began to shift towards him and away from Jean Gascon, who was increasingly ignored as yesterday's man. Naturally all actors wished to be part of Phillips' future company, and went out of their way to endear themselves to him. Particularly assiduous were the attentions of Galloway, Pennell and Hutt, who used to be referred to by our technical director Bob Scales with splendid aptness as 'the Royal Family'. The family had its eunuchs too, and its jesters and its knaves. And Phillips, I realised, had married into them, simply for social station and security. I knew well how they were disliked by the younger company, with whom I was still able to talk, and who were many of them thoroughly sympathetic to me. Phillips seemed to be fatally gummed up in politics and image.

I learned later that when Pennell and Galloway began to fret at the situation with Dawn, they had gone not to me, nor to their artistic director Jean Gascon, but to Phillips – who apparently had smuggled himself into my rehearsals and sat hiding behind the protective wall in the front row of the Gallery (!), listening to what went on. So when Jean was confronted by the whole group of them together, he was not strong enough to defend me or my direction. He also felt guilty at having failed to respond to my earlier concerns about Dawn, and having allowed the problem to fester. A year or two later, when both Jean and I had left Stratford, we met socially in Toronto. We were still close friends, but I accused him very directly of having deserted me during that time, and having allowed Phillips and 'the Royal Family' to ambush my production. He acknowledged this at once, and generously apologized. He said he had been entirely taken in by Phillips, and only much later realised the clever political goings-on that lay behind my shabby treatment. He also apologized for having committed the original mistake of saddling me with an actor who was not capable of playing the Princess.

Once *Love's Labor's Lost* opened I took off thankfully for New York, where I met up with Gene Feist and his colleague Michael Fried (co-founder of the Roundabout Theatre), and shared with them the news of my wretched experience at Stratford. Once again Gene invited me to join them in the running of their company, and even offered me a production of *The Rivals* in their coming season. Gene's warmth and friendship was astonishing, almost embarrassing. He and his wife Kathe invited me out to their cottage in the New England woods, where (apart from having to watch what seemed to be the wildly incompetent upbringing of their two daughters) I was able to spend time trying to pull myself back together.

I am... sitting in peace on a patio in Westport, Connecticut, surrounded by trees, blue jays waiting for food, children mercifully away swimming, Gene Feist resting, a stream curdling behind me among the rocks – a moment that only two weeks ago was out of all possibility. Still those stones in the stomach, but they come and go, and I have stopped cigarettes again, and begun to eat, and am putting a good face on the affair, but reluctant to go back.

I have never known so heavily wooded a place as here, the woods hiding retreats of such calm and loveliness.

It was indeed a blessed retreat: my self-confidence had received a wounding blow. In August I would be returning to Minneapolis to restart rehearsals for *Tartuffe*. But I still had two Stratford productions ahead of me: *Everyman* and *The Medium*.

I talked with Gene about the Stratford rupture, about the future, about Roundabout. 'There is always a job for you with us,' I remember him saying. And for the first time I began to consider a break from Stratford, a job in New York among good people, directing and helping to organize a new theatre. It was attractive. The small-town atmosphere of Canada began to suffocate me as I thought of it. 'USA Here I Come!' I thought.

Back home, and two or three days into the rehearsals for *Everyman*, I realized that I was still very shaky and easily overwhelmed. Since Jeremy Gibson had finished his work on *Lorenzaccio*, I asked him whether he would join me as my assistant, and he agreed to do so, to my great relief and gratitude. My production team also included Susan Benson, who had first worked with me on *Centralia* in Vancouver, and whom I had invited to Stratford – her first time there – to design the clothes for both my operas. I was enormously glad to be working with such a good friend, and someone who knew and was sensitive to what I had been going through on the main stage: 'sensitive' was Susan's middle name. It was a time when I needed to be with friends, and I was happy to be working away from the Festival Theatre and from what seemed its increasingly toxic atmosphere. Raffi Armenian was our highly competent and supportive music director.

Charles Wilson's *Everyman* is a somewhat literal work, with music that seldom rises above the pedestrian. But I had always responded to the famous story as a play, and there was enough of the original drama in the piece to bring out and enjoy.

While directing *Everyman* I was also preparing for *The Medium*, and had gone up to Toronto for my first lengthy meeting with Maureen Forrester. I was bowled over by the strength of her personality, and recorded some of her talk in my diary:

An onslaught to remember: the energy and outwardness and strength of an Ethel Merman, the Canadian grossness of Barbara Hamilton. BUT the refinement of a Yehudi and the sharp wit – NO to all this journalism – try again.

Blonde-dyed hair, big features and fat in the face, but with the nose and brow and jaw of a man, the side view sculpted almost like Jon Vickers. Gusto, speed of thought, easiness and warmth but strength of will. 'I hate arguing – I never do it myself because I know I am right.' In Texas she sang out of doors in 120°, and as she walked off stage her feet went crunch,

crunch over the bugs. A wealthy woman aged 92 drove from Houston to the concert. Her name: Ima Hogg. Her father had two daughters and named them Ima Hogg and Ura Hogg.

Of Otto Klemperer (a marvellous conductor, though 'he got a little senile towards the end') 'I noticed that his score had no markings in it. I said 'Why? You've been conducting this work for 40 years.' Klemperer replied: 'I start every time with a clean score.'

Casals was 'naughty'. I was singing a Brahms lied in Puerto Rico and he was taking it at an unbelievably slow speed. I didn't know what to do, and after two days decided to broach him about it, planning to say (diplomatically) 'singers tend to drag this, and it's all my fault.' And I came in to see him, and before I could open my mouth he looked at me and said, 'At last — someone who can sing this lied at my tempo.'

Rehearsals for *The Medium* started almost immediately *Everyman* opened. It was a delightful little cast, and we worked quickly and well. Maureen had thoroughly mastered her part by heart before we began, and was totally open to my direction, though still full of ideas. She thoroughly approved of the orchestra being hidden behind a mesh, and said that opera singers were usually much too transfixed watching their conductor – simply because he was right there in front of them – instead of using their ears. There were only three places in this whole score, she said, where the singers simply have to be able to see Raffi to get his downbeat for a *tutti* entry following a pause. I was happy to organize the staging to make this possible.

Stratford had rented a farmhouse some way out of town for Maureen to live in during the rehearsals and run of the opera, and when we were thinking about a cast party after the opening night she immediately invited us to hold it at her place. It would be a potluck affair, but she offered to make miniature pizzas as her contribution. It says something for the energy of this extraordinary woman that she got up early on the morning of the premiere and, before coming in for our final rehearsal, cooked two hundred and fifty-six pizzas for the party. 'I do everything well,' she used to say. 'It's just the kind of person I am.'

There was a great deal of interest in the production because of its distinguished star. Maureen at that time had sung very little in opera or musicals, and the 250 tickets for each of its four performances were all sold out well before we opened.

And I am proud to say that the first night was received ecstatically by the audience, and that the show was a great critical triumph. 'Forrester creates a stunning Medium' (*Vancouver Sun*); 'Forrester brilliant... skillfully directed by Michael Bawtree' (*Globe and Mail*); 'Another artistic triumph for Maureen Forrester... directed by Michael Bawtree with a great deal of sensitivity...' (*Montreal Gazette*); 'Forrester triumphant in opera at Stratford' (*Toronto Star*); 'The singer was greatly aided by Bawtree's telling, fluid direction' (*Opera News*). The configuration of the stage meant that the spectators were almost in the room with Madame Flora and her wretched deaf mute, and from her first appearance Maureen, who was happy to wear the overdone lipstick, the unbecoming wig, baggy stockings, and the down-at-heel shoes, clothes and hat which Susan had given her, was indeed terrifying.

It can be imagined what a power of good this success did for my morale. I was also buoyed up by a conversation I had with the great JB Priestley, who was visiting that summer as a guest of the Festival.

30 July

J.B. Priestley has been here for ten days and goes tomorrow – I still had not met him, so last night went round to the Windsor Hotel and got Moya to rout him out...

Priestley arrives alone, small and bunched, slow-moving, heavy pouched face, with rheumy sharp eyes that occasionally dilate for a mad Robert Newton effect. He sits in an easy chair with a weak Scotch and a cigar. He liked Love's Labor's, *he told me, and Don Armado and Moth were the best he had seen. The comics in general were wonderful – especially Nathaniel (Richard Curnock) – but he thought nothing of the lovers, and the girls especially were without charm and without warmth. I warmly agreed.*

But the conversation moves on to other topics. 'People over here know only two of my books: The Good Companions *and* Angel Pavement *– as though I ceased work in 1931. But all my best books have been written since then.* Bright Day *is my best novel.'*

'I wouldn't live in Canada if you paid me a million pounds. I've been all over – Winnipeg, Edmonton, Medicine Hat, Calgary, everywhere – but there is a provincial surliness in the people – I have described them as 'Scots living in a cold climate.'...

*'Some men came up and shook me warmly by the hand, saying how much they enjoyed my '*Dr. Finlay's Casebook.*'*

I mention that I cannot abide the upper class English accent. 'Why do you think I talk the way I do myself, still? I've been fighting these people all my life... I was once going up from Portsmouth to London – when we lived on the Isle of Wight – and in the compartment were these two talking about the theatre – and do you know they couldn't remember anybody's name – actors, playwrights, nothing!'

'You've become a classic,' I say – suggesting why his plays were being done more and more after forty years lapse. 'I am a classic,' he corrects.

Why have the English produced so many good actors? 'They are a highly dramatic people. It is only crisis and drama that interest them... No people in the world are so readily bored. If I had been PM last year I would have introduced rationing and really engineered a crisis, because it's the only way of getting people to work together in England.

'I am a freeman of the City of Bradford. Bradford used to be called 'the comedian's grave' on the old variety and music hall circuit, because everyone is a comic in Bradford, and they're hard to please.'

'Excuse my not getting up. I'm fat and old.' He is 80 and will die soon.

Within a few days, I was making a life-altering decision. After the shattering events around *Love's Labor's Lost*, and after seeing the way Robin Phillips disported himself during the summer – he never once consulted me after that play opened – I realized that my position as associate director had become meaningless, and that I could not continue.

August 12th. I resigned from Stratford last Thursday. A nasty business, and I suffer the usual anguish of the dispossessed. But I could not ever work for that cold, elegant angel-fish, his cards held so close to his chest it must hurt. He has been beautiful and charming so long that perhaps he needs our sycophantic warmth and admiration like Danegelt. I would not move first. He would not trust me. I became for him the Judas to his Jesus – 'the greatest possibility for good, and therefore for evil.' And when I resign with a trumpet-call of reasons why, he congratulates himself that he was right not to trust me; and yet he could have persuaded me no doubt from all my reasons why, had he shown care towards how I felt. He is passionate for trust and loyalty – and I am passionate for them too, but they are to be found in the event and not before it.

So what of Phillips' extraordinary reputation in the theatre? I recently saw him described as 'an actor's director', and it reminded me once again of those days. It was the same phrase that people used of Phillips when he took over some of my rehearsals of *Love's Labor's*. A director that makes his actors feel good, that dazzles them with his cleverness, and cradles them in the security of his touch, is exactly the kind I do not want to be. Should not the director work towards being an <u>audience</u>'s director? Rehearsals do not have to dazzle. Actors do not have to be given the impression that risks are to be taken not by them but only by the director. They should share the ache, the difficulty, the decision-making that is creation. Why on top of the overall responsibility must the director build an image of security, play-acting assurance and knowingness? Did this not lead to exactly the kind of performance that was Phillip's stock-in-trade – the choreographic campery of his work for me in my play?

I wrote my resignation letter to the Board of Governors, with a copy to Phillips. In it I made clear my reasons, somewhat circumspectly if I remember, but leaving no doubt that I questioned the values of the new artistic director and that I did not feel I could support him or them. To my astonishment I received next day a personal letter from Phillips – with a copy to the Board – which began:

'Dear Michael,
When I asked you to resign, I did so because…'

The cheek of it! My decision to resign was my own: he had never asked me for my resignation, or even hinted at it, and was now trying to suggest to the Board that my initiative was prompted by him! I immediately wrote a second letter to the Board, making clear that my resignation was entirely my own decision, and that I had never been approached to resign by Phillips. I went further, saying that Phillips' trying to claim responsibility for my action was another example of the kind of unethical behaviour that I had already detected in the man. There would be some six years more of Phillips' hegemony before the Board would seem to reach more or less the same conclusion.

Many, many years later, in the nineties, I was in New York, and discovered that John Hirsch was staying in the same hotel. We arranged to have breakfast together, and within a few minutes started talking about Robin Phillips. To my amazement I found that John's estimate of the man was exactly the same as mine. 'When you sup with the devil,' he quoted, 'use a long spoon.' He felt that Phillips had come close to ruining Stratford; that when John had succeeded him as artistic director in 1980 he found an organization which was totally demoralized, in which for six years no one but Phillips had dared to make any decision on their own. He could not understand how seasoned actors like Martha Henry (a particular protégé of John's) had been so thoroughly taken in. "She's gone mad," he said.

I told John of my experience when I had resigned, and how Phillips had tried to claim responsibility for my action. John was astonished – he said he had always understood that I had been fired. I said it would have been impossible for Phillips to fire me, since when I resigned in mid-August Jean Gascon was still my boss. John became enraged and pointing a finger at me said 'you must bear witness! You must bear witness!' He asked whether I still had the letters. I said I thought I had somewhere. 'Find them!' And again – 'You must bear witness!' And here I am, bearing witness.

August 16th. And now four days later I am flying again, to Minneapolis again, for Tartuffe again, having left the Festival for the last time, desk emptied, heart something torn, with a two-fold pull of delight at liberation, at the prospect of not being a Responsible Person for a bit, and yet anguish at leaving, especially leaving under a cloud... Sorriest of all to leave behind the house (with its beauty that keeps striking me every time I fetch a cup from the kitchen or a book from the study. In all lights, at all angles it is hugely satisfying) and Pushkin, and of course Colin, who drives me to the airport and who once again is left on the tarmac to wave and smile. Te quiero, Colin.

I heard that Joel Kenyon – an actor I brought to Stratford to play the Tsar in '66 – has said that I was 'power-tripping, and totally unethical.' Searching my conscience, I find myself guilty in wanting to hang on to the influence and responsibility that I had under the old administration, but don't blush much at that kind of guilt. Having participated in choice of repertoire, auditions, casting, publicity style, souvenir programme, workshop, library, archives, for all three theatres, and having now been appointed 'Associate Director' of Festival and Avon Theatres, as well as Director of Third Stage, I naturally had hoped to be involved continuously as before, but was not. Guilty too of speaking behind Phillips' back, but to whom? In unguarded terms only to John Hayes and Jean Gascon, and fully reciprocated by both. In guarded terms (mentioning mainly my belief that the Love's Labor's *situation did not have to happen) to many, to some of whom I mentioned that there was a difference of style between the sections that he rehearsed and those that were mine, and that they didn't gel. Tactless maybe, but considering the humiliations visited upon me by Jean's indecisions earlier, and by Robin's alacrity to fill a breach and 'save' the actors, it was surely not an impeachable offence to express other than profound gratitude for Robin's help. How tiresome all this is – was. For now, high in the sky, a new world is beginning again.*

And there, high in the sky, just three days after Richard Nixon resigned the US Presidency, I left that now faraway self of 1974, battered by the stresses of the summer, and quitting Canada and my loved Colin with a sad heart, but still buoyed by the promise of new possibilities and new horizons south of the border. *Tartuffe* is to come, and after that *The Rivals* in New York. What might not follow?

CHAPTER FIFTEEN

TO THE USA

My departure from Stratford in fact signalled my own sense of having come of age as a stage director. Though I continued to learn and make mistakes, I now felt confident enough to bill myself as a professional, and for the next three years my work kept me continually in the United States, directing productions in Minneapolis, New York off-Broadway, Westport, Cincinnati and Chicago. As soon as *Tartuffe* had opened at the Guthrie Theatre in the fall of 1974, I headed to New York to begin work for my production of *The Rivals* for Gene Feist at The Roundabout. Once in New York I took a room at the Chelsea, and looked for an agent to represent me both as director and – why not? – as an actor. I still have the absurdly sexy portrait shot at the time to accompany my resume, though I never took the idea seriously enough to bother with the wretched round of auditions that is the daily work of so many actors. It was far more satisfying to be on the receiving end, and I prided myself on having a good eye and ear for talent.

Minneapolis had been a delightful interlude. After the maelstrom of Stratford politics I enjoyed being part of a company that seemed genuinely happy, and spending time once again with

Michael Langham – now living with and married to Ellen Gorky – had been a chance to further our close friendship. Sam Kirkpatrick was my mischievous and talented costume designer for *Tartuffe*, and it was at his suggestion that we chose the French painter Chardin as our inspiration for the look of the piece. The domesticity of Chardin's portraits, his interest in a house's servants as well as their masters, his tender care with domestic objects and his sense of the easy relationship between people and their things: all this helped us discard the fussy and over-dressed look of Molière's own time, and make a genuine household of Orgon and his family. Larry Gates was once again my splendidly befuddled if sometimes a little too uncontrolled Orgon: I was astonished, knowing of his long and distinguished career as a character actor, by his nervousness. I noted in my diary:

Today lunch with Larry Gates, and early evening drinks with him, the drinks opening the floodgates of talk still wider. Interesting: he talks with great assurance, and yet with the obsessiveness of a nervous man who talks for fear. And then every half-hour, 'Am I boring you?' He describes how nervous he is approaching 'Tartuffe', because he has come since last winter to the realization that Orgon has to be believable. But that is exactly what we discussed and agreed upon last November: Orgon must believe, and be seen to believe. So why repeat it with an air of discovery? Only, it seems, for confirmation, for which he has an insatiable hunger – and yet which comes across as no more than a conversational gambit. 'Am I boring you?'

For all Larry's oddities we became good friends, and he was kind enough to introduce me as his guest to The Players Club in New York City when I went to work there later in the year.

My Tartuffe had been Ken Ruta, who had taken over the lead from Bunny Behrens after the cancellation of the winter tour. Tall, arch, saucer-eyed and with a healthy strain of iron behind the fawning, Ken's Tartuffe didn't entirely avoid the showy campery of the character, but it came close. Mark Lamos (later to become a distinguished artistic director) was my handsome Damis. The production played in the Guthrie's repertory through the winter, alongside Michael Langham's *The School for Scandal* and *King Lear*, and received good local notices: 'Gorgeous fun' (*Minneapolis Star*); 'A brilliant production of clarity, grace and firm ensemble, which moves with unflagging upbeat rhythm' (*St. Paul Dispatch*); 'Molière's 1644 comedy, "Tartuffe", will probably be the surprise hit of the 1974 Guthrie season' (*Mankato Free Press*). I remember that I myself was not entirely happy with my ending of the play – I had not realized how in just a few lines, when Tartuffe is suddenly unmasked, that scene has to balance in force the whole of the rest of the piece. I would like to have had another go at it, but sober second thoughts are not often possible in professional productions.

And now, at the Roundabout Theatre with Gene Feist, I was to enter a whole different theatrical world. Gene had founded the Roundabout ten years earlier, and its first home was the converted basement of a supermarket down on the West Side. His colleague Michael Fried had been around since the early days, and by the time I became involved he was being billed as Executive Producer to Gene's Producing Director. I had met with them both when accepting Gene's invitation to visit him in New York the previous year, and had soon become puzzled by their close and apparently loving relationship. Gene had charm and a powerful personality, whereas Michael was articulate, even verbose, but had an enigmatic air about him. That summer in Stratford Gene had invited me to New York to become a co-director with him, but I now saw that this would involve a troika with Fried, and I was not at all sure how

I would fit in. I had dinner with Michael alone just before returning to Canada that time, and my diary from that visit showed me trying to work things out:

I asked Michael: 'Could Gene fire you?' – Apparently a wound, this one. He tells me he and Gene have a symbiotic relationship, that the Roundabout Theater is their joint creation – 'I have gained as much from it as I have given to it, and so has Gene.' I try – first to myself and then, on his rather distrustful urging, to him – to pinpoint my unease when talking to him… It is to do with a warmth and flattery that means nothing and leads to nothing. I say he puts up a smokescreen between me and himself, and – I believe – between himself and the facts. It is in his case simple pomposity, never using one word where ten will do. It is also the obfuscating generality of his talk. 'You ask, what is our aim? We believe essentially that the kind of theater we believe in as contributing importantly etc. etc. etc.' and I am floored by the contaminatingly high load of uplift. He is an evangelist of the best-worst kind – and I cannot imagine him talking business in simple, direct phrases 'Lenore [their business manager] has commendable capacity in her relationships with the staff' – e.g. she's good with people. Michael, it seems, is a continual presentation: 'I don't choose to…' ; 'my response to that is . . '. Ah, yes. He doesn't respond but reports his responses ostensibly post rem. *Which implies some embarrassment about direct feeling, about spontaneity. Does he love Gene? Not in a possessing sense, but in a cleaving way that will do him damage if Gene leaves or dies. 'Do you ever think of leaving and setting up your own theater?' 'Roundabout is my own theater.' 'Does Gene ever think of… etc?' 'Roundabout is Gene's theater.' The word 'organic' is thrown around as if we were market gardening.*

It was soon clear that my production of *The Rivals* was to be something of a test: if I could deliver them a hit then the future with them would be assured. My challenge was considerably increased by the fact that they were just moving their operation into a somewhat awkward site, converted from an old movie theater: *The Rivals* was to be the first production in their new home, and we were attended with the usual stresses of settling into an untried space. Gene was warm and wonderfully helpful as we held auditions, drawing similar conclusions in most cases. But with his colleagues he was amazingly different. I was reading Machiavelli's *The Prince* at the time, and I suppose this made me particularly observant of the ways of both Gene and Michael as they went about their business. I was astonished at how nasty they could be:

Watching Gene Feist and Michael Fried at work, I see the survival aggression carried to almost absurd lengths – shouting down the telephone, brutal, impulsive treatment of staff. Yet they only just made it into the new theatre, as though with only an ounce of gumption less they wouldn't have made it. Gene says 'you seem to be shocked sometimes by the way we do things, but otherwise we wouldn't be here. Anyway what else do you expect from a couple of Jews?'

And then the two of them would take me out to dinner at Marni's, with Gene so loving I had no heart to quibble about his strange ways: even Michael was at his most charming. During the meal Gene went so far as to describe me as 'after Michael, the best friend I have in North America.' Well!

This was in fact my first close encounter with the cut and thrust of New York's theatre scene. Though Gene was running a not-for-profit theater, and was keen to present the classics, his values were commercial. He was driven by the need to associate celebrities with the Roundabout, and keen to employ Big Names in his productions. He was insistent that *The Rivals* should be drastically cut in order that the audience could catch a ten o'clock train – but also required me to write a new scene into the final act so that his wife Kathe (Elizabeth Owens), who played Mrs Malaprop's maid Lucy, would have a reason for sticking around for the curtain call. (After appearing there the first few nights, she would often call in to the stage manager to say that she wouldn't be able to stay to the end today because she had some shopping to do, and would the cast mind going back to the original text?) He cosied up to John Lindsay, Mayor of New York, to Hermione Gingold, to Arthur Miller and many others while I was working for him, and when they came to his theatre he would entice them on to the stage to have their photographs taken with him, with Michael Fried, with me, with our lead actors. I could never quite reconcile this embarrassing behaviour with my own sense of the proprieties, and remained a reluctant accomplice.

It was not easy to assemble an American cast that could handle the intricacies of Sheridan's text, but after auditioning some hundred and fifty actors, and meeting with a few of them who were too distinguished to submit to an audition, we put together a talented bunch, with Christopher Hewett (fresh from *The Producers* movie) to play a powerful if somewhat over-the-top Sir Anthony Absolute, and Jane Connell to appear as a very funny Mrs Malaprop. Canadian actor Richard Monette (later to be artistic director of the Stratford Festival) was also in New York at the time and out of work, and we were able to hire him as a graceful and fiery Jack Absolute. I was also able to invite my good friend and colleague Susan Benson to make her New York debut, designing our clothes with her faultless good taste.

Our stage was a straightforward proscenium with curtains, but as a thrust stage habitué I was unwilling to separate scenes with curtains continually opening and closing. Gene's set designer Holmes Easley did his best with my demands, designing a painted surround to represent the city of Bath and then incorporating a revolve in the centre of it, to enable us to prepare interior scenes in advance. He told me he was in love with the colour of Bath stone, and determined to reproduce its golden tones on our stage. Unfortunately he chose altogether too pungent a tint, and Christopher used to refer to the final rather lugubrious result as 'Dogshit City.'

We opened on December 3rd, moving off to Sardi's for the traditional reception while waiting for the morning papers, which came in just after midnight. The results were mixed. *The Times's* Clive Barnes, who had so praised my *She Stoops To Conquer* at Stratford two years earlier, judged this production to be 'not so solid', but was pleasant if unenthusiastic in his assessment: "Mr Bawtree has made the play move rapidly, with clarity, and has made some decent surgical cuts in a text that does call for an operation. Everything has been done tactfully and with skill." Emory Lewis of the Bergen Record called it "a sparkling and beguiling romp". *The News* was less fulsome. Though it was not a complete failure, we certainly did not have a hit on our hands. In my diary I wrote:

I went to bed at one, full of Scotch and champagne, and wide awake at 5.30. Finished [Aldous Huxley's] Eyeless in Gaza *by 7.20. Dressed and breakfasted out. Back to the Chelsea by 9 am, expecting at any moment to be ready again for bed. But there is too much exhilaration in me for sleep – so elated at the final end of work on* The Rivals *after nine or ten weeks' rehearsal and performance and being subject to the continual irritations of the Roundabout Theater.*

I enjoy sitting here waiting for Michael and Gene to make the next move. Will they want me to stay after I failed to get them a rave review?

They will discuss it from every publicity angle, with their usual misdirected paranoia. And I am in the happy position of not caring a damn what they decide. I can stand a lot about them but least of all their personal lying – through lack of moral courage in facing people with truth, and through an engrained habit of mistrusting the truth.

I attended the first few performances of *The Rivals*, and gave notes, coping with the realisation of just how much a director's work is so heavily supported by the lavish infrastructure of a place like Stratford, and how much I had missed that support. I had a happy lunch with the kindly and generous Christopher Hewett at his apartment, enjoying his company, though I had realised early on in rehearsals that he did not have a light touch in his acting of Sir Antony Absolute. In fact he was mainly responsible for the review in the *New Yorker* of January 27th: 'Under the direction of Michael Bawtree… the Roundabout company plays "The Rivals" with a broadness that the Amazon itself might envy.' Not for nothing, with his eyes popping out as he mugged amazement or anger, had Christopher been long ago nicknamed 'Eggs Benedict'.

The dying days of 1974, after a tumultuous year, found me for the first time with no directing tasks ahead. I was taken on by the theatrical agent Joel Pitt, and with his help worked hard to open up new possibilities. I was also encouraged by Maureen Forrester's New York agent Harold Shaw, and he arranged me to meet with Michael Kahn with the idea of my directing *The Winter's Tale* for the Shakespeare Festival in Stratford Connecticut. But meanwhile, thanks to Michael Langham, I did pick up one commission. PBS-TV had chosen Michael's Guthrie Theatre production of *The School for Scandal* for their classical drama program. The play, which was to be shot in a studio at Minneapolis, had to be heavily cut to fit the two-hour limitation dictated by their programming, and Michael asked me to come up with a text for the adaptation. Having worked so closely on the play with Michael back in 1970, I was more than happy with the idea, and had several sessions with Michael in New York to plan the project: the version had to be delivered early in January, which gave me time for something of a working holiday over Christmas and New Year. Colin and I decided to return to Jamaica for two weeks.

Getting in touch with Joyce McLeod, whose Great House hotel we had stayed at in 1970, we discovered that she had now purchased a small estate close by: it was a luxurious modern house with steps down to the warm ocean, in a garden riotous with poinsettia, bougainvillea and Jamaican firebird bushes, and exotic fruit trees like rose apple and ackee. She had just two guestrooms, and we were able to secure one of them. We could not have imagined a more paradisal setting for what amounted to a reunion after so many months apart, and we both returned much refreshed, Colin to his third term at the University of Guelph, I back to New York with a truncated *School for Scandal* under my arm, and a plan to settle into New York for at least the next few months. I sublet an apartment for February.

Our revisions of the *Scandal* text at Stratford had been retained in the Guthrie production, but for television a new approach was needed. Not only was it necessary to cut at least an hour from the running time, we felt that the long-drawn-out exposition of the play's beginning would never succeed in holding a television audience. So we reshaped the start of the play entirely, beginning the action on a coach bringing Sir Oliver to London from Southampton, where he had just landed off his ship from India. We took Sir Peter Teazle's right-hand man Rowley down to the docks to meet Oliver on the quay, and inside the coach as they travelled home we had him bringing Oliver up-to-date on the situation of the Surface brothers and of his old friend Sir Peter's tempestuous marriage. This gave us an opportunity to bring the audience swiftly into the story. With steady English rain pelting on the coach's roof as it jolted along, it was a lively and visually attractive scene – with images of Joseph, Charles and Sir Peter, in characteristic cameos, cut into the action as Rowley described them.

The lengthy gossiping scenes of Backbite, Candour, Crabtree and Sneerwell were rigorously tightened, and the scene where Sir Peter joins the gossips – and finds himself the butt of their jokes about old husbands married to young wives – was removed entirely. There was also a fairly drastic rearrangement of the middle section of the play.

Michael was happy with the version, with a few minor changes, and before long we flew out to Minneapolis to rehearse for the television production and to oversee the sets designed by John Barkla and constructed at the studio. I felt somewhat at a loose end, having completed my part in the proceedings:

Clearly I am here only on guard duty. Michael does not need me at all – my work is done but for the odd phrase – WNET keeps me here 'in case' – but I can't think they're right. But where else can I go? Home is sub-let and the New York apartment doesn't come free until February 7. From Monday I shall spend time writing.

I had returned to 'Minn' in time to witness the last performance of my *Tartuffe*:

A good and instructive time – to see the show as I left it but working – to see again what I noticed in The Rivals *– that the difference of timing and tone to make a laugh work is almost too small to measure. 'The audience* *tells you.' – And confidence is the trick, which can come only of knowing you are playing the instrument correctly.*

While still in Minneapolis I received a call from the University of Illinois at Evanston: their Shakespeare Conference was being held in a few days, and they had just had news that Jonathan Miller had had to drop out of their roster of speakers. Could I come in his stead? Yes I could, and being at something of a loose end, I was happy to do so. I recall little of the proceedings, but was interested to meet Charles Marowitz, who was becoming famous for his 'cut-up' versions of *Hamlet* and other plays, and also New Yorker Herman Buchman, who had recently written his book on stage make-up, and was to become a good friend over the next years. From there, with *Tartuffe* over and shooting completed for *The School for Scandal*, I returned to New York City, and took over my two-month sublet apartment on 72nd Street.

I had no sure work ahead. My possible future with the Roundabout Theatre had evaporated, with no regrets. But I had a few other irons in the fire, and with a few dollars still in the bank I viewed my prospects calmly. Best of all, Maureen Forrester was in town for her debut with the Met the next day, and had arranged a ticket for me – sitting next to her husband Eugene and her agent Harold Shaw. The performance was something of a disappointment: Maureen was singing Erda, who pops up in the last scene of *Das Rheingold* for a single aria before fading back out of sight. The director had set her far away upstage in the murk, where she could barely be seen, and where her splendid voice, unamplified by the downstage microphones, had little chance against the full orchestra. Eugene was incensed, and Maureen disappointed to say the least: she knew she had had no chance to shine, and that her debut had fallen short. But she soldiered on with her contract, opening two or three weeks later and more successfully with the same role in *Siegfried*.

A day or two later I met up with Maureen and her assistant Irene Bird to go to see the Canadian movie *Lacombe Lucien*. It had snowed heavily that morning, and after trudging through the uncleared streets we discovered that I had got the date wrong. Trudging back, we decide to have dinner at Maureen's apartment ('I can put a Polish sausage in my oven'). Over the meal Maureen revealed a secret. She was leaving Eugene Kash, her husband of many years. She had fallen in love with a Toronto businessman called Doug Annett.

Apart from its effect on Eugene and her young family, the news was to have long-lasting repercussions for my work with Maureen. Ever since our production of *The Medium* at Stratford the previous year, we had been cooking up the idea of launching a Canadian music theatre company. We had decided to invite Gabriel Charpentier to join us, in order to link up with Quebec music. We would be a board of three, with Gabriel and Maureen as Vice-Presidents and myself as President, but we needed a financial person to help us with that side of our operation and to give us credibility for granting agencies. It wasn't long before Maureen suggested Doug Annett; so that when we registered the Company, and finally launched COMUS in September of that year at the Royal York Hotel in Toronto, Doug had become our Treasurer. He even made an office available in his small suite on Adelaide Street. We had not only a Treasurer but an address.

The times when Maureen and I got together in New York in the early months of 1975 were in fact instrumental in our planning of COMUS Music Theatre of Canada. I was well aware that Maureen's involvement would attract considerable public interest, and was continually amazed and delighted that she was keen to devote her high, quick intelligence and her imagination to developing the project. But then we had forged a real friendship since those days working on *The Medium* in Stratford. We laughed a lot, and at the same things. And our seriousness was about the same things too: our mutual enthusiasm was contagious. Maureen was also – for all her single-mindedly classical career as a singer – very catholic in her musical tastes. She loved jazz. She loved musicals. She loved theatre. She saw at once how a company that covered the whole range of music theatre, from opera to musical revue, could break down barriers, explore new ground, and grab people's imaginations. And it would be, we believed, the first exclusively music theatre company in North America. Why COMUS, people asked? I got tired of recounting the history of Milton's masque COMUS – which could be thought of as an early piece of music theatre. So I started telling them that it was an acronym, and that is stood for 'Canada Ought to Make Use of its Singers.' This went down well.

For myself, I was beginning to knit together a theoretical rationale for the whole idea of music theatre. I saw it as a breakaway from the grand opera in which Maureen was becoming immersed at the Met, where a production could cost millions, where a conductor could be paid $50,000 for a single performance, where social ostentation in attendance and sponsorship was so significant an issue. Why not music theatre pieces like the ones we had presented at Stratford's Third Stage, where five or six, or eight, or a dozen performers participated as soloists like actors in a play; where the orchestra could similarly be small and intense, and where serious social issues could be dealt with as well as comedy or melodrama? It was a way of thinking which continued to develop, and eventually to shape my working life for the next twenty years.

It was ironic that just at the moment when we were planning our Canadian project we were both launching into new American phases of our careers. Maureen was of course widely known and acclaimed in the United States as a concert singer, particularly for her Mahler performances with Bruno Walter and others, but she was now finally having her debut at the Met. And in an infinitely more humble way I was beginning to build something of a career as a director, helped by my Stratford pedigree and my Guthrie Theatre connection. In my own case, this tug between Canada and the USA became more and more stressful over the next years. I managed to land some more productions – in New York, Cincinnati and Chicago. But at the same time I was running back to Canada when I could, in order to advance the COMUS project – and also of course to return to my beloved Colin and our dog Pushkin and our delectable apartment. The fact that our home was in Stratford was of course something of a disincentive; I had no desire to be there and to meet my old colleagues at the Festival – least of all Robin Phillips. Amazingly, in the many years that followed, I never set eyes on him again.

I was still waiting for a final decision on *The Winter's Tale*. Michael Kahn continued to seem positive. He drove me out to Stratford Connecticut one day, to see the huge and cumbersome Shakespeare theatre there. He had even taken me to dinner at the then highly fashionable Joe Allen's, where Michael caught sight of his friend Tennessee Williams sitting alone, and we moved to his table to finish our wine. (Tennessee was fairly drunk, and I have no memory of the conversation – if indeed there was one.) But still the invitation did not come. I eventually called and asked him where we stood. He told me that William Gaskell had been invited to direct the piece, and that if he turned it down I was next in line. With this I had to be content.

So with no immediate work prospects in sight, I flew back now to Ontario, and was able to spend time both at home and also in Toronto – where to my great joy I hooked up with Helen Burns again, after a two-year gap. Although she was still endlessly bitter at Michael's desertion of her, and even hurt knowing that I was still seeing and working with him, our friendship re-blossomed almost at once. I took her out for dinner at a smart fish restaurant on Bay Street. We were treated snootily by the manager and shown huffily to a table, where our order was finally taken by a waiter who was clearly bored and unhappy. After sitting for another ten minutes, Helen had had enough. "Let's leave," she said, and got up and walked out, murmuring icily as she passed the manager's desk: "It's all that Swiss training." We found another place, much more simple, with check tablecloths and a fiddler, and had a high old time, laughing uproariously as in the olden days. How good it was to be with her again!

It was during that time that I emerged one lunchtime from a restaurant on Spadina just in time to watch a helicopter lifting up the final section of the CN Tower and dropping it delicately into place. A fine historical moment.

CHAPTER SIXTEEN

BRITTEN TO BERNSTEIN

I returned to New York in the middle of March, in time to join Maureen for a performance of *Falstaff* at the Met. While talking with her I mentioned that I was having to give up my short-term sublet at the end of the month, and since she was leaving as soon as her Ring Cycle appearances were over, and not returning until the fall for *Un Ballo in Maschera,* she offered me her own apartment for the next few months. This was a modest one-bedroom studio – with a small grand piano – on the 10th Floor of an elderly 12-floor building on 74th Street West, just a few steps east of Broadway. A week or two later I was more than happy to move in with my sparse belongings, and was once again grateful to Maureen for her spontaneous generosity. It had come at a timely moment, because it was just then that I heard that my directing *The Winter's Tale* at Stratford Conn. was definitely off. I wondered at the time whether my *crise* at Stratford Ontario the previous year had something to do with it. I would never know.

As I stepped into the elevator one day, shortly after moving, I met an elderly and very genial-looking man with a bald head, a slight stoop, and thick-lensed glasses. I have often said since that the United States of America is the only place in the world where you meet someone in an elevator on the tenth floor, and by the time you have reached the ground you have been invited to dinner. We got talking… My fellow rider was Oren Brown, who I learned was a distinguished voice teacher, and who – besides teaching private students here in his studio – held a faculty position at the Juilliard School. Oren lived with his fairly new second wife, named Juliska, in an apartment in The Astor, a massive and historic building at Broadway and 75th. My dinner with them there was the first of many, and the old couple became two of my closest friends for the next ten or twenty years. Oren was fascinated with my plans for music theatre, and was to become not only an ally but also a colleague – as will be seen.

It was not long after I moved into Maureen's place that I had a close brush with personal danger. A month afterwards I wrote a letter to the *New York Review of Books* describing the incident, since it raised an ethical question. The letter was published in October, many months later. Here is what I wrote:

To the Editors:
Some weeks ago I was held up in my apartment by a man (let us call him Jack) who, masquerading as a police-officer, handcuffed me to the toilet and made off with a tape-recorder, a radio-recordplayer, and $42.00. Jack's act was convincing, his manner charming and regretful, and the spontaneity of his invention remarkable. While we "waited for the police-car" he even made me tea to calm my outraged astonishment, and it was only five minutes before he left that my suspicions began to simmer. Only when he was gone ("I'll be back in five minutes") and I made out the word JAPAN on the handcuffs did I know for a certainty that I had been had.

As it happens Jack stupidly left evidence behind him – he dropped a Social Security card. The name was checked by the police (through their own records, not through Social Security) and was found to belong to a twenty-five-year-old man on probation for illegal possession of a weapon, and with a record behind him that included charges of robbery and first-degree rape. Eleven days later a photograph of this man was produced and I identified it positively as Jack. We must now wait for a finger-print check (three weeks so far) and then some days after that it will be arranged that I try to identify him in person, either outside his house or in the probation office. If I identify him as Jack he will be arrested, and we shall presumably move at the same leisurely pace through trial, and quite possibly to conviction. And if convicted Jack will almost certainly go to jail.

Now, because I am the prosecution's only witness, I am able at any time to stop proceedings by deciding to drop the charges. And this situation brings to a sharp focus for me the problems posed by Garry Wills in his review of Tom Wicker's A Time To Die *(NYR, April 4). Thanks to Jack's strange way of doing things I know him not as a "young hood" or a "masked gunman (Hispanic)" but as a person. What then is my motivation for allowing things to take their course?*

Revenge? Absolutely not. "Society", whatever that is, may feel vengeful at such things, but I can honestly say I feel no wish at all for revenge – no more, say than after being beaten at pool: I would of course jump at the chance of a return match.

Rehabilitation? Well, I saw enough of Jack in the hour we were together to be sure that jail of itself will have no rehabilitative effect whatsoever. His imaginative faculty is so complete and so dazzlingly effective, and so obviously the only thing he has, that it is without question a necessary food for his personality, like piano-playing to a pianist. The time behind bars will be spent honing his gift, perfecting the fine tissue of his lies, and writing out ten thousand times in his mind "When visiting, I must not leave a visiting-card." The only way to try breaking the compulsion of his behavior would be to integrate him in a social group where his artistry could be seen as art: where he could step back from himself enough to see the behavior not as himself but as performance. I have been feeling that theater, my own profession, could well do with such a talent.

It is also clear, for the reasons that Mr Wills gives, that the deterrent value of a jail sentence would be negligible. In the view of any delinquent friends he might have, Jack would be paying not for his crime but for his incompetence.

My only personal reason for proceeding with the charges is the chance of recovering the stolen goods. But at the snail's pace of the investigation – it is now over four weeks since the crime took place, though the police had tracked the man's name within forty-eight hours – the expectation of recovering the stuff is minimal. Furthermore, without being melodramatic about it, there is always the possibility of reprisal. Jack had a gang symbol tattooed on the back of his hand.

Do I then drop the charges?

Let us be clear: Jack was almost certainly armed (he told me was, and though that means nothing I find it hard to imagine he left himself with no safety margin beyond his wit); and if I had not been a little frightened and almost infantile in my naiveté there is a fair chance I might have been threatened and possibly wounded or killed. His previous record (if it is Jack's) is not savory, and my friends tell me I am lucky to be alive. But will the next catch be as lucky? Will he make Jack laugh as I did, will he play the piano for him as I did – with handcuffs on? This clowning probably saved me, but someone so pathologically out of touch with the difference between truth and lying is surely almost as insensitive to the reality of death. "Just trust me," he kept saying: "may my mother die if I'm not speaking the truth." I fear for the old lady's health, but I fear still more for the life of anyone who defies him. "Zapping" is child's play, like making up stories.

I have the chance, then, of getting Jack off the streets and into jail where he will by all accounts be brutalized beyond recall, or of dropping the charges and so being indirectly responsible for the possible maiming or even death of an innocent person, or two, or three. Multiply this dilemma by the number of crimes on New York State (fifty to a hundred a day in this precinct of New York City alone) and you have the "tragedy of Attica," and the whole monstrous prison system. It is fine for us to reject the system as Wills and Wicker do – as I do myself. But what is to be done at this moment, now?

Michael Bawtree
New York City

By the time the letter was printed I had identified 'Jack' in person (The police hid me behind a pillar at the probation office!), but the court date was set for months later, on a day when I would no longer be in town. The case lapsed, and how Jack's life turned out I never knew.

After another few weeks in the city I was still without work, and once again returned home to Canada. And during that month of May one of those life-changing calls came through: Niki Goldschmidt, artistic director of the Guelph Spring Festival in Ontario, had seen my production of *The Medium* at Stratford the previous year, and invited me to direct *The Beggar's Opera* at his Festival in 1976. This was not an offer to be passed up. Not only was I very familiar with the piece, having been involved in two productions in earlier days, but it was also in many ways just the kind of 'music theatre' piece I had been interesting myself in. And Niki was keen to present the Benjamin Britten arrangement of the opera, a version that I did not know.

I immediately hit on the idea of visiting the Aldeburgh Festival that June, and possibly even of meeting with Britten. Britten was not well, having barely survived a heart operation in 1973, so the chances of talking to him were slim. But I was lucky enough to have an *entrée* into Britten's world: when Arthur Harrison, the headmaster of my old preparatory school, retired in the 'fifties he had moved to Snape, just a few miles from Aldeburgh. He had subsequently become a Festival governor. He had often invited me down in earlier days. I now wrote asking whether he could possibly arrange a visit to the following month's Festival. He immediately wrote back that I must come, and that I would be the Festival's guest.

5 June. Over a month has passed and once again an air journey calls out the black book – flying this time from Toronto to London for a visit to the Aldeburgh Festival et alia. Just taken off in a misty late spring evening, leaving Colin with so much sense of tearing loss – imagining him climbing back into the car: Pushkin sitting in the back, perhaps walking with Pushkin a little, then deciding whether to go back into town or to head for home and the monastic life to which he has given himself. He says 'you go away and I feel so terribly sad: I know you're coming at the weekend and my whole life is filled with sun and purpose. I suppose that's what love means,' he says, putting on a voice for that phrase to show his awareness of the cliché, but knowing the truth of it. I wish he was with me. After nine years – no difference.

After a day or two with my old friend John Weston and his wife Sally at their newly-acquired house in Richmond, I took the train to Saxmundham, where Arthur met me. We sped back to the coast, in order to arrive just in time for a matinee performance of Bach's *Mass in B Minor*, to be conducted by Norman del Mar. It was the first course in an astonishing feast of musical and literary riches over the next ten days. Just imagine! I heard Sviatoslav Richter in a solo concert at Orford Church, where a day or two later I also heard New York's Beaux Arts Trio. I attended concerts given by aged but still lively pianist Clifford Curzon, and by Victoria de los Angeles. I saw *Death In Venice* with Peter Pears at The Maltings in

Snape. I heard Janet Baker in the premiere of *Phaedra*, Britten's last completed work, with the Queen Mother in attendance. I heard guitarist Julian Bream in concert. And at the Jubilee Hall I heard Stephen Spender give a talk on his friend WH Auden, who had recently died.

Aside from this superb sweep of performances, I was able through Arthur's good offices to meet many of the Festival's great stars. I met and talked with Spender, with Imogen Holst, with Julian Bream, with Norman del Mar, even with Joyce Grenfell, beloved comedienne and longtime friend of the Festival. I caught up with my dear Stratford colleague from *Cymbeline* Tanya Moiseiwitch, who was visiting the Festival and staying with friends. And on one of those perfect English summer afternoons I was able to join Arthur at a cocktail party given by Britten and Peter Pears in their garden at the Red House. I chatted with Pears, and when a frail Benjamin Britten put in a brief appearance – with his nurse alongside – I was brought up to be introduced and we talked for a few moments about *The Beggar's Opera*, about the Stratford Festival in Ontario (where he had visited and performed with Pears) and about Tyrone Guthrie, the first director of Britten's version of the opera.

There was one other person I was keen to meet. This was Colin Graham, the director of *Death In Venice*. Colin had recently launched the English Music Theatre Company, and with my mind full of COMUS Music Theatre I knew I would be able to benefit from his advice. It was duly arranged, and on my last day in Aldeburgh I sat with Colin somewhere out in a garden among the roses. Colin's story was a sombre one. He and I very much shared a vision for Music Theatre, but he warned me of the enormous difficulties he had had when setting up his company. He had an especially hard time dealing with the Arts Council, whose departments of Music (Opera) and Drama were firmly separated, and which simply did not know how to deal with the whole concept of a hybrid animal like Music Theatre. Is it high art, or is it popular? Is it music, or theatre? Is it hostile to legitimate opera? Does it have high standards? What will happen to the produced voice? And so on. Within a year or two I was going to understand at first-hand what he had been experiencing.

While in Toronto the previous month, Maureen and I had been prospecting various possible sites for a music theatre home. We had looked at the old Music Building in the Exhibition grounds – and discussed a possible conversion with architect Ron Thom. With the blessing of the Toronto Harbourfront Foundation we had also visited a disused building on the waterfront at Bathurst Quay, once a foundry and now known as Loblaw's Warehouse, and wandered several times into the vast, empty, industrial cathedral, where Maureen launched into a Handel aria, and pronounced the acoustics 'superb'. Now, in Aldeburgh, I was particularly interested in the Maltings Hall, converted into a theatre and concert hall by the celebrated Ove Arup Engineers (design engineers for the Sydney Opera House) from its original role as a centre of the local malting industry. Through Arthur I was given an introduction to Arup, and later met with him at his office in London. He expressed interest in our project, and we communicated for a while. But the Foundry Music Theatre was not to be: it was altogether too ambitious a project for our new initiative.

I took advantage of being in Europe to fly to Italy for a visit with my parents. The stay was not happy. As I noted in my diary flying back to England:

20 June.
Twenty days later – days in which I have wanted so many times to pull out this notebook and record a wealth of pleasures – in Aldeburgh, in

London, in Italy. But it is leaving the parents on the station at Bucine that haunts me – the long slow curve that keeps me and them in sight, and before I reach the tunnel Dad has said 'that's enough' and Mum has bowed to him, and they've walked over the line and gone out like a light through the station gate. Always this moment is the tearing one – with them that slight thought that I will not see one of them again, but more that sense of resignation as they get into the car and recommence the lifelong grapple, the binary politics of a marriage of 43 years. Which, I wonder, has the darker thoughts? – Mum, who must cope in solitude again with playing the cracked double bass of Dad's temperament – someone whom you cannot say you love: or Dad, facing that perpetual race between the revelation of his inadequacy, and death – a race he has to hope death will win. Almost no contact this time. I tell them at the last lunch of my debacle over Love's Labor's Lost. And at a pause Dad, leaning over the table to rest his hernia, says 'Mum, do we have any stain-remover?' His revving car-driving exhausts me, and the sweet voluntary helplessness of Mum tears my heart. What a heart she has, while he lives through a glass darkly. Her hunched walk and slight mix of grey in her brown hair the only signs of age, his signs many – the wheeze, the stance, the glaze of eye. Does he begin to face the futility of his recording of temperature, weather, birds and debts in graphs, in diaries, in account-books? The extraordinary lack of easiness I had forgotten – as though embarrassed by casual human contact. Compare Arthur Harrison, 73 and bursting with zest.

Back now to Rome and to Jo: to Paris on Friday, to London on Monday, to Toronto on Tuesday.

On my last night in Rome Jo gave one of her wonderfully international dinner parties, with the usual cocktail of languages:

Claudio, a Brazilian who speaks a private esperanto of his own, French-English-Spanish-Italian: an economist;

Gloria, his wife – about to leave for Mexico to set up a Third World Information Centre;

Mahomet, Moroccan, Director of Information at FAO, quadri-lingual, sharp as a spear, malin, smiling, dangerous;

Carol, his wife, American;

Donatella, Italian;

Franco, Jo and I.

The Moroccan speaks of Arabs and the Moslem and Turkish empires. 1) The Turks gave nothing to the lands they conquered – were always parasitic on the cultures of their subject peoples – Greeks, Moors etc. 2) It was Napoleon when in Egypt in 1803 who first sowed the seed of nationalism in the Arab world: 'You are all Moslems, but you are Egyptians and they are Turks.'

And so to France.

In so many ways so tiresome a place, Paris. So why each time that I'm here do the fireworks explode in my mind? I try, always adumbrating, I try to put the sensation to work. I stare out of my window in the Hotel Colbert at the south façade of Notre Dame to decide why it is and can only be French. It is to do with large masses finely connected. The masses though are formally cut and sliced, giving evidence, unlike say the sculptures of Henry Moore, of a knife bigger than the cheese – and so of a maker holding the knife. English cathedrals have the air of being built from below by an army of pigmies, the French of being assembled from above, the work of a geometric God. And this same confidence in form follows through to Haussmann – throwing up Descartes on the way to set it down on paper...

As I cross Pont Neuf and look west into the sharp silver fish scales of the Seine – it is evening, cloud and breeze – and I watch people crossing the iron footbridge to the west, little figures crawling pleasantly through a skein, flies happily in the divine web. Look, no spider! Again the geometric God.

Jardins du Luxembourg. 6.35 pm. A Sunday evening, my last touch of quiet before London (tomorrow) and Toronto (Tuesday) and heaven help us New York (Thursday or Friday). A day spent at Chartres with Jane Russell's nephew. We tacked on to lectures in morning and afternoon. Mr Malcolm Miller exegeticised four of the windows and the north door. And back with a rush came the emblems and the typology of le moyen age – *Joseph, Melchisadek, David, Solomon as Ur Christs. Ravished above all by Joseph's window in which every incident foreshadows Christ. It was surely not the dogma but the exegesis that held the allegiance of the literati. This elaborate four-dimensional system of interconnections, parallels, allegories, symbolic* gestes. *The falling of that structure was like the falling of a cosmic cathedral of mind.*

In London I was a guest at the home of my friend from Worcester College, Iain Mackintosh, and his wife Jan. (It was here that I noticed that in a discussion all his English friends kept preceding their comments with "I would say..." In what circumstances would they say it? Were they not saying it now? It was a very un-Canadian turn of phrase, and I wonder if it is still part of the English idiom.)

On my final day I was taking an afternoon plane back to Canada, and by previous arrangement was able to meet up that morning with Oren and Juliska Brown, who were paying their first visit to the city and knew nothing of it. I had only a couple of hours, but the gods were with us. After meeting for coffee at Fortnum and Mason, we walked down Piccadilly to Green Park. It was a sparkling morning, and as we strolled through the Park the flowers were riotous and dancing. Approaching Buckingham Palace we found we were there just in time for the Changing of the Guard, which they watched and drank in. I then took them to

Downing Street – which you could still walk along in those days – and just as we came to Number 10, lo and behold! – a cabinet meeting was breaking up, and there was Prime Minister Jim Callaghan and his colleagues on the steps. I finally left the Browns at Westminster Bridge so they could take a boat down the river to Greenwich. In after years they often remembered their miraculous introduction to London.

When I got back to Canada, I discovered that while I had been away a message had arrived inviting me to direct the summer stock production of a four-handed play called *In Praise of Love* by Terence Rattigan. It was to rehearse in New York and then open at the Westport County Playhouse, with a couple more touring dates in New York State. These summer stock productions were often able to snag well-known stars who had their summers free, and I was pleased to find that our leading actor was to be Tammy Grimes. Tammy had made an early name for herself in *The Unsinkable Molly Brown*, and had recently won a Tony Award for her performance in a revival of Coward's *Private Lives*. I had known of her for years as the former wife of Christopher Plummer, and as the delicious, breathy, plaintive voice on a song album owned by Helen Burns. I was happy to sign on.

Before leaving for New York I took part in an important ceremony in Toronto: I became a Canadian citizen. Though I had been now thirteen years in the country as a 'landed immigrant', I had never felt the need to go through the formality of citizenship, since British subjects were entitled to vote in Canadian elections after a year's residency. But this had now changed as part of Britain's entry into the Common Market, and if I was to be a functioning Canadian I had to change with it. For all my forays into the American scene, I was very much content to do so.

As soon as I returned to New York, I met with Tammy at her

brownstone house in the 50s on the West Side. She was quick, sharp, funny, and a little terrifying: I was not particularly encouraged to hear from an acting friend that she had been known to hit or bite her fellow actors, and that she "ate young directors for breakfast". But I had learned something since my *contretemps* with Carole Shelley in 1972, and was determined not to be browbeaten. In the event the rehearsals were good fun and a pleasure. Tammy was used to having her own way as 'the star', but I found myself standing up to her and found she accepted it. She was always ready to take advantage of any perceived weakness, however. On a blisteringly hot August day in the un-air-conditioned rehearsal rooms on Broadway we worked through till mid-afternoon, when I said "I suggest we stop here for the day. It's so hot, and my mind's porridge." As she picked up her things to go, Tammy blew me a kiss and said, "Bye-bye Mr Porridge". It was a name she used again from time to time – even dedicating her first-night present to me with "To Mr Porridge" on the flyleaf. The show opened successfully in Westport, and I saw it through to their second date at the Tappanzee Playhouse on the Hudson River.

I then returned once again to Canada. Through a great deal of lobbying and persuasiveness, Maureen, Gabriel and I had been able to raise $10,000 for a feasibility study of COMUS's prospects: funded by the Floyd Chalmers Foundation, the MacLean Foundation, the Ontario Arts Council and the Canada Council. We now decided to host a public launch of 'COMUS Music Theatre of Canada'. The press conference took place one hot August evening, in the Alberta Room of the Royal York Hotel. Many of Toronto's music leaders and critics were there and were plied with food and drink, along with brave speeches by the three Founders. It was the beginning of an enterprise that would engage and almost engulf me before I was through. It goes without saying that although I was the company's artistic and executive director, there was no salary involved. So my freelance directing career had to continue.

A few days later I received a call: a producer wanted to take *In Praise of Love* to Chicago, to the Arlington Heights Playhouse. Everyone else was available: was I? Yes. There was only one snag: the Arlington Heights Playhouse had an arena stage, and we would have to restage the play in the round.

This was as much as anything a challenge in design, and the producer had his own preferred designer: I was put in touch with him, and for the first time ever found myself conducting major design discussions over the phone, with a designer I had never met. To my surprise I found that he seemed to understand completely my feeling for the London living room that was our set, with its eclectic mixture of antique furniture and ultra-modern plexiglass, book-cases and clutter. He assembled our needs from second-hand stores in Chicago, while we re-rehearsed in New York. When we arrived, we found that his taste, and his feel for the play, was flawless. That designer's name was Neil Peter Jampolis. He was to be my colleague and friend for the next forty years.

As we assembled for the final rehearsal run of the play in Chicago, we realised that Tammy had not returned from lunch. We waited, and she arrived ten minutes late munching a hamburger. We had to start the run immediately, and when it came to her entrance Tammy walked on stage still clutching her lunch, and speaking with her mouth full. I stopped the rehearsal, and said, "You can't do that, Tammy. We'll wait until you've eaten and then start again". This we did. At intermission I went up to her where she was seated beside the stage, and growled "Tammy, don't ever do that again". I said it with mock ferocity, baring my teeth. She looked up and said, "What beautiful teeth you have for an Englishman". A neat deflection, and I couldn't help laughing – she was so quick, and so determined to remain on top. For all her aggressive-defensiveness we remained chums. She was even good enough to put in a good word for me with her agent the fabled Milton Goldman – the only person I have ever seen conducting a meeting with you while simultaneously conversing with two other people on two separate telephones, one in each ear.

While in Chicago I received a phone call from Bob Kalfin, artistic director of New York's Chelsea Theater Center. They were in a fix, and wondered whether I might be able to help them. This was the situation, as Bob told it to me:

A young composer-director had come to them with a unique property called *By Bernstein*, a cabaret-sized musical revue written by the legendary team of Betty Comden and Adolph Green, authors of many Broadway shows, including Bernstein's early musicals *On the Town* (1944) and *Wonderful Town* (1953), and – with Jule Styne – the great musical movie *Singing In The Rain*. Betty and Adolph had had the idea of making use of the 'trunk songs' of their friend and longtime collaborator Leonard Bernstein – songs that for whatever reason had been discarded from his musicals – and incorporating them into a cabaret musical revue. Bob and his colleagues immediately saw the potential of such a titanic line-up of composer and book-writers, and happily put the show into their subscription season. But as the production approached they realised that there were problems: they began to see that the script needed fairly radical work. Unfortunately, when this was put to Betty and Adolph, they replied: 'But Lenny *loves* it', and they would not consider changes. However Lenny confided to Bob that he agreed the script was weak, but that he didn't feel he could possibly say so to his old friends. *Impasse!*

This needed careful handling, and Bob decided that the bright young composer-director whose project it was would simply not be able to exercise enough authority to sort things out. The young director accepted the decision, and agreed to serve as assistant to a more experienced hand. Bob had heard from my agent Joel Pitt that I was a music theatre director, and also that I was maybe sensitive and adroit enough to be able to pull things together. Would I consider the mission? I agreed to come to New York and discuss it with them, and a week or two later I had agreed to take on the project, realising that I was being hired as a diplomat as much as a director.

Rehearsals and performances were to take place in a cabaret-style space – tables and chairs around a small stage – at the Chelsea Theatre Center, a former Baptist church on 43rd St. Auditions were naturally well attended for a show with such credentials, and we were able to select a talented cast of seven, including Kurt Peterson and Patricia Elliott. It was agreed with the producers that we would start rehearsals and then see how the wind lay.

Trouble did not take long to blow up. On the first day we read through the script, and music director Clay Fullum played through the songs. Everyone warmed to most of the music, but the actors were almost incredulous at the clunkiness of the show's book. It's not hard to explain why. Responding to the 'trunk song' motif, Betty and Adolph had set the show in a cafe-bar in New York's Village, with a large trunk in evidence. The bar was called 'The Cafe of Lost Songs', and was run by a philosophical barman who served as the host of the show. How did it work? Well, at the start the sailor Gaby from *Wonderful Town* enters in a wretched state and orders a double martini. The host makes it up for him, but asks him why he is so low. He replies that they have just cut his favourite song out of the musical. "Oh dear," says the host. "Look, why don't you sing it for us now?" "Really? Can I?" "Sure! It's Bernstein Night!" And so Sammy pulls his music out of the trunk, hands it to the band. The introduction starts up and he launches into his song.

It had seemed to me all along – as it had to Bob – that this was a feeble set-up, and one that was incapable of development, since a second character would come in similarly upset, and once again be cheered up by singing his or her number in the Cafe of Lost Songs. Was our actor playing the stage character Gaby, or was he playing the actor playing him? Either way, there was no further use for them after they had sung their song.

I suspected that the actors would have difficulties with what they were expected to do and say, but I hadn't bargained for their almost total rejection of the whole premise of the piece. The lines were so stagey, so artificial, that they more or less refused to say them. I reported back to Bob that evening, and it was agreed we would tell the cast that the script was going to be re-written, and that meanwhile we would concentrate on learning the music. Bernstein – 'Lenny' – would be showing up in a few days, and we would then discuss the whole thing with him in person.

The days went by, the script was set aside, the music was learned. And on the day appointed Lenny strode in, accompanied by a retinue of agent, wife, friends and attractive young chauffeur. Bob introduced us, and then led Lenny to a table, which (on advice) he had prepared by placing on it an expensive bottle of Scotch whisky, a carafe of water, and a glass. Lenny and his entourage sat down. Lenny helped himself to a liberal dose of Scotch, while Clay put the cast through their paces, in both chorus and solo numbers. Lenny seemed reasonably happy with what he heard (though afterwards he insisted to Bob and me that the bartender sang out of tune and must be fired – which he duly was). But then he asked:

"But where's the book? Where's the script? Where's the staging?" This was the moment Bob had been waiting for. We dismissed the cast and stage management, drew chairs up to Lenny's table, and told him the sorry tale: that we knew from the beginning that Betty and Adolph's script – the whole idea of it – was poor and unworkable, but that the writers refused to believe us because they insisted that Lenny thought it was a masterpiece. We had now reached the point when our talented cast simply refused to speak the lines: the whole basis of the 'Cafe of Lost Songs' was simply not viable. The only solution was for Lenny to tell them straight out that he agreed with us that the script did not work, and that the whole thing had to be drastically re-written.

Lenny was torn, but after a few more belts of Scotch he agreed to go to Adolph and Betty that evening. Meanwhile he posed for publicity shots, standing on the piano stool and offering his profile with evident pleasure. He also sat at the piano and gave the cast some musical notes, and I will never forget his playing.

That evening, instructed by Bob, and after dinner with the two of them, I even accompanied Lenny all the way to Adolph's apartment – I suppose in order to be sure he didn't run out on us. Lenny went through with his difficult task, and the immediate crisis was solved. But of course the hard work had only just begun. The next morning I met with Adolph and Betty in their writing nook at the back of the theatre: Betty at the typewriter, Adolph pacing. They were shell-shocked. Betty was on the edge of tears. They then asked the inevitable question: "So what do we do now?" I found myself sitting with Broadway's most distinguished book writers/lyricists, brainstorming possible new approaches, and even proposing new lines. It was the first of several sessions with them.

I remember little of the subsequent going-on. Somehow we cobbled together a re-arrangement of the script, changing it almost daily, with Betty and Adolph reduced to responding to director's and actors' suggestions with new re-writes. Lenny repeated his staged entries two or three times, each time unhappy. For weeks he refused to allow the show to have an official opening with critics, so the first three or four weeks of the limited run were billed as previews. He once sidled up to me and said "Michael, why don't we call the whole thing off? It was a nice idea, but it can't work". I was naturally loyal to the Chelsea, who had sold most of the tickets to their subscription audience and would be put in serious jeopardy by a cancellation. But in my heart I knew the whole thing would never be more than passable. Moreover, with my director's contract long expired, I had other engagements in Toronto and could not continue with *By Bernstein*. So I left it in the hands of Bob Kalfin himself, who continued to tinker with it, and — if I remember — eventually gave it an official opening shortly before it closed. The critics were kind: Clive Barnes called it "exceptionally bright". But I never felt any sense of personal ownership of the piece. There were simply too many hands at work, with too much last-minute improvisation, and always the heavy weight of Lenny's disapproval of the whole venture.

It was not a happy time. But I was fascinated to have had the chance to meet Bernstein, and to watch something of his character at work. I was also honoured to get to know and work with Comden and Green, and we became good friends in the way that theatre folk do in while working on a show. I wrote of the whole experience in my diary:

[I was] strongly opposed to the pathological foxiness of Lenny's attitude. The ineradicable impression remained of his musical and creative brilliance: he sat down at the piano and his hands held the notes as though grabbing, almost eating them. But I remember wondering too about the springs of his

creativeness. The music seems strongly manipulative, always audience-aware, theatrical and dancey, never a chance message from some inner city of thought or feeling. The same is true of many lesser composers, but then the pretensions – the hopes– are not there either: Harry Warren never wrote a symphony. So Bernstein is all dressed up and nowhere to come from. A D.P. of music, a lost child. And his awareness of the lostness, of the trappings of brilliance hiding a hole, is the source of the restless, vain melancholy of the man.

Betty and Adolph I grew fond of, like children but with less Wagnerian aspiration than Lenny, in fact with the attitude of simple wordsmiths plying a trade. They gave me dinner at Sardi's, and we joked and enjoyed. I shall never be able to cope very long with Betty's spikiness under pressure, but the bubbling gag-humour of both of them can be a delight, and watching them together on the sofa, after thirty years' collaboration, I saw a marriage: a testiness of familiarity you see only in old couples.

CHAPTER SEVENTEEN

COMUS MUSIC THEATRE: A SPLASHY LAUNCH

'Harry Warren never wrote a symphony.' So I had written in my diary, as I put together the note of my experience with Leonard Bernstein. But who was Harry Warren? A year or two earlier I would not have known the name. But some time in 1975, in talking to Toronto theatrical agent John Downey, I was told about a musical revue which was being put together by a friend of his, built around the music of this Harry Warren. The friend was Tony Thomas, originally from Wales, who after spending many years in Toronto as a producer and writer with CBC had moved to Los Angeles, where he began a new career as a film historian, putting out book after book about the film industry and some of its celebrities. He had a special interest in music written for the movies, and it was while preparing for his book *Harry Warren and the Hollywood Musical* (published 1975) that he got to know Harry as a personal friend, and to recognise him as one the great American popular songwriters of the mid-twentieth century. Harry wrote many of the hit songs of the Busby Berkeley movies of the 1930s, and won three Oscars for his film songs. But because he wrote only for the film

studios (who automatically owned the rights to his music) he never attained the celebrity of Broadway's musical theatre composer stars like Jerome Kern, Irving Berlin, Cole Porter and Noel Coward. It is by his songs that we know Harry: he had over fifty 'standards' in the universal repertoire. Who of later generations was not familiar with *Lullaby of Broadway, That's Amore, An Affair to Remember, The Girl from Kalamazoo, You're My Everything, Chattanooga Choo Choo, You'll Never Know, Forty-second Street, The More I See You, Shuffle Off To Buffalo, My Million-dollar Baby*, and so on, and so on?

I got to meet Tony Thomas on his next visit to Toronto and he gave me a copy of the show he had compiled, a simple musical revue with four singers, designed for a cabaret stage, and crammed with the best-known songs of the Harry Warren catalogue. I wondered about rights and royalties, but he told me that Harry had in fact bought some of the rights to his songs back from the studios, and that in any case the studios did not control 'small rights', ie rights to perform the songs in non-dramatic situations, on radio or on the concert or cabaret stage. It was these small rights that Harry had made available to Tony.

When I read the revue, I knew it could do with some extensive revision, but I immediately saw its potential for COMUS Music Theatre. If we could start off with a successful piece of popular musical theatre, we would rake in enough money to set us up for the less 'popular' work which we saw as part of our mandate: small operas, modestly-sized musical plays, new and adventurous music theatre pieces, and so forth. My fellow Board members Maureen and Gabriel went along with the plan, and I made a deal with Tony, who was luckily very much open to collaborating on a revision.

So while still nursing *By Bernstein* along, I was also developing ideas for COMUS Music Theatre's first production. This included the question of finance. It was clear that we would not be able to raise the $24,000 we guessed we needed to mount even a small music theatre production. But I was developing the idea of setting up a joint venture, in which COMUS would partner with private investors; COMUS would provide the 'sweat equity' in preparing and mounting the show, financed by the investor group. It was I think a new idea for Canada, with a non-profit organisation entering into a strictly commercial arrangement. But our lawyers could find no problem with it, and plans went ahead. The investors would receive their money back first, and then subsequent profits would be shared 50/50 between them and COMUS.

During this same period I received one day a call from Michael Murray, artistic director of Playhouse in the Park in Cincinnati. Would I be interested in directing Joe Orton's farce, *What The Butler Saw*? Set in a private psychiatric clinic, this was the last play Orton wrote, and had premiered in London in 1969. Yes, indeed, I would be very much interested – especially after reading the play and being bowled over by its manic brilliance. We talked some more, and he arranged to meet me in New York soon afterwards: the play was scheduled to begin rehearsals towards the end of the following January. I was particularly interested to know how Michael had hit on my name, and was gratified to learn that I had been recommended by the designer I had so recently worked with – Neil Peter Jampolis. In fact it was Neil who was going to be my designer for the piece. I could not have been happier.

Meanwhile I returned to Toronto and during the month of December was able to spend a blessed chunk of time at home in Stratford with dear Colin and our gorgeous and aristocratic Afghan, Pushkin. It had been a tumultuous and exciting year for me, and I was very much aware of the slogging tedium that Colin had been suffering in his art history studies at the University of Guelph. He was now in his final year, and just hanging on: he was not a natural writer or even a natural student, with his flitting attention and his impetuous emotions. The only bright spark in his time there was his work in the sculpture studio with his professor John Fillion, who detected in Colin's pieces a real gleam of talent, and who no doubt responded to the beautiful mania of Colin's personality at that time. Another more bewildered professor told him: "You're either an idiot or a genius". He took this as a special compliment.

The New Year began with a flurry of activity that makes me tired just to recall it. Neil Jampolis came up to Stratford for a working visit, and he and I settled on a set for *What The Butler Saw*, inspired by Jacques Tati's film *Mon Oncle*, all shiny and fake, with a fountain on stage turned on to welcome visitors. Back in Toronto I spent a day or two auditioning singer-actors for the Guelph Spring Festival production of *The Beggar's Opera*, and worked with designer Brian Jackson on the *Opera*'s set. We had a COMUS board meeting in the middle of the month, following which I made a quick visit to Guelph to attend Niki Goldschmidt's press conference announcing his 1976 season. I was also able to take a side trip to Niagara to direct the Canadian Brass Quintet in the premiere of a comic 'Horse Opera' called *Hornsmoke*, which they had commissioned from PDQ Bach creator Peter Schickele, who flew in to perform as narrator for the premiere at the Shaw Festival theatre. Somehow along the way I also fitted in a two-day trip to New York to cast the women for *What the Butler Saw*. I had already secured my good Canadian friend Eric House to play the psychiatrist Dr Prentice , and had engaged a bright young actor named Philip Anglim for the male *ingénu* role of Nicholas: it was Philip's first Equity part, for which he was always grateful. (He went on to make his name in the title role of *The Elephant Man* – a play for which he had been astute enough to secure the American rights after he saw it in London. Philip was fresh out of Yale, and enormously handsome, intelligent, warm and witty. We became good friends, and continued in touch for many years.)

Finally, on the 22nd of that hectic month of January, I flew to Cincinnati to begin *Butler* rehearsals. After the furore of the previous weeks it was a blessedly tranquil time; and after the ferocity of the Ontario winter I remember being amazed by our mild and sunny days in the Ohio River Valley.

I like Cincinnati, never cease to get an Italian thrill from watching the hillside of Mount Adams. There is little to do, and no friends to do it with, though young Philip Anglim has been fun to dine with. The play is at its best stage – gone as far as it can go on the rehearsal floor – two runthroughs yesterday, and bounding along. Now we start a week of trials – no Mrs Prentiss for two or three days (she is attending a trial in the UK) and not until Wednesday do we get on to our set. There are 140 entrances and exits in the piece and every one of them has to be accurately timed. It is certainly the funniest play I have ever worked on, but we'll need luck to survive the transfer in time for a Friday preview.

I'm annoyed with myself for having made so little effort to keep these notes going during the fall and winter. And once again a sense of need to write is building. I feel it's time to make thoughtful contributions to the cultural life of Canada. Who has written anything on Canadian theatre which isn't either a) bitchy, b) historical/critical or c) about money? I would like to explore the whole crux of it: what does the theatre of an ex-colonial country do for its living? Who are the leaders? Where the future plans? What are the penalties of regional fragmentation – and the glories? When did you last read anything about it, in fact, which wasn't just politics? Or telling other people what they should be doing? I'd like to give people some ideas and inspirations: create a loosely sketched blueprint for the next years.

J'ai tellement envie de trouver quelqu'un qui... je... je suis tellement fatigué... j'

A night later and the same in English. But readying for the Big Push I am in bed soberly at 2.30 a.m., up in time for a squash lesson at 10.15. Then, at 1 pm, the first time on that splendid stage set. Mon Oncle *rides again.*

February 15. Sunday pm.
On Thursday the sound equipment failed. On Saturday the stage manager stepped into air from a 15-foot platform at the back of the auditorium, and amazingly fell between the seats and was only bruised and cut. That same evening the costume designer had a miscarriage. From some conjunction of Friday the 13th and a full moon sprang these mysteries. The Friday preview was cancelled. Saturday's drew 500 people and more. Only one sound cue misfired. And this afternoon, after another two-hour rehearsal, the play rode high. Tomorrow's a blessed day off – presents for the actors. And Tuesday we open. I think it is very fine.

We opened in a violent rain and thunderstorm, which reduced our first night audience. However, the critics came and were warm in their approval. A few more days to check and tighten things, and it was back to Toronto - overnighting in New York, where I had the rare pleasure of going to theatrical agent Milton Goldman's home for cocktails, joined if you please by Douglas Fairbanks Junior: somewhere I have a photo taken by Milton's partner Arnold Weissburger, to prove the fact! If I had settled in New York I think Milton might have helped shape an American career for me. But I was already loosening my ties to the great city, and developing a new commitment to Canada through COMUS Music Theatre.

My return to Toronto found me up to my ears in moving our fragile company along. I had to report to the Arts Councils and Foundations on our progress with the feasibility study. I had to plan the raising of funds for the Harry Warren show. And most exciting of all I had to arrange a trip to California to work with Tony Thomas and to meet Harry Warren.

I flew to Los Angeles in mid-March, flying via Cincinnati so that I could see one more performance of *What The Butler Saw*:

How happy it was last night to meet with the cast and to go back with them to their house for Scotch and beer, and a delicious omelette cooked for me by Philip. So close to returning home, and they are a family. Eric got cantankerous about being dominated by the set. He later apologised, but got drunker and drunker, talking morosely of suicide. He makes the mistake of regretting, always regretting – even his own words and acts of half an hour before – so he squirms with remorse. He blames his father – a grey, timid failure. Why this shouldn't push Eric to the opposite extreme I can't imagine, but his father's lack of nerve must have coloured every experience during an age of trauma.

Today was quiet – I lay in bed till twelve hoping to still a restless stomach that's been with me since Sunday. Then to my wondrous Acres of Books bookstore for two hours – I bought the second volume of John Rothenstein's autobiography, and also his father's Men and Memories – 2 vols for $7.50 – which I got them to ship back to Canada. Then by bus up to Mt. Adams hoping to catch the last of the matinee – I missed it by a few minutes to hear it was marvellous. Back to the actors' house to see them cooking dinner – four of them in the kitchen, all waiting for their different dinners to be done in the oven – the weirdest spectacle. We fantasised a play about a group of actors who have been playing a family play for some time, and are living together. They even call each other Mum and Dad, and for some time the audience has no idea that they are other than an 'Odd Quintet'.

I flew on to California the next day, and recorded much of my subsequent stay in my diary:

And now in Los Angeles – all asphalt and palm trees at the airport, but then the sudden blush of green grass and shrubs, even under a heavy sky, assaults you like technicolor after the bloodless northern winter. I've just lunched with Tony Thomas, and we shall start work together tomorrow, and visit Harry W. after lunch. Tony's a peasanty little dark Welshman, with a soft voice and a wry understated talk. Hair so black and brushlike I suspected a wig: arching Edith Sitwell eyebrows, and that strange embalmer's rosiness of complexion that happens with no ruggedness of weather. He is embittered in his sardonic way by Canada, and I think with justice, because he's a doer, and has come up against that same grudging of recognition that so bedevils us there. No pleasure in ambitious energy – how opposite from the USA.

March 12th. 9.20 am.
Waiting for breakfast with sun streaming through the windows of the Hollywood Roosevelt, where I am staying on Tony's excellent recommendation.

March 13th. 9.50 am.
Waiting for breakfast downstairs, having slept late after a particularly long and fruitless night of trawling. Yesterday, after a morning's talk with Tony, and a quick lunch together, we drove along Sunset to call on Harry Warren. A Rolls-Royce and Mercedes nestle cosily in the double garage. A pretty garden with pool and blossom. We find Harry in his garden studio. He's getting over 'flu and is feeling weak, but is warm and welcoming. To Tony: 'Someone has been trying to call you and had no luck. I told them you were a bachelor, so were probably out fucking.' 'Would it were true,' muttered Tony. Harry is very short, his face and hands California-blotchy, and wears thick spectacles. His wit is quiet and subtle, but mischievous and continuing. And his face reflects it, sunny and mobile and holding still some of the startling good looks of his youth. Of his music: 'I always thought "That's the end of it, I'll never be able to write another song." But I did – I went

on for thirty years!'

We listen to a turgid tape of the TV version of his Shangri-la [the one stage musical for which he composed the music] *and to many sound-track recordings of the songs we shall be working with. I am confirmed in my feeling that we have a strong piece on our hands... We go into the house and have a drink together. His wife joins us. They have been married over 50 years. He shows me his pictures, enjoying my enjoyment. We sit on a long sofa. Tony asks about the huge Chinese screen on the wall behind the sofa. 'I don't know,' says Harry, 'I've never looked at it. We've had it 20 years.' He didn't want us to go, and we arrange to meet again Monday, to 'mangiare italiano' somewhere. The house is in pleasant unostentatious taste – none of the pictures quite right, given his income – except a Dufy drawing called 'The Mother', hand over brow. The other hand was for me the only Dufyesque feature, made up of those rounded arc-ing curves, almost calligraphic.*

March 14th.
Breakfast again. Yesterday morning Tony and I worked again in the hotel – we engineered a totally new order of songs. Lunch by the pool. And in the afternoon we drive down Sunset to the coast, turn up to Malibu, walk on the fishing pier, have a drink at a crazy horse saloon, and back by the Santa Monica freeway. He leaves me at 5.30 pm and I lie down for a sleep; awake at 10, undress, sleep again till 1 am, read, sleep till 7 am, making up for three five-hour nights.

Tony tells me that Harry has strong likes and hates and is famous for his one-line summaries. When it was announced in the war that the Allies had bombed Berlin, he said 'Yeah, the wrong one.'

...And today after another morning session we took ourselves over to Harry Warren who treated us to Italian lunch at Villa Rosati. Back to Harry's in the afternoon, joined later by Gene de Paul (composer of Lil Abner, Seven Brides and Seven Brothers etc.) who has had in the last six

years two heart attacks, two strokes and a tumour removed from his brain. Only 56. He played the piano occasionally, lifting his right hand (which had been paralysed by the stroke) and clenching it in anger at itself for not obeying his orders. Harry was splendid, alert like a bird.

Story [of Harry's] of the old Lord in his manor-house ringing for the butler, who comes upstairs to find his Lordship in the bath with a huge erection. 'Shall I call for Her Ladyship, my Lord?' 'No no: fetch me my baggy tweeds. I'm smuggling this one into London.'

They talk of the old days in Las Vegas – what fun it was when it was run by the gangsters. It struck me that a film on early Las Vegas was a worthwhile project – the gambling (small and big-time) a splendid paradigm of a jittery age. They described one rich old couple sitting gambling with $100 bills, a security attendant (armed) behind them, and being fed all the drinks they wanted – free of course. Quel image – light on the green baize – a kind of economic jacking-off. The black déprivé watching over.

Tony tells of Harry coming out of the Bel Air club last month saying, 'I'm getting so weak in the knees I can hardly walk. Must be falling apart. I hate to see it happen.' It's this detachment and alertness which is so engaging. 'It Pays Not To Advertise' – his motto.

March 16th.
My last day in California and a heady one. Tony picked me up at 10.00 at the hotel. We work a couple of hours, finishing off the new draft of 'To Harry With Love'. Then a sandwich and a pear, and we're off to the Huntingdon Library at San Marino, Pasadena. I'm not overly excited by the big formal portraits of Gainsborough, Lawrence and Romney – and their imitators. Though 'The Boy In Blue' and 'Pinky' exerted their fascination, and Mrs Siddons too, I couldn't help feeling dutifully 'I am seeing the original' rather than having the experience of seeing a remarkable picture. I found the convention of rich dresses in a shady glade cumbersome and fakey. The Constable 'River Stour near Dedham' is a splendid work,

but the Salisbury Cathedral is not inspired – isn't there another version? And the Turner of the Grand Canal with Shylock clutching his knife and scales did not attract me at all – gingery tones are never my preference. A nice Stubbs 'Baronet with Sam Chetney up'. A Queen-Motherish 'Diana of Hendon'. One of the most startling was the 'head of a young man' of Sebastiano Mainardi. And of course the books – the Ellesmere Chaucer, the Gutenberg bible, the Shakespeare first folio, etc.

And from there out into the garden – sumptuously laid out – Japanese, Desert, Palm, Australian, Shakespeare gardens. A feast.

We left at 3.30 to return to Hollywood for tea with composer Miklós Rósza. He reminds me of someone I can't place. Small, slightly bowed man with drooping navy-blue cardigan, a fine head of grey hair with slavic peak and prominent brow, thick glasses, strong nut-cracking chin. We sit in his castle living-room, surrounded by second-grade Dutch and Flemish masters and some not very distinguished Roman heads. – Notice Marcus Aurelius though, with a mop of curly hair and a plaster nose. His three Oscars – one for Ben Hur, one for Spellbound, one for A Double Life… nestling on a table in front of the fireplace with a bunch of plastic grapes like a mock-offering before them.

The tea is Chinese, excellent, from Fortnum and Mason's. 'One of my little luxuries,' he says: 'the other is San Pellegrino.' This from a man surrounded by treasures on this high hill with his summer home in Santa Margarita. He used often to see Max Beerbohm walking in his white suit, but never spoke to him. 'What would I say?'

He spoke at length of the forger van Meegeren – he suggested to Edward G. Robinson that a film be made of him. But this was 1946 and 'no one was interested in painters…' I think he's right.

We talk of Toscana, of Munich ('one of the beautiful cities of the world') He has charm and knowledge and a splendid clutter of pleasant things – a little too much chosen for age rather than beauty – the result of European homesickness perhaps. It was difficult to believe sitting there looking out through the cypresses at the blue hillside the other side of the valley that down below, out of sight, was the Hollywood Freeway. Just before we left, he showed us his autographs. He has most of the famous musicians of the nineteenth century – Mendelssohn, Wagner, Liszt, Brahms, Debussy, Ravel, Puccini, Verdi spring to mind, as also GBS and Max. A pleasant John nude, a Rodin nude – watercolour; and some Durer and Rembrandt and Cranach engravings that I didn't much enjoy. We leave after six – he opens the gate and waves farewell. 'Come again.'

I returned to a torrent of work in Toronto. I had to write out and design an investor's memorandum for the Harry show – now for the moment called *Harry Who?* – to be ready for a Backer's Presentation at the beginning of April. There was work still to be done in preparation for *The Beggar's Opera*, due to start rehearsing later in April. And to stress things still further we had decided – with Colin's degree program at Guelph nearly completed – to make the move from Stratford to the city. I had been prepared to rent or sublet - in fact I was just moving now for six weeks into the apartment of Raymond O'Neill, who had been one of my fine servants in *She Stoops To Conquer* at Stratford. But Colin was determined we should buy. We had already scouted out a shabby old townhouse on Gerrard Street East, and now put an offer on it ($55,000 if I remember), knowing that if the offer were accepted we would have to say goodbye to our lovely Stratford place. It was, and we did, although we did not make the move until July.

So began a period of extraordinary stress, which as I recall it wakens nightmares even now. The events and episodes of the rest of that year swim in and out of my memory. But first I must briefly record a momentous evening spent with two dear, dear friends –

Helen Burns and Michael Langham:

Strange the night before last – stranger than strange – to be sitting at dinner with Michael – and Helen – who themselves had met the night before for the first time for four years. We had a leisurely and fine dinner at the Auberge Gavroche, and I felt impelled to pay for it. And all the time it was being on a ship where random electrons of people are briefly captured. It was a dream of ten years ago – endless eye-meets and laughs – and again now other laughs and talk about ourselves. We looked occasionally in astonishment, frowns and smiles mixed, at one another – at least not Michael, but Helen and I – Michael performing calm, but agitated inside.

Michael's marriage to Ellen Gorky had become increasingly unliveable (though still perfectly good-tempered), and Ellen had gone to settle in California. At some point after that, Helen had been in touch with Michael, and they had begun a correspondence. Now, finding themselves both in Toronto, they had met. Though we none of us knew it at the time, their friendship and their love would blossom in the next years, and in 1978, ten years after they split up, they would be remarried in the presence of their son, daughter-in-law and grandson.

Memories jostle together:

– Our Backer's Presentation for COMUS took place in late April. I spoke with my astonishing confidence and determination, and Maureen sang Harry Warren's *Chattanooga Choo Choo*. We were pleased to raise as much as half of the investment money we needed...

– I rehearsed *The Beggar's Opera* with a talented and agreeable cast, led by the splendid Judith Forst as Polly Peachum and Emile Belcourt as Macheath, and with Calgary singer Alex Gray as Lockit. I recalled only recently that the elderly actor cast as the Beggar could not remember his spoken lines, and that we finally had to release him, with the result that I had to stand in for him, just a day or two before we opened for our two performances at Guelph. The critics were pleased, though aware of the limitations of the high school auditorium where we played: "Michael Bawtree moved his players with considerable skill to avoid cramping the stage." The production went on tour to Montreal and Ottawa. I accompanied it and directed the restagings – the Beggar by this time replaced by my friend Eric House.

With the stresses of our forthcoming Harry Warren production I remember little of all this. But I do recall a fateful meeting following the Guelph premiere. Alex Gray (our Lockit) served as head of the Musical Theatre summer program at the Banff School of Fine Arts in Alberta, and had been looking for a director for the program's 1977 production of *Gigi*. During our rehearsals he developed the idea that I might fill the bill, and so had invited the director of the School's arts programs, Neil Armstrong, to attend the performance, and to meet me afterwards. At that meeting the possibility of my working at Banff in 1977 was raised, and within a month or two I had been contracted. I had little idea that this one meeting would change the course of my life – and of Colin's…

– One very full day in July we drove down to Stratford, and within an hour of arriving had sold our duplex on Birmingham Street to our tenant, for $49,000. We packed up some of our furniture and belongings, drove back, took possession of our house on Gerrard St., picked more things out of storage in our real estate agent's basement and dumped them back in the house, until at midnight we dossed down on a mattress in the middle of the living room surrounded by the accumulated mess. Somehow our beautiful Pushkin was with us through all this, and gracefully adapted to his new home.

But the major life event of that year of 1976 was the effort to mount COMUS's first production, and to that we now turn.

There was little precedent at that time in Toronto for mounting a 'commercial' show: theatres were almost all non-profit affairs, dependent on charitable donations, and on subsidies from the Ontario Arts Council or the Canada Council, to keep their doors open. COMUS, on the other hand, was a non-profit company entering into a commercial production venture with a group of private investors. During the summer we worked at finding the balance of the $35,000 which we had now determined we needed to mount the production, by this time renamed *Harry Who?*. Some of my investors were friends and acquaintances. Maureen Forrester and Doug Annett brought in some, I sweet-talked others, and somehow all the money was raised by mid-June.

A critical question was still to be answered. Where could we mount the production? Like any New York venture, it was going to have to run long enough to make money, which meant that its run had to be open-ended. This immediately put most of the city's theatres out of consideration. There was one empty theatre though, known as the Bayview Playhouse. It had been bought some years earlier by one of Toronto's real estate czars, David Mann, who had converted it from its original cinema format into a working theatre with small stage and orchestra pit, and 400 seats. He had done this in order to make a working space for his son Peter, who was a composer of film and television music. Peter however seemed to have little interest in the project, and as a result the building had languished and been closed for the last two or three years.

The Bayview seemed a possible answer to our needs, and I was able to set up a lunch with David Mann at his favourite restaurant Murray's, at Yonge and St. Clair. We were not long into our chicken pot pie before I realised that I was dealing with a very tough customer indeed. David's interest was certainly piqued by our project, and especially by its commercial aspect. He had not heard of Harry Warren, but he was of a generation that had been brought up on Harry Warren's 'standards', and knew them all. He saw that here was a very real possibility of creating a success, and within a day or two we arranged to meet at the Bayview theatre. Maureen came with us, impressing David further, and certainly adding *cachet* to our enterprise.

The space was adequate, though the backstage area was minimal. It would do.

Then came discussion of the terms. We wanted to set up an open-ended lease, to accommodate a potential run of our show. But David dismissed this idea: he would not rent the theatre to us for less than a year. Second, he set a high rental fee, though I now forget the figure. But third, and most controversial, he insisted that he would only rent us the space if we agreed to appoint his son Peter as the production's music director.

To say that I was getting out of my depth would be an understatement. But David was cannily aware that we had no alternative up our sleeve. It was arranged that Peter and I should meet. Peter was affable enough, though very much his own man: a self-taught musician with a strong jazz interest, he came out of quite another world from mine. He showed some interest in our project, though I was aware that he had initially been persuaded (bullied?) into it by his father. I left him a copy of our latest script. Within a few days, it was clear that he was taking up the idea in a big way: when I met him again, I found he had already begun to conceive a much more elaborate show. It was certainly exciting, and at some point I had to accept that Peter would be our collaborator and called Tony Thomas in Los Angeles to tell him of our situation, getting his rather bemused blessing.

Peter and I then sat down together to map out a whole new scenario, setting our seven-member cast in New York in the early 1930s, then having them travel west in search of work after the depression, and finishing up in Hollywood. The first section allowed us to use Harry's New York songs like *Lullaby of Broadway*, *42nd Street*, *Fifth Avenue* and *Lulu's Back In Town*, and then the *Gold Diggers* songs like *We're in the Money*. The travel westward opened us up to the railroad songs: *Chattanooga Choo Choo*, *The Atchison, Topeka and the Santa Fe* and *Shuffle Off to Buffalo*. A night in the desert gave us *That's Amore* and other open country songs. And with their arrival in Hollywood we could complete the Harry Warren canon. The company's shifting personal relationships throughout gave us opportunities to fit in many of Harry's most famous love songs, like *Million Dollar Baby*, *The More I See You*, *You'll Never Know* and *An Affair to Remember*. Altogether, the scenario made some use of over fifty of Warren's numbers. Though very much a contemporary musician with an intimate knowledge of rock and roll, Peter was also a film buff, and his knowledge of – and admiration for – Harry's music came from his interest in the movies of the 1930s and 40s, and the fact that Harry had written songs sung by Judy Garland, Bing Crosby, Gene Kelly and Frank Sinatra. It has to be said that Peter was a fine collaborator, imaginative and inventive, and that with my theatrical experience and ability with dialogue we made, I believe, quite an effective writing team. As his involvement became greater I also realised that I was taking on not only Peter but also his father, who got us together at his apartment one evening to insist that *Harry Who?* was a negative title. I can't remember who finally came up with it, but we settled on *Harry's Back In Town!* – clearly a far more lively and hustling name for our show.

When it came to auditioning singer-actors, Peter's knowledge of the music and television scene was also invaluable. The famed

Toronto production of *Godspell* had played for some months at the Bayview Playhouse two or three years earlier, and Peter had become friends with some of its talented cast, including Victor Garber, Martin Short and Andrea Martin. Victor and Andrea were unavailable, but we were happy to sign on Martin Short, still barely at the beginning of his illustrious career in show business. We also brought in Marc Connors from the singing group *The Nylons*; Nora McLellan, fresh from the Shaw Festival, Judy Marshak, Ruth Nichol, Michael Fletcher, and the splendid African-Canadian dancer-actor Len Gibson – well on in his career but still with splendid gifts as a tap-dancer and as our choreographer.

We had also hired a business manager, a gentleman called Peter Hanley, who was introduced to us by Doug Annett. He seemed enthusiastic and assured, and keen to help.

Meanwhile, our stage design was beginning to run us into trouble. Wanting a 'New York' look, I had asked my new friend Neil Peter Jampolis to design the show, and he had accepted, but then had to withdraw. He recommended another young and emerging New York designer called David Mitchell, who accepted the contract. David engineered a brilliant but very complex set, depending for its changes on the use of five projectors hidden above and behind the proscenium, projecting back on to mirrors which would cast the projected images on to the back of a rear-projection panoramic screen. I knew at once that this would involve us in all kinds of extra expense, but it was too late to turn back.

On the first day of rehearsals, with the cast assembled, we introduced our company to the show. Obviously the whole motivation for the show's creation was the music of Harry Warren, so it was something of a shock to realise only that day that for all his musical gifts, our musical director was quite unable to read music! In the end it was I, the stage director, who sat down at the piano and played through most of the numbers.

Our trials grew and multiplied. I had all along assumed that as musical director Peter would be in charge of all musical rehearsals. But it was immediately evident that we would have to hire a rehearsal pianist. The budget was already strained but there was nothing for it, and we were soon joined by a competent keyboard man. (It has to be said that with the support of the accompanist Peter showed his brilliance in improvising vocal arrangements of the songs, and ran group rehearsals with great competence and assurance.)

The next problem arose when Peter decided that the four pit musicians we had budgeted for were not enough, and we would have to have a minimum of seven. I assured him that we simply couldn't afford to do this, however desirable. But Peter insisted that we simply could not make enough of an impression without the larger group. And that evening I received a call from Peter's father to say that if we did not enlarge the band as Peter requested he would not let us have the theatre. We had of course completed a contract with him for the rental of the building, but he had not yet signed it. He had us, as they say, over a barrel. There was no alternative but to give in, though it was to add $1000 a week to our running expenses.

Hard on this discovery came the news that Peter would not be able to write the orchestral arrangements of the music. My assumption had been all along that Peter would undertake this in his role as Music Director – but no, we would have to find someone else. We were extremely lucky to be able to engage the eminently capable Jerry Toth (first arranger of the 'Hockey Night in Canada' theme, among much else) to take on the work at very short notice. It was to cost us a cool $5,000 that was not in the budget.

Meanwhile, our appointment of Peter Hanley as our Business

Manager turned out to be a mistake. Peter was something of a romancer, and talked proudly of the small collection of vintage cars he kept at some garage north of Toronto. For all this he was strangely short of money, and at one point I foolishly lent him $2,500. In the first or second week of rehearsal, when we were already installed in the Bayview and trying to come to terms with Peter Mann's expensive demands, Hanley came up to me in the lobby one afternoon with tears in his eyes, handed me his keys, and said he was leaving. It soon turned out that he had been keeping absolutely no record of our financial situation – the books were blank. When they were taken over and brought up to date, we found we were in a very tight financial corner indeed, and would be lucky to be able to pay our actors up to the first night. (I continued for over a year to pursue Peter for the repayment of my personal loan, but without success.)

And now, as we started putting our designs together, the technological demands of David Mitchell's set were beginning to overwhelm our technical director. We just did not have the equipment or the expertise to line up the mirrors at the precise angle that was needed to project accurately - the slightest degree out of true and they would mess up. Then in the midst of these anguished technical efforts David was suddenly called back to New York: he had just landed the design contract for a new musical called *Annie*. (Incidentally the producers of *Annie* had the resources to ensure that David's same complex projection arrangement was made to work, and helped to seal the musical's remarkable success. We all felt that poor COMUS had been used as the unwilling guinea-pig.)

By now we were in serious trouble. We were running out of money, and fast. I shared our problems with Peter Mann, whose demands had generated a good part of the mess we were in. But I was unprepared for what came next. The following day David Mann asked for a meeting with me, told me that he knew of our difficulties, and advised me that he was preparing to take over the show lock, stock and barrel. He wanted to separate COMUS completely from the project, and said my services as director would no longer be needed. When I had recovered from my astonishment I told him that this could not happen without the permission of my investors – whom he was preparing to dump unceremoniously, so that they would lose their whole investment in the process. He asked for a meeting with them, at which he would make his proposal.

It will be obvious to any reader of this sorry tale that I must now have been in a serious state of panic and dismay. It was worse than that: I was in the early stages of a complete nervous breakdown. Everything that could have gone wrong was going wrong. I had a momentous failure on my hands. My optimism, my articulate assurance, my confidence that all problems were soluble, had crumbled. I began taking a drop of whisky with my breakfast. And driving up to the theatre each day, I found– not for the first time in my life – that I would dream of driving into a tree. I had no desire to kill myself, but simply to put myself in hospital and so be removed from the hornets that were now swarming around me.

It's worth recalling that my personal life was also under stress in another way at that time. One evening I received a call from a friend whom I will call Joseph. A day or two earlier, thinking he must be going mad, Joseph had signed himself into the Clarke Institute, Toronto's mental hospital. But he was now feeling much better, and from something his live-in girl-friend had said to him, he guessed that she might have put Speed into his food 'to cheer him up', and that was why he had been turning crazy. To sort all this out in his mind he had stepped out of the Institute that afternoon and gone for a coffee in a little place opposite the hospital. He had not been there long when two men in white coats entered the café and forced him back into the institution, where he was at once 'committed'. He was now no longer there voluntarily. In a subsequent interview with a psychiatrist, he told her that he had finally worked out what his trouble had been – that he had been given Speed by his girlfriend. Unfortunately this story was simply seen as evidence of serious paranoid delusion, and the staff had now decided that he should receive shock treatment the next day. "Michael, I beg you, you've got to get me out of here! If I get shock treatment my life will be ruined!"

I told Joseph to get hold of his doctor. But he had only recently moved to Toronto, and had no doctor. I told him I would try to do something, and immediately went to see my own doctor and told him the situation. He was splendid. He got in touch with the hospital and managed to talk to the head physician, who talked to the psychiatrist. The psychiatrist then phoned to me to say, in her ominously sinister South American accent, that she was very reluctantly turning Joseph over to my care, and that I would have to come to the hospital and sign a document accepting full responsibility for his behaviour. This I did, and that evening Joseph came back to live with us for some weeks, even following us to our new house when we moved in. He was still shaky from his experience, but he has told me since on many occasions that I had saved his life.

Colin meanwhile had decided to apply to the Ontario School of Education, and rather to his surprise was accepted for the fall term. Poor fellow, he found that one of the two people he was living with had recently gone bananas, and the other was moving rapidly the same way. Every evening he would precede our supper with a grace, asking for help with our multiple problems. Evening followed evening, and the graces would get longer and longer, while our meal grew colder and colder. And then one evening, as Joseph and I braced for what had become a five-minute prayer, Colin said "O Lord…" he paused, and finally came out haplessly with "Help us get our shit together." There were not many laughs in those dog days, but this was certainly one of them.

With our continuing financial crisis, David Mann's request for a meeting with the investors had to be honoured. I got in touch with each of them and told them what was afoot, and on the appointed evening we all met in a room above the theatre. I outlined the financial problems of the production, and made it clear that we would need to double the amount of funding we had already secured. I then told the investors that David wanted to speak to them about a way to rescue the situation, and handed him the floor. David outlined the proposal he had made to me.

There was silence when he had finished. One or two of the investors asked for clarification, and David made it quite clear that COMUS and I would be out of the picture. Silence again. And then one investor spoke up. She was outraged, she said. She and the rest of them had come into this venture out of friendship for Michael and Maureen, and to support a really exciting project. This was their show – and David was now proposing to take it out of their hands. It was intolerable. Since the whole problem was a question of money, she was quite prepared to double her stake in the show, from $5,000 to $10,000. She stopped there. But to my amazement the investors all spoke up and agreed, one after the other, to double their stakes. They would have nothing to do with David's proposed take-over. This was their show, and they would not allow Michael to be pushed out of it.

I can still remember the swell of gratitude and relief that followed this turn of events. David was clearly taken aback by the group's loyalty to me, and soon retired from the field. The risk of collapse had been averted. But of course we were not by any means out of trouble, and our business manager had decamped. One of the investors, an accountant, then offered to take over the finances until we could find a replacement, and his offer was warmly accepted. The legal details of the new investment were then gone through. Perhaps cheques were even written that very night; I don't remember.

I also had an artistic crisis to deal with. Faced with our vertiginously multiplying financial and technical woes and living on less and less sleep, I had been finding it increasingly difficult to function as director of the show, and was frankly fumbling from one day to the next. Many times I was called out of rehearsal to field another curve ball, and the production's needs had once again to take a back seat. I was also trying, not quite successfully, to shield the cast from the truth of the situation, and in my wretched state I had the acute sense that they were beginning to trust more in Peter Mann than myself: after all, he must have been very much aware of his father's attempted *putsch*, and even behind it. Having no doubt known of the plan to oust me, he now had to carry on working alongside me. It has to be said that he was professional in this, but it was clearly a tense and unpleasant situation.

It was in this state that I decided to call on my friend Jeremy Gibson to join me as my assistant director. Jeremy happened to be in Toronto and available, and was happy to help, refusing to take any kind of fee. His presence in rehearsal was a godsend for me, and I was slowly able once again to take hold of the show, which in spite of everything was beginning to come together in a very promising way. Jeremy's sharp eye was everywhere, and with him beside me I started slowly to believe in myself once again.

Somehow things began to knit. A solution was found for our

design snarl-up. We hired the splendid Helga Stephenson (later to head up the Toronto International Film Festival for many years) as our publicist. A fine poster was created. Advertisements were placed. A box-office manager was brought in. Tickets were being sold, bringing in much-needed revenue. The musical arrangements were delivered. The orchestra was hired – and there came that wonderful dress rehearsal day when all seven of them joined our pianist in the pit and brought the music heart-stoppingly alive. We even managed to find the funds to fly Harry Warren and his wife over from California for the premiere.

The show opened in the first week of October. The house was full, both of our investors and all their friends, of many invited guests, and a good smattering of general public. The response was warm: "A fashionable and critical first night audience jumped to its feet in an immediate spontaneous standing ovation when the curtain fell the other night on *Harry's Back in Town*, the long awaited new musical at The Playhouse Theatre ... The show is a knockout . . ." (*Toronto Telegram*). And when the diminutive Harry Warren walked on to the stage to take a bow at the end of the show, the crowd cheered for three or four minutes. "You know, Michael," he told me afterwards, "That's the first stage bow I have ever taken in my life." He was ecstatic. Having written all his songs for the movies, and got used to seeing his name in tiny print at the end of film credits, he was suddenly the hero of the hour.

The reviews were in general equally positive, and the telephone began to ring off the hook. Out of the jaws of hell we had plucked what looked like a success.

In the first weeks that followed our opening, audiences continued to flow in and our optimism was high. But it was not long before *Harry*'s strained finances began to take up more and more of our attention. Commercial theatre, after all, has two financial goals. The first is to raise the funds to be able to prepare and mount a production. The second is to meet the weekly 'nut': to take in enough revenue at the box office to cover the weekly expenses *and* to begin to pay back the original production outlay. With our crisis re-financing in September we had managed to mount the production. But our weekly expenses, swollen above all by our enlarged band, were just barely covered by the sale of tickets in a good week. This was where we needed the ruthless hand of a commercial manager, who would care far less about the artistic values of the show than about the bottom line: someone who had the authority to tell Peter and his father to go to blazes, and who would cut and cut – without totally destroying the show – until the situation could be brought into line. New York was full of such people, but Toronto was not. We eventually took on Gary Goddard as our Business Manager, and he did his best. But 'the nut' remained elusive.

Colin, who was unhappy all fall with his studies at the School of Education, was also having to cope with my bouts of despair. His support and encouragement were tremendously valuable to me, but I often asked myself whether my ambitious plans with COMUS had been pursued at the cost of our relationship and our life together. I will go further and say that for one reason or another Colin's moods had been becoming increasingly difficult and even mean-spirited during all this time. There were still wonderful moments of fun and happiness, but there were moments when everything suddenly changed and he became red in the face, manically angry, and even physically violent. I endured these episodes, but was terribly saddened by them, wondering why they came on so unpredictably, and how our loving relationship might survive them. Our Christmas was a strained affair. The dog

Pushkin, like a shared child, played his endlessly sweet-natured part in keeping us together.

Meanwhile the ghost of *Harry* continued to haunt us. It had done good business through the fall, reaching an amazing climax in the weeks before Christmas and into the New Year. But then came January with its wintry weather. With all our tapped-out citizens recovering from their holiday extravagances, audiences fell off drastically, and by the middle of the month there was no alternative but to give our performers and our staff their notice. My diary was neglected these many months, but I note one forlorn entry:

A long gap again, while I have contemplated suicide, died several hundred deaths, lived (lived?) through enough crises, horrors, counter-crises, counter-horrors, to drain a shallower swamp. Now February 1st, 1977, and the flotsam and jetsam stays only in the memory while I battle with after-mathematics: $39,000 or $51,000 in the red, what's in $10,000?

Yes, the show was over. Our investors had not been repaid a penny, and though they went into it fully prepared to lose their money, I continued to be deeply remorseful about this because many of them had become my friends. On top of this we still had seriously unpaid bills. Worst of all, we were still contracted to operate the Bayview Playhouse for another eight months, and to pay our weekly rental to David Mann. It seemed that the nightmare was to continue forever.

Details of the next months are hazy. Somehow I was able to find producers – including the composer-producer David Warrack – who were prepared to mount shows at the theatre, and we continued running it until June, when we finally informed David Mann that we could go no further. David knew our situation and realised there was no point in coming after us for the remainder of the rent. He changed the locks on the theatre that same day, and I don't think I ever saw him again.

One great joy in these months of anxiety and stress was that my friendship with Maureen Forrester stayed constant. She never upbraided me for the difficulties that *Harry* had got us into. In fact early in the New Year she said that we needed to get up on our feet immediately, and offered to be available for a re-staging of *The Medium*, which had first brought us together at Stratford in 1974. This was a noble offer indeed. We succeeded in renting the Edward Johnson building at the University of Toronto for dates in June, and started to apply for grants to make it possible. Neil Jampolis agreed to design the stage set, and Susan Benson to revise her costumes. Stratford agreed to lend us whatever we needed from the original production. We were in business again.

My summer foray with the Banff School of Fine Arts was also beginning to take up time. I had been flown out for a weekend in November to join meetings of the 1977 summer staff. I was also able to sit down in Toronto with the music director of Banff's summer musical theatre program, who was none other than the highly distinguished Canadian band-leader, conductor and arranger Howard Cable. Howard's easy professionalism and genial manner was irresistible, and it was immediately clear that we would get along.

Then, early in February, I took off for a country-wide audition tour with faculty from Banff's Musical Theatre, Opera, Drama and Music programs, to select students for our summer sessions. The tour, well organised and advertised in advance, flew us from Halifax through Montreal and Toronto, Winnipeg, Regina and Vancouver, finishing in Banff. My fellow auditioner for Musical Theatre was our dance teacher Joyce Gray (wife to Alex), and together we were able to audition well over a hundred young singer-actors aged between 16 and 24, choosing from them just 36 successful candidates. The whole caper was an extraordinary pleasure. It was my first experience of Banff's bringing together artists from different disciplines, and our little team of auditioners, eating and drinking in a group as we moved across the country, became good friends. Besides, I have always enjoyed holding auditions, particularly with the young. I still get a real thrill out of seeing each new prospect: cheering up and encouraging the terrified, advising the hopeless, applauding the talented. It was a privilege to meet these young folk from all over Canada, so full of hope and doubt, and so keen to follow a life-dream. The Banff summer school, which had been in existence since 1932, had clearly established itself in the minds of talented young Canadian artists as the place to be.

There was another particular reason for enjoying this swanning cross-country journey: for the first time since Stratford I was able to forget my endless and often agonising search for money and instead concentrate on deploying my artistic skills. It was amazing to me that such an expensive ten-day tour, involving six or seven faculty from four departments, flying from city to city and staying in the best hotels, was effortlessly bank-rolled by the Banff School. It was my first experience of the School's easy way with funds – but by no means the last.

Back in Toronto I had once again to take hold of the COMUS situation. One possible way through was to try and get an American producer to mount the show in New York. I paid several visits to the city, and once even to Boston to follow up a possible lead. None of these efforts was successful. Meanwhile we applied to the Ontario Arts Council for a one-time grant of $50,000 or so, to be able to dig ourselves out of the hole we were in. I can't even remember whether we received it, but I guess not; our troubles seemed to continue.

Some time that year we also brought in a new administrative director, Jane Holland. A fairly recent immigrant from England, Jane was highly intelligent and an extremely hard worker. She brought some much-needed stability to COMUS, for all its financial stresses. Later in the year we also hired the talented singer Billie Bridgman, on a six-month apprentice contract, as an assistant to myself. These were both good appointments, and Billie was to stay with COMUS for several years, becoming a close friend and succeeding me as artistic director. Her wit was a great tonic in those stressful times: after one of our more than usually manic days at the office, her version of Descartes' pronouncement "I think, therefore I am" kept us laughing for days:

"I see myself ceasing to exist
Therefore I was."

For our production of *The Medium* we started by trying to reassemble the cast that had performed so successfully in Stratford three years before. They were not all available, and our replacement for Mr Gobineau was a handsome young baritone called Gino Quilico. It was his first professional opera engagement, for which he had to join Actors Equity. He sang and acted beautifully. He was of course to go on to be one of Canada's most distinguished singers, performing at the Met, Covent Garden, La Scala and almost everywhere else.

Our four performances were well reviewed, both Maureen and the production receiving splendid notices. But these were summer nights in the hot city, and we were unable to fill the large house. We established COMUS as a continuing force, but lost a few more thousands in the process. Life as Canada's first music theatre company was still hard, it seemed.

Colin's year at Ontario Teachers' College was finally over in May, and he had emerged with a Bachelor of Education degree. He had not had a good time, having fallen out early on with his supervisor, who appeared to be something of a racist and misogynist. When Colin told him that he would like to concentrate on elementary school teaching, the man simply snorted and said: "Women's work". He made some applications to schools, and was offered a private school position, which with its paltry salary he turned down. But when our friend John Sime, founder and director of 'Three Schools of Art', offered him an acting course at the school, he readily took it, and at once found himself in his element. John went on to engage him for more courses in voice as well as acting, helping him to begin his slow climb to distinction as an acting and voice teacher. The one teaching aid he had taken away from Teachers' College was the need to create a 'lesson plan' before every class. He did this religiously for the rest of his career, though often neither looking at it nor following it once the class was in progress. Colin was totally energised by his classes, and his wild yet centred approach won him many adherents. But outside his work he continued to have bouts of near madness, which put us both under strain; it was to be another few years before we were able to trace the problem to its source. Meanwhile it was not surprising that both of us continued to look elsewhere for pleasure and calm. Yet he was even more furious when I left on my many trips away. It seemed that the brutal loss of his parents still made him so ready to feel abandoned, and so full of seething, vituperative anger. I was caught, spell-bound, by both the power and the stress of my love for him as a human being. It was some time around then that I wrote in my diary:

Who could ever tell the wonder of Colin, whom I have known and not known for ten years, who stands like a tower of white flame, who is shining water and priest of darkness, who is a child and witch and panther, beside whose bloody and sweet will mine turns to the foggiest dew?

Somehow that difficult spring and early summer passed by, and I found myself looking forward more and more to my sojourn in the mountains. I had also picked up something from Howard Cable in his chat with me: he had told me that the air in Banff is so pure that when a car goes past you can smell its exhaust for a whole minute afterwards. I had been wanting to put an end to my smoking habit for years now. I decided that I would stop the day I left for Banff.

The day came. Colin drove me to the airport, where I left him waving goodbye with a huge sense of sadness and loss – on both our parts.

It is July 3rd, 1977, and another notebook. And again written in air, this time between Toronto and Calgary, bound for six weeks in Banff, and the day of a new turning. I can't remember when I last recorded something this way – perhaps a few scribbles in New York before or after Christmas. Nothing since then, certainly.

But then it has been the same with letters, with friends, with everything that has not been part of the struggle to hold on to COMUS. And still the struggle limps on – I believe I have left behind me some possible new directions, but still money is being its evasive self. So these six weeks are simply furlough, no less welcome for that.

With the journey, as so often with my journeys, I make as I say a new turning. The 18-month fight has made me careless of myself – of anything that is not 'the cause'. Smoking has become an unthinking habit, eating irregular, exercise non-existent. Now as we nose towards the Rockies, I can smell already those pines on the cold high air that I remember from the Troodos mountains in Cyprus, and call back now with Proustian trails of people and times. And I resolve to be a mountain monk, to live a St. Jerome, to put back together my abused bod, to write my daily piece and letters too, and generally to be impossibly good.

Writing here reminds me how long I have written nowhere but in letters, reports and applications on behalf of that perverse organization of mine. The words now cumber and clot. So a new day and a new light air each day, as I rise with dawn and write first by candlelight, in my horsehair robe watch the eastern rim, mutter prime and clutch at the cross on its stone wall, and write, and break off black bread and bless it, and write as I eat – hungrily – and eat as I write.

I have become more and more irked in Toronto at my lack of friends – no, I have friends, but I seem never to be part of a society of friends. Directors are busy being generals – does this make for friends?

How much it has to do with my life with Colin is another question I find hard to tackle. There is an incipient infantilism in our loving life together: like the squirrels at the end of 'Look Back In Anger' we turn our backs on the world outside. This is as evident to C. as to me and we have in the last week discussed more seriously the possibility of breaking our 11-year liaison. There is this anti-societal thrust of our lives; and then there is the sheer competitive difficulty of sharing a life in which both wish to shine, or at least to make light waves, and where each to some point hampers the other. Marital partnership – at least of the old-fashioned kind despised by the newspapers – offered a system of complementary support. I sometimes think how much more I could do in the lap of such a luxury, casting myself immediately of course in the role of bread-winner not bread-maker.

– After months I suppose I am bound to pick up my threads of consciousness with a piece of self-embroidery.

So, as once again I headed west on a new venture, with Canada's waters and uplands unrolling far beneath me, I found myself reviewing all that I had accomplished since I had sailed into Montreal fifteen years earlier. There was much to be proud of, much to be thankful for. There was also, it seemed, a disquietingly recurrent theme in my recent professional life. This was now the third time that I had gallantly put out to sea with all sails flying, only to see the ship beginning to founder beneath my feet. Was there some defect in my character that led me to launch breezily into grand projects and then find myself adrift? There was no doubt I was a risk-taker: my vivid imagination could see the excitements ahead; and I was able again and again to communicate that excitement to others, getting them to see what I saw, with a steady tenacity that brought me friends, allies and supporters. But somehow on these separate occasions I had not won through: each time I had got myself into a state of *angst* beyond bearing. Why was this? Was I accident-prone? Bad at forcing my will against opposition? Or so blind to danger that I ploughed into the thick of things without even contemplating failure? They were questions I would continue to ask myself in Banff as I moseyed towards my fortieth birthday. I wondered whether I might have inherited my father's abiding fear of failure. It has taken me a long time to embrace the fact that failure goes hand-in-hand with adventurousness, and that all I needed was to develop the capacity to lick my wounds and pick myself up again for the next fray.

Yes, I saw my summer in Banff as a chance to do just this. There was no way I could have known, as we thrummed westward and I smoked my last cigarette ever, that in fact I was heading by slow degrees to a major shift in my life, to a place where – both for Colin and myself – our gifts and temperaments would find a happy home for the next years. The story of our decade among the mountains of Alberta, followed by yet another trek back cross-country to plant our home for the last quarter of a century beside the oceans and bays of Nova Scotia, will have to make its way into a final volume. The rough and tumble of our life in the sixties and seventies gave way at last to opportunities for exciting creative work within institutions, with their comfortable financing – though often uncomfortable politics. And near the close of it all a great grief, as the redoubtable, the one and only Colin 'moved softly to his own end.' Without his light and his life, these many years would have hung a lot more heavily on my hands.

INDEX

Any titles and ranks are listed here as they stood at the time. One or two names are incomplete and irretrievable. The author's name is abbreviated to MB.

Allen, Woody 242

Almond, Paul 90

Anderson, Dame Judith 58

Andrès 2

Anglim, Philip 315-6, 318

Annett, Douglas 288, 326, 329

Applebaum, Louis 54, 58, 60, 114

Armenian, Raffi 258, 268-9

Armstrong, Malcolm 207

Armstrong, Neil 325

Arnold, Trish 56-7

Arrau, Claudio 54

Arup, Ove 299

Attridge, Bruce 71, 87, 91-5, 101, 110, 161

Auden, W.H. 298

Baker, Janet 297

Baker, Ron 101

Ball, Bill 43

Barkla, John 286

Barnes, Clive 240, 283, 310

Basie, Count 43

Baxter, Iain 101, 156

Bawtree, Jennifer: younger sister of MB: 46, 83, 98

Bawtree, Josephine Victoria: elder sister of MB 23, 45-6, 54, 81-3, 96-9, 127, 300

Bawtree, Michael (MB): passim

Bawtree, Raymond Francis: father of MB 45-6, 82, 127, 258-9, 260-1, 300

Bawtree, Tessa: mother of MB 45, 64-5, 127, 258-9, 260-1, 300

Beckett, Samuel 163

Behrens, Bernard ('Bunny') 201, 218

Behrens, Jack 201, 254

Beissel, Henry 250

Belcourt, Emile 324

Bennett, Alan 47

Bennett, 'Wacky' 109

Benson, Susan 145, 268, 270, 282, 339

Berkeley, Busby 312

Berlin, Irving 313

Bernardi, Mario 202, 210, 214

Bernhardt, Colin: partner of MB 138-9, 142, 155, 160-3, 165-9, 170-9, 180-9, 190-7, 199, 200, 203, 207, 209, 214, 217-8, 221, 226-9, 230-2, 237, 239, 245-7, 255-7, 265, 275-6, 285, 290, 297, 314, 323, 325, 333-4, 337, 341-6

Bernhardt, Sarah 231

Bernstein, Leonard 306, 308-9, 310-2

Bettis, Paul 143-6, 208

Bird, Irene 225

Blake, Mervyn ('Butch') 48

Blakemore, Michael 256

Bolt, Robert 104

Bond, Timothy 159

Boretski, Peter 23

Bouissac, Paul 43, 92-3

Brassard, André 232

Bream, Julian 298

Bridgman, Billie 341

Britten, Benjamin 54, 296-8

Brook, Peter 191

Brookes, Chris 193

Brown, Jeremy 86-, 90,

Brown, Blair 201, 209

Brown, Brenna 94

Brown, Juliska 293

Brown, Oren 293, 302

Browning, Norman 112

Buchman, Herman 287

Buchman, Nahum 252

Buenaventura, Enrique 149, 150-4, 159, 160-2, 171, 174, 179, 185, 187-8, 194, 196, 224

Buenaventura, Jacqueline 171, 185

Buenaventura, Nicolas 171

Burge, Stuart 54, 58

Burgess, Michael 232, 243

Burns (Langham), Helen 25-7, 29-30, 32, 33-7, 46, 41-2, 62-9, 70, 72, 78, 83, 94, 117, 123, 129, 140-1, 163-5, 291, 303, 323-4

Burroughs, Jackie 209

Burton, Richard 47-8

Bury, John 117

Cable, Howard 339, 343

Caldwell, Zoe 163

Callaghan, Barry 90

Callaghan, Jim 303

Campau, DuBarry 90

Campbell, Norman 9, 255

Carey, Helen 200-1

Casals, Pablo 211

Casson, Jane 201

Castro, Fidel 149, 144, 184

Chalmers, Floyd 119

Chardin, J-P-S 217

Charpentier, Gabriel 52, 205, 222-3, 232, 234, 242, 288, 304, 313

Chilcott, Barbara 16, 17

Churchill, Winston 84

Chusid, Harvey 226

Ciceri, Leo 37, 198, 207

Clark, Greg 89

Clarkson, Adrienne 43

Clarkson, Stephen 43

Clutterbuck, Ursula 232

Coe, Peter 29, 31

Cohen, Nathan 124

Coldwell, Zoe 128

Cole, Beth Ann 209

Colicos, John 31, 37, 40, 62-4, 60

Collins, Patricia 26, 196, 249

Comden, Betty 306, 309, 310-1

Connell, Jane 282

Connors, Marc 329

Cook, Peter 23, 20, 47-8

Cornwell, David (John le Carré) 73

Count Basie 54

Coward, Noel 303, 313

Crane, Hart 191

Creley, Jack 225

Cronyn, Hume 48

Crosby, Bing 328

Crowe, John 58, 67

Csato, Tibor 41

Cullen, Don 44

Curnock, Richard 212

Curtis, Tony 141

Curzon, Clifford 297

Davies, Robertson 40-1

Davis, Donald 16, 198

Davis, Murray 16-17, 88

de los Angeles, Victoria 297

de Musset, Alfred 231

del Mar, Norman 297

de Paul, Gene 320

Diefenbaker, John 25

Dobbs, Kildare 19, 43, 90

Donald, James 200

Donat, Peter 37, 40, 52

Donat, Richard 209

Donkin, Eric 201

Dos Passos, John 135

Downey, John 312

Drake, Alfred 48

Dryden, John 155

Duke, Daryl 9

Dwyer, Peter 154

Easley, Holmes 283

Elizabeth, the Queen Mother 298

Ellington, Duke 31, 33-4, 54

Elliott, Patricia 307

Erickson, Arthur 91, 102

Evans, Gay 25

Evans, John 25

Evans, Ron 90, 124

Fairley, Barker 42

Fairbanks Jr., Douglas 317

Fairman, Blain 112

Fales, Herbert 39

Feist, Gene 253, 266-7, 277, 279, 280-4

Ferrer, Mel 142

Feydeau, Georges 224

Fillion, John 314

Fitzgerald, Maureen 209

Flannery, James 218

Fletcher, Michael 329

Foran, Owen 112

Forrester, Maureen 54, 258, 268-9, 287-9, 290, 292-3, 299, 304, 313, 324, 326-7, 334, 339, 341

Forst, Judith 324

Foster, Paul 191-2

Fraser, Simon 156

Freeman, Brian 208-9

Fried, Michael 266, 279, 280-1, 283-4

Frye, Northrop 8, 28

Fulford, Bob

Fullum, Clay 307-8

Gaitán, Jorge Eliécer 149

Galloway, Patricia 205, 207, 237, 262-6

Gammell, Robin 200, 205-6

Garant, Serge 232, 243

Garber, Victor 329

Gardner, David 9, 27-5, 22, 151, 194

Gardner, Dorothy 194

Garland, Judy 328

Garrick, David 157

Gascon, Jean 51, 52, 195, 197-8, 200-3, 205, 218, 221-2, 231-4, 236, 244-7, 252-4, 256, 258, 262, 264-6, 275

Gascon, Marilyn 222,

Gaskell, William 290

Gates, Larry 254, 278

Gatti, Armand 149

George, Chief Dan 144

George, Len 144

Gerardo 172, 186-7, 189

Ghandi, Mahatma 62

Gibson, Jeremy 216, 231, 268, 335

Gibson, Len 329

Gielgud, John 47

Gingold, Hermione 282

Glassco, Benjamin 4

Glassco, Bill 2-3, 7-10, 25, 71, 90-1, 195-6

Glassco, Grant, 7, 10-11, 13, 24

Glassco, Jane 2, 7, 8, 25, 71, 90

Glassco, Willa 7, 90

Goddard, Gary 337

Gogol, Nikolai 57, 89

Goldberg, Bert 140

Goldman, Milton 306, 317

Goldschmidt, Niki 296, 315

Goldsmith, Oliver 54, 182-3, 187, 233

Gordon, Walter 7-8, 25

Gorky, Ellen 163-6, 278, 324

Gorman, Mari 224-6

Gould, Glenn 42, 54

Graham, Colin 298-9

Grant, Patricia 224

Gray, Alexander 324-5

Gray, Joyce 339

Green, Adolph 306, 309, 310-1

Greenhalgh, Dawn 262-3, 266

Grenfell, Joyce 298

Grimes, Tammy 303-6

Gropius, Walter 95, 157

Grossmann, Suzanne 210, 224

Grotowsky, Jerzy 149, 167, 196

Grove-White, Robin 19, 43-4, 85-6, 90, 92

Guevara, Che 163, 184

Gunderson, Keith 49

Guthrie, Tyrone 15-16, 36, 53, 59, 68, 104, 298

Hall, Amelia ('Milly') 121, 249

Hanley, Peter 329, 330-1

Harbage, Alfred 58

Harewood, Lord 244

Harrison, Arthur 297, 300

Hayes, Helen 42

Hayes, John 119, 126, 195, 222, 232, 247, 253, 262-3, 275

Heeley, Desmond 64, 184-5, 188, 234-6, 240

Helpmann, Robert 59

Hendry, Tom 199, 200-1, 218, 222-3

Henry, Ed 224

Henry, Martha 17, 19, 37, 60, 274

Herbiet, Jean 210

Hessey, Wilma 46, 97

Hewett, Christopher 282-4

Hillman, Serrell 90

Hirsch, John 197-8, 222, 257, 274

Hoeniger, David 11, 24

Hogan, Dominic 209

Holiday, Billie 43

Holland, Anthony 139, 144

Holland, Jane 341

Holst, Imogen 298

House, Eric ('Nick') 24-5, 27, 67, 87-8, 225, 315, 318, 325

Hovenkamp, Henry 17

Hume, David 108

Huot, Guy 154

Hurry, Leslie 58-9, 64, 114, 123, 201

Hutt, Jack 64-5, 154-5, 197

Hutt, William ('Bill') 37, 114, 120-2, 125, 231-2, 246, 253, 263, 265

Hyland, Frances 37, 60, 114, 121

Isaacs, Jorge 186

Iseler, Elmer 20

Israel, Charles 'Chuck' and Verna, 90-2

Jackson, Barney 58, 66

Jackson, Moya 212

Jackson, Brian 30-1, 315

Jampolis, Neil Peter 305, 314-5, 329, 339

Johnson, President Lyndon B. 49, 89

Jones, Sandra 258

Jonson, Ben 206

Joseph 259-60

Juliani, John 117, 129-30, 143-5, 163, 183, 193

Jungh, Esse 9

Kahn, Michael 284, 290

Kalfin, Bob 306-9, 310

Kareda, Urjo 226

Karsh, Jousuf and Estrellita, 42

Kash, Eugene 287-8

Kelly, Gene 328

Kelly, Mona 214

Kelly, Red 25

Kennedy, Edward 49

Kennedy, President John F. 43, 49, 106

Kenny, Sean 149

Kenyon, Joel 122, 125, 275

Kern, Jerome 313

Kerr, Tom 104-5

King, Martin Luther 49, 163

Kinsolving, William 114-6, 121

Kirkpatrick, Sam 254-5, 278

Klemperer, Otto 211

Kott, Jan 58

Labiche, Eugène 224

Laing, Alan 226, 232

LaMarsh, Judy 148

Lamos, Mark 279

Langham, Christopher 41, 46, 69, 129, 140-2, 164

Langham, Michael 16, 26-9, 30-4, 36-7, 40-2, 46, 51-57, 60-9, 70, 78, 94, 105, 114-9, 120-1, 123-6, 140-2, 163-6, 195-8, 200, 203, 206, 231-2, 238, 240, 254-5, 278-9, 284-6, 323-4

Lasdun, Denys 149

Lawson, Bruce 130

Lebensold, Fred 149

Legrand, Michael 141

Leech, Clifford 125

Leigh-Fermor, Patrick 79

Lewis, Emory 283

Likos, Georgios 74-9

Lindsay, John 282

Linklater, Kristin 57

Littlewood, Joan 87

lo Jacono, Geppino 81-383

Loney, Martin 155

Lyndon, Joan 19, 92, 94

Lyndon, Patrick 19, 44, 71, 92, 161-3, 183, 193

Macchiavelli, Niccolo 220

MacEwan, Geraldine 122

MacFarlane, Doug 90

MacGregor, Barry 121, 237

MacKinnon, Archie 92, 101, 157

Mackintosh, Iain and Jan 302

MacPherson, Hugo and Louise 90

MacPherson, Jay 45

MacMillan, Sir Ernest 42

MacOwen, Michael 263

Maddox, Diana 60

Mahler, Gustav 290

Mailing, Phyllis 101, 182, 232, 242-3

Major, Leon 17-18

Malcolm X 49

Mallinson, Tom 101, 110, 157

Mann, David 326-7, 330-1, 334, 338

Mann, Peter 326-9, 330-1, 335

Marc-Michel 224

Marowitz, Charles 287

Márques, Gabriel Garcia 152, 172

Marshak, Judy 329

Martin, Andrea 329

Marx, Groucho 141-2

Massey, Vincent 42

Maud, Ralph 105, 125-6, 154

Maugham, Somerset 70

McAlpine, Mary 19, 94

McAnuff, Des 142

McCance, Larry 195

McDowell, Paul 43-4

McEwan, Geraldine 155

McGowan, George 9

McGreevy, John 71

McGuire, Dorothy 142

McLean, Prof. 28

McLellan, Nora 329

McLeod, Joyce 285

McLuhan, Marshall 92, 96

McTaggart-Cowan, Patrick 101, 86, 156

Menotti, Gian-Carlo 258

Mill, John Stuart 43, 108

Miller, Arthur 87, 282

Miller, Joel 217

Miller, Jonathan 47, 287

Mills, John 105, 107, 109, 118, 132-5

Milton, John 226

Mirbt, Félix 250

Mirvish, Ed 13

Mitchell, David 329, 331

Moiseiwitch, Tanya 36, 205, 298

Molière 256, 278

Monette, Richard 282

Monk, Thelonious 23

Moore, Dudley 47

Mortimer, John 155

Mrojek, Slawomir 223

Munro, Neil 209, 250

Murray, Michael 314

Negret, Edgar 181, 191

Needles, William (Bill) 249

Neruda, Pablo 181

Newton, Christopher 23

Nichol, Ruth 329

Nichols, Jack 90

Nikos 72-4

Nixon, Richard 275

O'Brien, Maureen 198, 206

Olivier, Laurence 51, 155,

Olson, Charles 105

Ondaatje, Michael 250

O'Neill, Raymond 323

Orton, Joe 314

O'Toole, Peter 164

Owens, Elizabeth (Kathe Feist) 267, 282

Palmer, Kevin 87-8

Pannell, Raymond 237, 240, 250-2

Pannell, Beverly 250-2

Parker, Brian 43

Parker, Dorothy 43

Peter Pears 54, 297-8

Pearson, Lester 8, 25, 148

Peck, Gregory 140-2

Peck, Véronique 141

Pennell, Nicholas 237, 262-6

Penson, Art 226

Peterson, Kurt 307

Peterson, Robert O 140-1

Phillips, Robin 257-8, 261, 263-6, 272-5, 290

Pinter, Harold 87

Pitt, Joel 284, 307

Plato 107

Plummer, Christopher 52, 303

Pollock, Sharon 258

Porter, Cole 313

Porter, McKenzie 90

Porter, Stephen 224

Pound, Ezra 95

Pownall, Leon and Sharon 68, 209

Priestley, J.B. 270-2

Prisek, Mario 9

Quilico, Gino 341

Quinn, Anthony 141

Rain, Douglas 37, 40, 42, 60, 64

Rattigan, Terence 303

Redfield, David 47

Reineke, Gary 197

Richter, Sviatoslav 297

Ricks, Christopher 19

Riel, Louis 156

Robson, Jack 43

Rogers, Clarke 194-5

Rose, Leonard 54

Rósza, Miklós 322-3

Rosemond, Perry 9, 71, 87

Ruta, Ken 278-9

Sampson, Antony 187, 190, 224

Sanchez, Rosita 171, 180-2, 189, 190

Savidge, Mary 17, 186, 236-7, 249

Scales, Bob 265

Scarfe, Alan 186-7, 237-8

Schafer, R. Murray 92, 95-6, 101, 103, 148, 156, 158, 193, 232-3, 237, 242-3

Schechner, Richard 191-2

Schickele, Peter 315

Schurmann, David 224

Scofield, Paul 37

Sharp, Mitchell 25

Shaw, Harold 284, 287

Shaw, Joseph 17, 19

Shelley, Carole 237-8, 304

Sheridan, Richard Brinsley 54, 153, 183, 233

Short, Martin 329

Shrum, Gordon 91, 101-3, 106

Shumsky, Oscar 54

Silverman, Bob 209-10

Silverman, Stanley 201

Sime, John 342

Simpson, N.F. 24

Sinatra, Frank 328

Smith, Harrell 49

Smith, Joel 157

Southam, Hamilton 202-4, 214-5, 217-8

Sparshott, Francis 43

Speaight, Robert 58, 66-7

Spender, Stephen 298

Sprott, Eoin 242, 254

Stephenson, Helga 335

Stewart, Ellen 191

Stewart, John L. 140, 142

Strauss, Claude Levy 210-2

Stuart, Eleanor 109

Styne, Jule 306

Swerdfager, Bruce 198-9, 232, 252-3

Swerdfager, Mary 199, 221-2

Tati, Jacques 315

Taylor, Elizabeth 48

Thom, Ron 299

Thomas, Dylan 105

Thomas, Powys 37, 125, 206, 249

Thomas, Richard 254

Thomas, Tony 312-3, 317-9, 320-1, 327

Toth, Jerry 330

Town, Harold 90

Traversi, Derek 58

Trotsky, Leon 92

Trudeau, Pierre Eliot 161

Twain, Mark 191

Tynan, Kenneth 149

van Bridge, Tony 37, 60, 64, 125, 236, 239, 256

van Meegeren, Han 253

Vanier, General Georges 42

Vickers, Jon 211

Visscher, Jan 82

Wagner, Richard 96, 158, 233

Walter, Bruno 290

Warhol, Andy 191-2

Warrack, David 338

Warren, Harry 311-3, 318-9, 320-1, 324, 326-9, 335

Watson, Patrick 44, 148

Weaver, Bob 9

Webster, Hughie 60, 62, 67

Weinreb, Lloyd 49

Weingarten, Romain 210

Weissburger 249

Welsh, Norman 17

Wesker, Arnold 223

Weston, John 23, 73, 297

Weston, Sally 297

Whitehead, Paxton 210, 224

Whittaker, Herbert 124

Wiggins, Tudi 17

Wilkinson, Col. Cyril 19

William, David 231, 245, 252-3

Williams, Tennessee 87, 290

Wilson, Charles 258, 268

Wilson, Edmund 89

Wilson, Lanford 192

Winterbottom, Ian 45

Wiseman, Joseph 23

Wood, John 232

Wycherley, William 54, 153

Wylie, William ('Bill') 198, 222, 232-3, 247, 252-3

Wylie, Betty Jane 232, 249,

Yaroshevskaya, Kim 122

Zaslove, Jerry 105, 107, 109, 113-4, 130, 132-3, 147